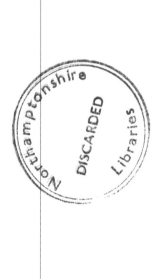

Nature's Cycles
The Water Cycle

Sally Morgan

WAYLAND

First published in 2008
by Wayland

Copyright © Wayland 2008

Wayland
338 Euston Road
London NW1 3BH

Wayland Australia
Level 17/207 Kent Street
Sydney, NSW 2000

Series editor: Nicola Edwards
Designer: Jason Billin

Picture acknowledgements:

Cover: Main image: Reinhardt Dirscherl/ Ecoscene;
river Wayne Lawler/ Ecoscene; cloud Sally Morgan/
Ecoscene; glacier Graham Neden/Ecoscene

Title page: Reinhardt Dirscherl/ Ecoscene; p2 Wayne
Lawler/ Ecoscene; p3 Robert Pickett / Ecoscene –
Papilio; p4 Neeraj Mishra/ Ecoscene; p5 Fritz Polking/
Ecoscene; p6 Graham Neden/ Ecoscene; p7 (t) Paul
Thompson/ Ecoscene, (b) Robert Pickett / Ecoscene –
Papilio; p8 NASA; p9 Wayne Lawler/ Ecoscene; p10
Peter Hulme/ Ecoscene; p11 Photographer/'s name tbc
Ecoscene; p12 (t) Paul Thompson/ Ecoscene, (ml)
NASA, (mr) Robert Walker/ Ecoscene; p13 (t) Sally
Morgan/ Ecoscene, (m) Robert Walker/ Ecoscene, (b)
Paul Thompson/ Ecoscene; p14 Fritz Polking/
Ecoscene; p15 Mike Whittle/ Ecoscene; p16 Wayne
Lawler/ Ecoscene; p17 Wayne Lawler/ Ecoscene; p18
Andria Massey/ Ecoscene; p19 Alan Towse/ Ecoscene;
p20 Kieran Murray/ Ecoscene; p21 Alexandra Jones/
Ecoscene; p22 Alan Towse/ Ecoscene; p23 Tony Page/
Ecoscene; p24 (t, m) Vicki Coombs/ Ecoscene, (b) Alan
Towse/ Ecoscene; p25 Chinch Gryniewicz/ Ecoscene;
p26 Mick Blowfield/ Ecoscene; p27 NASA; p28
Angela Hampton/ Ecoscene; p29 (t, b) Wayne Lawler/
Ecoscene

British Library Cataloguing in Publication Data

Morgan, Sally
The water cycle. - (Nature's cycles)
1. Hydrologic cycle - Juvenile literature
I. Title
551.48

ISBN: 978 0 7502 5358 1

Printed in China

Wayland is a division of Hachette Children's Books,
an Hachette Livre UK company.

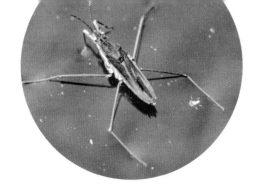

Contents

Water for life

Water is essential for life on Earth. Without it life could not exist. Earth is often called the blue planet because more than two-thirds of its surface is covered by oceans.

▼ Animals, such as these monkeys, need clean water.

Every living organism contains water. Water makes up about three-quarters of our bodies. That's about 35 litres in a teenager. Some organisms contain even more water, for example, jellyfish can be more than 95 per cent water. Water is an important habitat too, for animals such as fish, seals and whales, and plants such as seaweeds. Animals and plants that live in water are called aquatic.

In Focus: Plants and water

Plants need water. They obtain their water from the soil through their roots. Water is carried through their stems to the leaves. Then water evaporates from the leaves. If plants do not get enough water from the soil, their leaves will droop. This is called wilting. Without water the leaves will shrivel and the plant may die.

The world's water

Most of the world's water is salt water. This is water that contains salt and which cannot be drunk. The water that occurs in rivers, lakes and glaciers is fresh water. Fresh water makes up less than 3 per cent of all the Earth's water. Fresh water is virtually all water with just a few natural minerals. This is the type of water that comes out of taps and which people need for drinking and washing.

The amount of water on the Earth is constant, so it is continuously recycled between the atmosphere, rivers and seas. This forms the water cycle or hydrological cycle. The cycle starts with water falling as rain and snow onto the ground. The water seeps into the soil and into streams and rivers. Then water evaporates from all surfaces back into the atmosphere.

○ Fresh water pours over this waterfall. Waterfalls occur on rivers where there is a sudden change in height of the river bed. Here fresh water cascades over rocks to reach the lower part of the river.

Investigate: How much of an apple is water?

See if you can find out how much water an apple contains. Take a fresh apple and weigh it. Record its mass. Now cut the apple into slices and place the slices on a plate on a sunny windowsill, so that they dry out. When the slices are dry and leathery, weigh them again. How much does the apple weigh now? How much mass has the apple lost? The difference in mass is due to the loss of water.

Why is water special?

Water is the most common liquid on Earth. It is odourless and colourless. Water is made up of one type of molecule that is formed from one atom of oxygen and two atoms of hydrogen. Its chemical formula is written as H_2O.

Changing state

Water can exist in solid form as ice, as a liquid, and as a gas called water vapour. Earth is the only planet in the solar system that has the right conditions for water to exist in all three states. At $0°C$, water changes from solid to liquid and at $100°C$ it boils and becomes a vapour.

Ice is made from lots of water molecules that are bonded or joined closely together so they cannot move. When water freezes, it expands and it becomes less dense. This means that ice floats on the top of liquid water. This is why a layer of ice forms over ponds and lakes during cold weather. Icebergs are formed from solid ice and they float on the oceans.

All three states of water can be seen in this photograph. There is water vapour in the air, liquid water in the sea and frozen water in the glacier.

Investigate: Water's colour

If you hold up a clear container of water you see that water is transparent. It has no colour. But when you look at the sea on a sunny day it looks blue. This is because of the way light reflects off the surface of the water. Part of the colour is a reflection of the blue sky. But some of the colour comes from tiny particles floating in the water. They absorb red light and reflect blue light.

Water temperature

Amazingly, the temperature of the water that makes up the oceans does not alter much. This is because water can absorb a lot of the sun's heat energy without becoming much warmer. That is why the sea can still feel quite cool in the middle of summer. However, the seas can hold on to heat and do not cool down quickly either. So in winter, the water can feel quite warm compared to the land. This creates a very stable environment for marine organisms.

⬆ Water in a glass looks clear.

⬇ Surface tension prevents the pond skater from sinking into the water.

In Focus: Surface tension

A pond skater can walk on water. This is possible because of the property of water called surface tension. The molecules of water at the surface grip each other tightly and form a sort of skin. This is strong enough to support the weight of an insect such as a pond skater, enabling it to skim over the surface.

Fresh and salt water

Thousands of millions of years ago there were no oceans on Earth. The Earth was so hot that any water quickly boiled away. The atmosphere was full of steam pumped out by the many volcanoes. Then, as the Earth cooled down over many millions of years, the steam turned to water and rain fell. The water level rose and mountains disappeared under water. Large depressions on the Earth's surface filled with water and became oceans. The water was salty because the steam from the volcanoes was rich in salts.

Deep oceans

There are five oceans in the world; Atlantic, Pacific, Indian, Arctic and Southern. The depth of the oceans varies, but on average it is about 3.5 kilometres. Beneath the waves are mountain ranges, active volcanoes, and long, seemingly bottomless trenches. The deepest ocean trench is the Mariana Trench in the Pacific. At its deepest point it is just over 11 km deep and it could easily swallow the Himalayas.

◀ Two-thirds of the Earth's surface is covered by the oceans.

Within the oceans, the water is moving. Warm water is less dense than cold water so it rises above the cold water. In the oceans there is a layer of warm water that lies over cold water. There are currents of water moving through the oceans too. For example, there is a flow of warm water called the Gulf Stream that forms off the coast of North America and travels across the Atlantic to Northern Europe. There are cold currents too, such as the current which flows from the Antarctic up the west coast of Africa.

Fresh water

Most of the Earth's fresh water is locked up as ice in the polar ice caps and in glaciers. Some forms rivers and lakes and the rest is found in the ground. When rain falls, it runs off into streams and rivers. Some water seeps into the ground. This is ground water and it drains down through the rock until it reaches a layer of rock that it cannot pass. The water collects in the rock above this impermeable layer.

⬇ Water pours out of a well that has been dug down to an aquifer.

In Focus: Aquifers

An underground layer of water-filled rock is called an aquifer. An aquifer is an important store of water. Water may remain trapped in an aquifer for a long time. In Egypt there are aquifers where it is estimated that as many as 40,000 years may have passed between the time water fell to the ground and the time it reaches the surface again.

Evaporation and condensation

Evaporation and condensation are two key processes in the water cycle. Evaporation is the change in state of water from a liquid to a vapour. Condensation is the change from a vapour to a liquid.

Evaporation

Evaporation is caused by liquid water being heated and given heat energy. The heat causes the molecules in the liquid water to move around more quickly and bump into each other. Some molecules have enough energy to break away from the other molecules and turn into water vapour. This is called evaporation.

Water can evaporate at almost any temperature above freezing point. For example, after rain there are puddles on the ground. When the sun shines, the water evaporates into a vapour and the puddle disappears. Water also evaporates when it is boiled in a kettle. The steam emerging from the spout contains a lot of water vapour.

◀ A geyser is a spout of hot water and steam that escapes from a crack in the ground under very high pressure.

Sea water contains about three per cent salt. Salt is obtained from sea water by trapping the water in shallow salt pans. When water evaporates, the salt is left behind.

Condensation

Water vapour rises into the atmosphere. As it rises it cools. This causes it to condense, or change state back into a liquid. The water droplets fall back to the ground as rain.

Often condensation can be seen on windows. In winter for example, the air outside a house is colder than the air inside. When water vapour inside comes into contact with the cold window glass, it condenses and droplets of water form on the inside of the window.

In Focus: Antifreeze

Water usually freezes at 0°C. However if there are other substances in the water, such as salts, the freezing point is lower.

Water circulates in a car's radiator to stop the engine overheating. When temperatures fall below freezing, there is a chance that the water could freeze. Water expands when it freezes and this could crack the pipes. To prevent this, people add antifreeze to the radiator water to lower its freezing point and make it less likely to freeze.

Some animals can make a sort of antifreeze too. For example, the ice fish that lives under the ice of the Antarctic creates a substance that stops its cells freezing.

Investigate: Make your own water cycle

Create a mini-water cycle on a windowsill. Take a small pot plant, water it and place it in a large plastic bag. Tie the bag so the air cannot escape. Place the bag with the plant inside on a sunny windowsill. The heat causes water to evaporate from the leaves and soil. The water vapour condenses on the inside of the bag and runs down the sides to collect at the bottom.

Clouds and the water cycle

When water vapour rises in the atmosphere, it cools and condenses. This forms clouds. The clouds are made up of droplets of water which get bigger and bigger. Eventually these droplets become so heavy that they fall as rain. Clouds vary in their shape and appearance. The three main types of cloud are cumulus, stratus and cirrus.

Water vapour cools and condenses, forming clouds.

The Water Cycle

Water evaporates from all surfaces.

Rivers and oceans fill with rainwater.

Water droplets fall from clouds as rain.

Cumulus clouds

Cumulus clouds are puffy and they look a bit like clumps of cotton wool. They tend to form when warm moist air is pushed upwards. As the air cools, the water condenses and a cumulus cloud forms. Summer thunderstorms are usually caused by cumulonimbus clouds. These are large dark clouds that are not very puffy. They tower high in the sky and bring heavy rain, thunder and lightning.

Investigate: Clouds

Using the photographs on this page and on the Internet see if you can identify the different types of cloud that move across the sky. Can you link the clouds to the varying forms of weather?

Stratus clouds

The word stratus comes from the Latin meaning 'spread out'. Stratus clouds are horizontal, flat clouds that spread out across the sky like a blanket. These clouds usually form where a layer of warm, moist air passes over a layer of cooler air. When the warm air comes into contact with the cool air, water vapour condenses to form cloud. These clouds are associated with rain.

Cirrus clouds

Cirrus clouds are thin, feather-like clouds that form about five to seven kilometres high in the sky. At that height it is so cold that the water condenses to form ice crystals. Cirrus clouds are seen on fine, sunny days.

In Focus: Elephants and thunderstorms

Water is very important to elephants as they drink many litres each day and they use it to clean their skin. However African elephants live in areas where there are dry seasons with no rain, followed by rainy seasons. The start of the rainy season is marked by frequent thunderstorms. Researchers have discovered that the elephants can sense a thunderstorm more than 100 kilometres away. They can detect vibrations in the ground caused by the thunder. As soon as they hear the thunderstorm, they start walking towards it, because they know that it brings water.

Water and weather

The water cycle has an important role to play in our daily weather. It is responsible for rain, snow, sleet and hail.

Weather or climate?

Our daily weather is made up of a combination of wind, water and heat from the sun. The mix of different amounts of sunshine, cloud and rainfall varies from one day to the next. Climate is the usual pattern of weather that a particular place experiences. For example, areas near the Equator have a tropical climate that is warm and sunny all year round.

○ Blizzards are common in the Antarctic. The strong winds blow the snow around making it difficult for the Emperor Penguins to find their way around.

Investigate: Rainfall

The annual rainfall in the Amazon region of South America is a massive 1000 cm. In contrast, some of the driest deserts in the world receive less than 2.5 cm a year. See if you can find out the rainfall of the area in which you live. Can you research whether the rainfall has changed much over the last 100 years? Many public libraries have information on local history.

Extreme weather

Our everyday lives depend on there being enough water. In some parts of the world droughts are common, and there is no rain for months, or even years. This lack of water causes plants and animals to die. Crop failures can cause food shortages or even famine. In contrast, if there is too much rain flooding may occur. A storm can bring heavy rainfall in a short period of time. Soon, rivers swell and burst their banks and there is widespread flooding.

▶ Life goes on as normal in this Vietnamese town despite the heavy monsoon rain.

Monsoon rain

In some parts of the world there are periods of heavy rain called monsoons. The people have to cope with heavy rain falling almost daily for several months. Then there is little rain for the rest of the year. India has a monsoon climate. In summer, winds blow off the Indian Ocean and they bring rain. Heavy monsoon rain falls from June to September. At times the rain is torrential, causing widespread flooding and land slides. In winter, dry winds blow from the north east, and the weather is hot and arid.

In Focus: Stopping floods

Millions of people live near rivers and their homes can be at risk from flooding. Floods can be prevented by building barriers along river banks to stop water flowing over low lying land. Some towns are protected by flood barriers that close at times of flood risk. Sometimes the flood water can be directed onto farmland beside the river so that homes are not damaged.

Rivers

Much of the water that falls to the ground drains
into a river. The rivers run across the land
and empty into the sea.

River stages

When rain falls on hilly ground, some of its soaks into the ground, but the
rest runs downhill. First, it forms a stream that tumbles down the slope.
As more water enters the stream it becomes a river. Fast-flowing river water
is powerful and has lots of energy. It wears away the banks and the bed of
the river. Small rocks are picked up and carried downstream. The rocks rub
against each other and are worn down. As they become smaller they form
sediment, which is made up of many tiny particles of sand, silt and mud.

Once the river reaches the less hilly ground, the water flows more slowly.
It may form bends, or meanders. By the time the river eventually reaches
the sea, it has dropped all its sediment.

🔻 The water flows slowly along this meandering river.

Animals that live in fast-moving water are specially adapted to this difficult environment. For example, freshwater mussels have sticky threads to attach themselves to rocks, while leeches have suckers to hang on to plants. Water plants have adaptations too, such as well developed roots so they do not get washed away.

▼ This delta with its network is islands and channels has formed at the mouth of a river in Australia.

Estuaries and deltas

Estuaries and deltas form where rivers enter the sea. An estuary forms where the currents are strong enough to move the sediment out to sea, keeping the mouth of the river open, for example the Thames Estuary in the United Kingdom. Deltas form where the sediment is not removed. Instead it builds up into marshy islands, for example the Mississippi Delta in the United States and the Nile Delta in Egypt. The river splits up into many small channels that wind their way around the islands to the sea. Over time the delta grows larger, until it extends into the sea.

Investigate: Sedimentation

A fast-flowing river has lots of energy and it can carry many particles. As the river starts to slow down, the water loses energy and the particles are dropped. The heaviest particles are dropped first, and the lightest last. You can see how the different sizes of particles settle in this simple investigation. Collect a mixture of sand, gravel and soil and pour it into a see-through plastic bottle. Add enough water to cover. Replace the cap and give the bottle a good shake. Leave the bottle on the side for a week to allow all the particles to settle. Which particles settled first at the bottom of the bottle?

Water for drinking

People need water for many different uses, such as drinking, cooking, washing and cleaning. This water is taken from streams and rivers, lakes and wells. If too much is taken, it can disrupt the water cycle.

⬤ Collecting water from a well on the street is a daily chore for women in many less developed countries.

Water use

People who live in more developed countries such as Australia, the United Kingdom and the United States use far more water than people living in less developed countries, such as Tanzania and Pakistan. The highest use of water occurs in the United States where each person uses about 600 litres of water every day. Each person in the United Kingdom uses about 150 litres a day. In less developed countries the figure is as low as 20 litres a day. Also, many people in less developed countries do not have water piped to their home. They have to collect their water from a standpipe in the street or a local well. Around the world, millions of women spend several hours each day just fetching water. Often the water is not safe to drink and it has to be boiled first.

Litres of water are used each day in this town in Florida, USA to keep the roadside verges green.

Investigate: Daily water usage

How much water do you use each day? Make a diary that records how much you use. If you have a water meter, you can take a reading and see how much water is used in a week. Can you work out how much you and your family use each year? Can you think of ways of cutting back on your water use?

Disrupting the water cycle

The water cycle can be easily disrupted and this can have widespread consequences. If too much water is taken from a well, the water seeping down from the surface may not be able to replace the water being pumped out of the ground. Gradually the water level in the ground falls. The well runs dry and a new deeper well has to be dug.

In Focus: Water and disease

Safe drinking water is essential for health. Water can carry disease-causing organisms such as bacteria, viruses, and parasites. If drinking water is not treated properly, the disease-causing organisms can enter the body and cause disease. A staggering 1.8 million people die each year from diarrhoea. Many of these people are children under the age of five. As many as half of all people living in less developed countries suffer from a health problem caused by poor quality drinking water and inadequate sewage treatment.

Polluted Water

For hundreds of years people have used rivers and the sea as a place to dump their waste. Untreated sewage from bathrooms was emptied into rivers along with chemical waste and rubbish. In London in the 1900s, for example, there was so much sewage in the crowded city that the stench hanging over the area at night was almost intolerable.

A lot of chemicals are used in farming. When pests attack their crops farmers may spray a pesticide to kill them, or use a weed killer to keep weeds under control. Water carries these chemicals from the fields into streams, rivers and the sea where they harm aquatic life.

Oil spills

Oil can pollute water. Oil may leak from storage tanks into rivers, and accidents may cause oil tankers to spill thousands of litres of oil into the sea. The oil spreads over the surface of the water creating a slick. It clogs the feathers of birds and smothers small animals. Cleaning up the oil is a mucky job. Often the oil is simply skimmed off the surface and washed off rocks. Detergents can be used to break up the oil, but the detergents can harm aquatic animals too.

⬤ This oil tanker ran aground off the coast of Shetland, UK in 1993, causing an oil slick that spread along many kilometres of previously unspoilt coastline.

Investigate: How clean is your local river or beach?

You can use the Internet to find out if your local river or beach is clean. Look up organizations that are responsible for water quality. Do you have a favourite beach? In Europe, the Blue Flag scheme identifies beaches that have safe bathing water.

Too many nutrients

Fertilisers and sewage are full of nutrients. If they enter a river, the nutrients cause micro-organisms, such as bacteria, to increase in number. These micro-organisms use up a lot of the oxygen in the water. This leaves little oxygen for other aquatic organisms, such as fish, and they die.

Sometimes, as a result of too many nutrients in the water, rivers become covered in a thick layer of fast-growing green algae. The algae spread across the surface of the river, blocking the light to the aquatic plants below and causing them to die.

As rivers become more polluted, aquatic animals disappear. First to go are the larger fish such as salmon and trout, followed by small insects and other invertebrates.

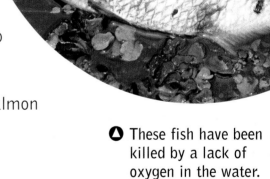

○ These fish have been killed by a lack of oxygen in the water.

In Focus: Cleaning rivers

Many countries now have strict laws that control the quality of water in rivers. There are laws controlling what substances can be put into the river, and how often. The quality of the water is tested regularly and industries have to make sure that their waste water does not contain harmful chemicals, otherwise they are fined. As river water has become cleaner, fish such as salmon have returned.

Down the drain

Do you know what happens to the water that disappears down the plughole or toilet? In many homes, waste water from kitchens and bathrooms empties into the drains and is carried along pipes to a sewage works where it is treated. This waste water contains sewage (waste from the toilet) together with soapy water and washing up water.

In the past, sewage and waste water was emptied straight into a river or sea without any treatment. Now, many countries have laws that state that sewage has to be treated before it can be emptied into a river or the sea.

The final stage of treatment for waste water in this area of Florida takes place in a marsh where the plants complete the cleaning process.

In Focus: Cruising and sewage

A cruise ship is a bit like a small floating town. The people on board produce a great deal of waste water. An average cruise ship produces 5,000 litres of sewage and 30,000 litres of grey water a day! Until recently this was dumped untreated into the sea. In 2005 new rules were agreed that all cruise ships would be fitted with a sewage treatment plant by 2010. However, raw sewage can be still be dumped in the sea so long as the cruise ship is 19 kilometres from land.

⬥ These huge cruise liners carry several thousand people, who all produce waste.

Recycling 'grey' water

In some homes, waste water from baths and washing machines is recycled. This water is called grey water because it contains soap. It can be used for flushing toilets. Some people pipe the water from their baths into gardens to water plants in summer. This helps to reduce the amount of water they use.

Industrial waste water

Some manufacturing processes generate a lot of waste water, for example every tonne of paper produces 40,000 litres of waste water, and for every litre of petrol there are 70 litres of dirty water. Waste water from industry has to be treated before it can enter a river or the sea. Many factories and industrial plants have their own water treatment centre.

Farmers have waste water too, such as slurry, the waste washed out of barns where animals are housed. This has to be stored in huge slurry tanks so it does not drain straight into rivers.

Investigate: Waste disposal

Some waste, such as cooking oil, bleach and paint should never be poured down the drain. It's not safe to pour away pesticides, such as garden sprays, either. All these liquids have to be stored in their containers and taken to a special disposal site. Often people store unwanted chemicals in a garage or shed. What does your family do with unwanted paint? Use the Internet to find out where to dispose of old paint pots.

Cleaning water

Most towns and cities around the world have large sewage treatment plants to treat the millions of litres of sewage produced every day.

Screening and settling

First, the raw sewage is passed through a screen that removes large objects such as plastic and paper. Then the sewage passes into a large settling tank, where the solids sink to the bottom. These solids are moved to another container where they are heated and then dried. The dried treated waste can either be burnt or used as natural fertiliser on farmland.

Raw sewage passes through a screen.

Sewage enters huge settling tanks.

Liquid from the settling tanks is sprinked over gravel beds to become clean water.

Sprinkled over gravel

The liquid from the settling tank is full of nutrients and bacteria, some of which are harmful. The liquid is sprinkled over gravel beds. The liquid seeps through the beds and comes into contact with bacteria that live on the surface of the gravel. These bacteria remove all the nutrients in the water and kill harmful bacteria. Clean water drains out the bottom of the gravel beds and is emptied into a river.

Investigate: What happens to sewage?

Some homes are connected to the sewage system and the sewage is piped away through drains. Other homes have a large tank in the ground, called a septic tank where the sewage collects. It has to be emptied regularly. Can you find out what happens to the sewage in your home? Is it piped away or is there a septic tank? Where is your local sewage treatment plant? Many sewage treatment plants have open days when people can visit to find out more.

Sewage ponds

Not all countries have sewage treatment plants. Some countries, such as Israel and India, pump the sewage into shallow ponds. The water in the ponds is heated by the sun and bacteria in the water break down the sewage. Then the water pumped through a series of ponds, where it gradually becomes cleaner.

Large fish called carp are often kept in the pond. They eat the sewage and when they are large enough, they can be caught and eaten.

⬤ Canna lilies can be used to clean water. These engineers are testing the water that drains out of treatment beds in India.

In Focus: Using plants to clean water

A natural way to clean water is to grow fast-growing grass that lives in shallow water, such as reeds or canna lilies. The planted are rooted in shallow beds and dirty water is circulated around their roots. Bacteria around the roots break down the sewage and the plants take up the nutrients. By the time the water drains out at the other end it is clean enough to enter a river.

Water for farming

Farming uses huge amounts of water every day. Crops need a good supply of water if they are to grow well and produce a large yield. If there is insufficient rainfall, the plants need to be watered by a process called irrigation. In some countries as much as two-thirds of the water used is used in farming.

⬥ A child fills watering cans to water his family's crops by hand.

Irrigating plants

Irrigation is common in drier parts of world such as California, Australia, Pakistan. Water is pumped from rivers and lakes and carried by pipe or channel to irrigate the fields. The water can either be sprayed over the crops, or dripped on the soil around the plants. It is important to control the amount of water that is taken from rivers. If too much is taken, the water levels in the river fall and aquatic wildlife suffers.

Investigate: Hydroponics

Hydroponics is soil-less farming where the crops are planted in tanks of nutrient-rich water rather than soil. The nutrient levels in the water are carefully controlled so the plants get everything they require. You could try this yourself. Buy some seeds of a fast-growing salad plant such as lettuce. Place a thick wad of cotton tissue in the bottom of a plastic container and sprinkle a few seeds on top. Add water so the paper is moist and leave on a sunny windowsill. Within a few days the seeds will germinate and grow into lettuce plants. Each day, add water to the paper so the lettuce plants do not dry up. Every few days add a few drops of a liquid plant fertiliser to the water.

Poor irrigation

Irrigation has to be carried out carefully, since poor irrigation is as bad as no irrigation. If too much water is poured over the crops, the soil becomes waterlogged, and the plant roots die. If too much water evaporates from the surface of the soil, salts are drawn from deep in the soil up to the surface. This leaves a salty crust over the soil which very few plants can survive. This problem is called salinization and it is affecting large areas of irrigated land, especially in Australia and Pakistan.

⬇ In 1960 the Aral Sea was the world's fourth largest lake. Now it is one quarter of its original size.

In Focus: The Aral Sea

One part of the world that has suffered greatly from too much water extraction is the Aral Sea, a huge inland sea that lies between Kazakhstan and Uzbekistan. Since the 1960s the Aral Sea has shrunk, and now it is a fraction of its original size. It may disappear completely by 2020. The Aral Sea receives most of its water from two major rivers, but most of this water has been diverted to irrigate fields of cotton crops. What little water that remains is heavily polluted from industry.

Water forever?

Water is an important natural resource. As the world's population increases, so too does the amount of water used each day. The activities of people are disrupting the water cycle and causing climates to change.

Trees, water and climate

Forests hold a lot of water. When a large area of trees is cleared, the ground is left bare and unprotected. When it rains the water runs straight off the ground into rivers. This may cause local flooding. The loss of trees means that less water is stored in the soil. Also, there is no evaporation of water from the trees' leaves into the atmosphere. The air becomes drier and there are fewer clouds. This means there is less rain. As a result, over time the climate of the area changes.

Investigate: Saving water

Some simple things that will help to save water:

- don't leave the tap running while you are brushing your teeth;
- have a shower rather than a bath;
- if you have to run the tap for some hot water, save the water you've used in a container and use it to water the garden;
- use the 'low flush' button on the toilet or pop a brick in the cistern of the toilet so that less water is flushed;
- use a water butt to collect rainwater for watering the garden.

◖ Dams are built across many rivers to collect water that can be piped to homes.

○ Deforestation removes the trees and leaves the soil exposed to the wind, sun and rain.

Climate change

The burning of coal, oil and gas, and clearance of forests is causing the temperature of the Earth's surface to increase. This is called global warming. One of the effects of global warming is climate change. Some parts of the world may become drier and warmer and suffer a fall in rainfall. The climate of southern Spain, for example, may become more like North Africa. Other areas may become wetter and suffer from more extreme weather events, such as storms and strong winds. These changes will affect the crops that can be grown and the types of industries in a region.

◆ In Focus: Recycling water

Its not just individuals that can help to save water, industry can help too. Manufacturing industry can use less water for cleaning, cooling and washing. For example, if an aluminium rolling mill reused the water it uses for cooling, it could cut its water use by 93 per cent.

Some factories may be able to re-use water and, with the installation of more efficient machinery, could reduce the amount of water they use.

The building industry can build new homes and offices that are fitted with devices to collect rain water from the roof so it can be stored in tanks underground for use in summer. New designs of taps could be used that limit the amount of water flowing out each time the tap is turned on.

○ This stream is full of soil that has been washed off the land by heavy rain.

Glossary

algae Simple plants found in water, such as seaweeds, and the tiny green plants that float near the surface of water.

antifreeze A substance that lowers the freezing point of a substance so that it does not freeze so readily.

aquatic Living in water.

aquifer A layer of rock that holds water.

atmosphere The layer of air that surrounds the Earth.

atom The smallest unit of matter. A water molecule consists of two atoms of hydrogen and one of oxygen.

climate The usual pattern of weather in a place.

condensation The change in state from gas to liquid.

delta A triangular area of silt and other deposits in the mouth of a river.

detergent A soap, a cleaning agent.

diarrhoea A gut problem, sometimes called 'having the runs', when the body passes watery waste.

estuary The mouth of a river where fresh river water mixes with salty sea water.

evaporation The change in state from liquid to gas.

famine A situation when there is not enough food for people and they suffer from starvation.

fertiliser Nutrients that are added to the soil to make crops grow larger and faster.

freezing point The point at which a liquid turns to a solid.

glacier A slow moving river of ice that moves downhill.

hydrological cycle The water cycle.

hydroponics Growing plants without soil.

impermeable Describing a material, such as a rock, that does not allow water to pass through.

irrigation The artificial watering of crops.

marine Relating to the sea.

meander A bend in a river.

molecule The smallest particle of a compound that contains one or more atoms.

monsoon Seasonal winds that blow in different directions at different times of year and which bring heavy rains for part of the year.

organism A living thing.

parasite An organism that lives in or on another organism and does harm to that organism, for example a tapeworm that lives in the gut of animals such as dogs and sheep.

pesticide A chemical that farmers use to kill pests such as insects.

pollute To contaminate.

salinization When soil becomes too salty for plants to grow in it.

sediment Particles such as sand, silt and clay that are carried by a river.

septic tank An underground storage tank for waste water from a home.

sewage Semi-liquid waste from the bathroom and kitchen.

slurry Liquid waste that contains faeces and urine from farm animals.

surface tension The attraction between water molecules at the surface of a liquid.

vapour A gas.

virus A tiny organism that can only be seen using the most powerful microscopes and which infects other organisms and causes disease.

weather The conditions that exist at a particular time, for example how rainy, windy or sunny it is.

wilting When leaves become floppy and lose support due to lack of water.

Further Information

Books
Water for All, Sally Morgan, Franklin Watts, 2000

The Water Cycle (Cycles in Nature) Theresa Greenaway, Wayland, 2006

Water Cycle (Nature's Patterns), Anita Ganeri, Heinemann Library, 2004

Websites
www.wateraid.org
The website of the charity Water Aid that is helping to provide water to poor communities.

www.unicef.org.uk
The website of the charity UNICEF that is helping children in less developed countries.

www.water.org
The website of Water Partners, an organization in the United States that is helping to provide cleaning drinking water to people in less developed countries.

Index

THE BRITISH MOTOR BUS

GAVIN BOOTH

IAN ALLAN LTD

LONDON

First published 1977
This edition 1986

ISBN 0 7110 1641 0

Published by Ian Allan Ltd, Shepperton, Surrey;
and printed by Ian Allan Printing Ltd at their works
at Coombelands in Runnymede, England

Previous pages: **A handsome 1930s coach for
longer-distance journeys — a 1933 Albion
Valiant PV70 with English Electric 28-seat body
in the fleet of Hebble, of Halifax.**
Robert L. Grieves collection

Below right: **Mayne of Manchester was a
dedicated AEC user in the 1930s. This 1937
line-up shows Regal single-deckers and Regent
double-deckers, and a solitary 1928 Reliance in
the centre, the bus, according to the original
AEC caption, that prompted Mayne 'to adhere in
future years to one make of vehicle'. At the time
Mayne's double-deckers were used on the service
in Manchester; nearly 50 years after, the service
still survived.** *Ian Allan Library*

Below: **In its attempts to find the most suitable
vehicle for its services, London Buses bought
small batches of experimental buses in 1984. This
Leyland Olympian with ECW body, one of three,
was followed by sizeable orders.**

Front endpaper: **The chassis assembly shop at
Daimler in Coventry in the 1930s, with COG
models on the production line.**
Ian Allan Library

Rear endpaper: **The biggest-selling single-deck
citybus in the 1970s and early 1980s was the
Leyland National, here in Mk 2 form with
front-mounted radiator. Although demand had
dropped sharply by the time National production
ceased in 1985, it remains the most familiar
single type of British bus. These National 2s were
delivered in 1983 to Brighton Borough
Transport; one wears BBT blue livery and the
other six wear Shuttle livery for the network of
services introduced jointly with Southdown.**
Leyland

THE BRITISH MOTOR BUS

Title page: **The Great Western Railway played an important part in the early development of the motor bus outside Britain's main towns and cities. This early postcard, captioned 'On the way to Beaconsfield by GWR Motor Car' shows a 1904 Milnes-Daimler on solid tyres and on the type of road that tested the durability of the early chassis.** *Robert L. Grieves collection*

Contents

Introduction

The shape of the British motor bus has changed greatly over the past 90 years, and even in the nine years since the publication of the original edition of this book there have been changes that could never have been anticipated: the dramatic rebirth of express coaching, the equally dramatic slump in the demand for new buses — and the political background that played its part in these developments.

1914 Guy Passenger Mail Car.

This book is about the motor bus — the vehicle. How it grew from a simple, rugged and unreliable machine into a sophisticated, expensive and usually reliable vehicle, in competition with tramcars, trolleybuses, railways, motor cars, television — and itself. Inevitably the story touches on the structure of the operating industry, and the legislative and political background, for all of these affected the shape, size and layout of the motor bus.

1921 30 seater Bus with double reduction geared back axle.

When *The British Motor Bus* was first published in 1977, the vast majority of buses operating in Britain were British-made. After the brief flurry of imports in the 1920s died out, imported bus chassis or bodies were almost totally unknown. Then in mid-1970s operators started buying increasing numbers of imported coach chassis and bodies — so much so that by 1984 more than 22% of new buses and coaches registered in Britain were imported. Although most imported vehicles have been coaches, the importers have also made a slight impact on the stage carriage market, but domestic

1926 First 6 wheeler petrol engined bus.

manufacturers, with their understanding of the peculiarly British service bus, have been able to cater more precisely for the needs of operators. Coaches tend to be more international.

But just as imported vehicles have become an accepted feature of the British bus scene today, the domestic manufacturers have a long and distinguished background of export successes. Often these were to countries with British connections in the days of the

1933 "Arab" — the first bus with Gardner oil engine.

Empire, a bond that was still strong in the infancy of the motor bus. As these countries have moved from British rule, so too have they moved from traditional suppliers. The manufacturers have reacted well to this, particularly when faced with a declining home market, and have broken new ground in new areas, particularly in the Far East, where the British double-decker has proved an ideal crowd-mover.

One of the first things any writer discovers when researching a book such as this is that historians often disagree in the way they record or interpret important events. This has certainly been my experience. Time has an irritating way of clouding precise memories, so where there was any doubt I have included my own interpretation of various events. Then there is the further danger of distortion, for a number of the available bus books have been primarily public relations exercises written for the greater glorification of the operator or manufacturer concerned. But

we are all guilty of prejudice, and it would be unrealistic to pretend that my own views might not colour my interpretation of certain events in this book.

The story of the motor bus almost fits neatly into decades, but events have really decided the way the chapters are split. It is widely recognised that 1905 was the year the motor bus really emerged as a serious form of transport, so the first chapter traces the background of horse and steam traction up to this date. The end of World War 1 is another obvious turning-point in the story of the bus, and the major

1941 Utility buses for wartime operation.

reorganisation of the industry in 1929-30 really relates to the decade that followed. World War 2 must be considered on its own, and the uncertainties of the early postwar years merit a separate chapter. Forty years after the upheavals of the 1920s came the 1968 Transport Act and its consequences, and 1969 is taken as the starting-point of the 1970s chapter.

The story of the bus can never really be up to date, of course. Events will overtake some of the developments in the last chapter, even before the book is published. This is inevitable, and readers will appreciate the practical difficulties of trying to be totally up to date. But this is a continuing story, and one that never fails to surprise all of us with an interest in buses.

Gavin Booth
Edinburgh

1950 "New Look" Arab Mk. IV

Guy celebrated 50 years of building passenger vehicles in 1964, and published these illustrations in an advertisement celebrating the event.

Various difficulties gradually surmounted
The years to 1904

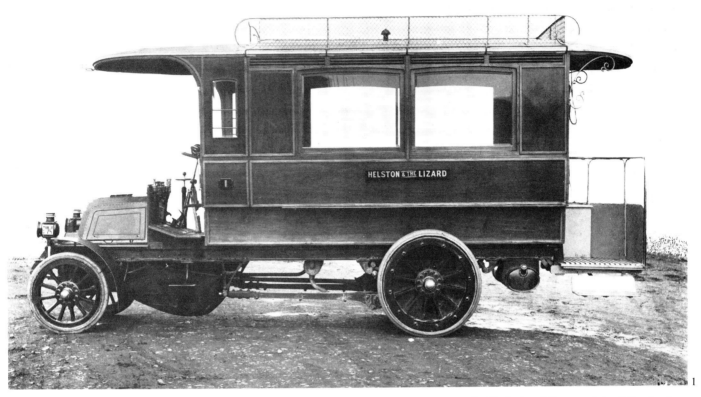

1   Displaying all the rugged simplicity of early motor buses, Great Western Railway No 1, a 16hp Milnes-Daimler of 1903 carrying its second body, complete with Parisian-style rear platform. It was used on the pioneering GWR bus service between Helston and The Lizard. *BR/OPC*

A report published in 1985 by the Adam Smith Institute forecast that the bus would be obsolete by the year 2025 unless competition among operators was encouraged and increased. Even if this pessimistic prophecy proved to be true, the motor bus would have given over 120 years' good service to the people of Britain, carrying millions of passengers every day to school, work, shops, leisure pursuits and holidays. If the heady days of the late 1940s have long since gone, busmen in the 1980s were witnessing a levelling out of the steady decline in passenger numbers — reflecting the continuing role played by buses in the lives of the young and the old, and even in the lives of the car-owning city-dwellers faced with the increasing difficulty and cost of car parking.

Man has always wanted to travel. Some more adventurous spirits, in previous centuries, have tried to travel faster or farther than anyone else. But the common man was always content to live, work and play within a tightly-bounded environment

— often because he had to. To him, transport was a horse or, more often than not, his feet.

The countryman, living by the soil, often lived and died without straying far from his birthplace. Even in the 17th century only the privileged few had personal transport, horse-drawn carriages to move them in relative comfort. Most towns were still small enough to render public transport unnecessary except, again, for the moneyed classes who supported the hackney carriages or used their own sedan chairs.

Paris and London were the exceptions, and for many years they set an example that other towns followed. In 1662 Blaise Pascal set up a service of *carrosses a cinq sols*, horse-drawn vehicles on regular services, but it was a venture which lasted only until 1675. A century later the French and English capitals had grown sufficiently to prompt men to consider new forms of regular public transport. The first mail coach, carrying both mail and passengers, was introduced between Bristol and

London in 1784, and though this was an expensive way to travel, within 50 years there were regular mail coach services all over Britain. By 1820 there were around 1,500 stage coach departures from London each day. This new mobility appealed to the citizens of Britain's fast-growing cities and short-stage carriages were soon to be found on the streets.

Once more the French led the way. In 1819 Jacques Lafitte introduced 18-passenger short-stage coaches on a number of cross-city routes. Four years later Stanislas Baudry, of Nantes, started running coaches between his public baths and the centre of the city. The central stance was outside a grocer's shop belonging to a M. Omnes, and gave the service the name *Omnes Omnibus*. The success of Baudry's service, not only with his bathers, prompted him to seek powers to operate a number of coaches on service in Paris. These were granted, and in 1828 his omnibus started on regular service in the Paris streets with a success that did not go unnoticed. Soon there were competitors for the business that Baudry had generated, and one by-product of this rivalry was the emergence of the man generally credited with the introduction of the omnibus to Britain, George Shillibeer. As a young coach builder in Paris, Shillibeer realised the potential traffic to be explored in his native Britain. He sold up and returned to London, where he built two 22-seat three-horse buses for a regular service between the Bank and Paddington Green or Marylebone Road. This service commenced in July 1829 at a fare of 1s (5p) all the way with an intermediate 6d (2½p) fare to Islington.

The fares, which were cheaper than those charged on stage coaches, soon attracted what Shillibeer described as the 'middling class of trades-people' as a convenient compromise between the hackney carriage and walking. As in Paris there were soon imitators. While Shillibeer had the foresight, his business sense was possibly not so keenly developed. He was bankrupt by 1835 and turned his transport talents to the business of funeral undertaking.

The others thrived and the horse-drawn omnibus went from strength to strength.

2   Cheap railway excursions brought people from all over Britain to the Great Exhibition in London in 1851, and horse-drawn omnibuses carried them to the Crystal Palace. The extra traffic prompted operators to introduce more double-deck buses, and they were of the knifeboard type, with a central back-to-back seat on the upper deck, as shown in this contemporary illustration.
Gavin Booth collection

For several decades the horse omnibus dominated urban passenger transport but its elder brother, the stage-coach, was threatened by a noisy newcomer.

Simple railways, wooden or metal tracks to guide wagon wheels and ease load-carrying, were common in industrial areas. Steam, the power behind the industrial revolution of the 19th century, was soon harnessed for stationary engines, and then for locomotives. The early, crude, locomotives were regarded primarily as an alternative to horse-power for industrial purposes, but George Stephenson and some of his contemporaries realised their wider potential. Stephenson's Stockton & Darlington Railway is widely regarded as the first passenger-carrying steam railway, yet the Liverpool & Manchester, opened five years later in 1830 was really the dawn of the new era — the first railway built primarily for passengers. The railways brought about a change in population distribution. In 1801 only a third of the population of England and Wales lived in towns; 50 years later more than half the population lived in towns, and by 1881 the figure had grown to over 70%.

The 1830s and 1840s were decades of tremendous activity as far-seeing speculators constructed railways all over Britain. At first many passengers treated the railways with some caution. Railway guides even advised the public to choose a coach as far as possible from the engine for 'should an explosion take place you may happily get off with the loss of an arm or leg'. But by 1850 this advice was no longer necessary, and the British public was discovering the joys of travel. The *Illustrated London News* commented at the time: 'One of the most prominent social characteristics of the present time is the growth and progress of pleasure travelling among the people. The working classes of 30 or even 15 years ago did not know their own country. Very few travelled for pleasure beyond a small circle around the places which they inhabited. But now

industrious men of the Midland counties whose forefathers never saw the sea that encircles these islands are enabled to gain physical as well as mental enjoyment by a view of its mighty waters'.

The birth of the railways heralded an end to the golden age of coaching. As the railways built up they bought over stage coach firms to link up with their trains. Stage coaches lingered on for many years in those areas not blessed with the new-fangled railways, but horse-drawn transport in its other roles was far from dead. Passenger transport in towns was to remain firmly horse-drawn until the 1880s, in spite of numerous attempts to change all that. There had been experiments with steam road vehicles, but these were never very successful. High tolls, bad roads and fierce legislation were the main factors against steam coaches, but men like Richard Trevithick, Sir Charles Dance, Walter Hancock and Scott Russell were undeterred by these problems and some of their vehicles were even used in service. Increasing resentment and suspicion, coupled with the appalling state of many roads, combined to dampen the enthusiasm of their inventors. Oddly enough, the steam railways played their part in killing steam coaches; with the disappearance of long-distance stage-coaches, as the railways spread thoughout Britain, the country roads fell into disrepair.

Back in the towns, horse buses were developing fast. In London there was great rivalry between operators, and competing coaches often raced each other for passengers. There were other abuses, too. Many of the buses were poorly built and badly ventilated; some operators overcharged; others misused the Shillibeer name. But 'Shillibeers' did not catch on, and 'omnibus' became the accepted term. The existence of 'Shillibeer's Funeral Carriages' may have hastened this change! The omnibus was a simple vehicle, a box-like structure with two rows of inward-facing longitudinal seats for 12

OMNIBUS'S to the Great Exhibition every ten minutes

EXHIBITION

3 Later horse buses were built to an improved layout with forward-facing seats on the upper deck, although the lower deck seating remained inward-facing because of width restrictions; this layout was adopted for the earliest motor buses. A London General garden seat horse bus of the late 19th century — a fine example of the signwriter's art. *Ian Allan Library*

passengers in all. The *Morning Post* wrote of Shillibeer's Omnibus that it was 'in the shape of a van, with windows on each side, and one at the end'. Entry was through an outward-opening door in the rear wall. A critic described the interior of the early horse bus as 'nothing but a couple of narrow shelves on which passengers are packed like trussed fowls on the ledge of a poulterer's window'. As traffic grew the operators looked for ways of packing more passengers into their buses. The extra bulk and weight, combined with the narrow streets, prevented bigger vehicles so passengers had to be carried on top. The first double-deckers of the 1840s had a longitudinal seat on the open upper deck, but by the Great Exhibition of 1851, held in London's Hyde Park, the 'knifeboard' bus had appeared. This featured a central back-to-back bench seat for an extra 10 persons.

The Great Exhibition was a much-needed shot in the arm for the horse bus. The extra traffic which was attracted into London spawned a whole host of new services and new operators. Among them was one man whose name was to become increasingly familiar over the years, Thomas Tilling who started 'The Times' horse bus service from Peckham to the West End. Right from the start Tilling insisted on civility and realised the importance of regular timetabled services. The Tilling family went on to operate motor buses, building up an impressive empire which was eventually nationalised, ultimately to form an important part of what became the National Bus Company. But we are jumping ahead.

Amalgamation in London
In the 1850s Londoners at least were becoming transport-minded, but once more the French led the way. The Paris horse bus system had been reorganised in 1854, and a similar exercise was proposed for London. The new Compagnie Générale des Omnibus de Londres was registered in Paris, and through British agents it set about amalgamating the existing London bus operators. The new association was welcomed by the public and press. After the Great Exhibition the reduced traffic provoked fresh competition and the poor state of some of the buses combined with the congestion which even then was clogging London's streets to disillusion and confuse the travelling public. The Paris enterprise had started to

take over existing businesses in 1855, ready to start operations in January 1856. There were only 27 General buses at this time, but by the end of 1856 there were over 600 in service. Not all of London's horse bus proprietors sold out to the new company; some, like Tilling and Birch, held out and remained familiar names in the transport world over a century later.

The General company went from strength to strength and became the basis for the giant that is now London Regional Transport. In 1859 the business had been transferred from Paris and became the more familiar London General Omnibus Co.

But while London General gradually improved travelling conditions in the metropolis, there was horse bus activity in most of the other large centres of population in Britain. By the 1860s enterprising businessmen had followed the London example and had set up horse bus services with varying degrees of success. In Glasgow, the appropriately tartan-clad horse buses of Andrew Menzies were described by one observer as 'dreadfully uncomfortable. Passengers on the top deck were exposed to the weather. Inside, there was no ventilation and on wet days the floor was covered by damp, smelly straw!'

There were efforts to improve these conditions, however. London General ran a competition with a £100 first prize for 'the best design of omnibus that, with the same weight as at present, will afford increased space accommodation and comfort to the public'. A Mr Miller of Hammersmith, a coachbuilder, won the prize, but his design was not adopted; instead London General pinched the best ideas from all the entries. They also examined buses acquired from Edinburgh, Glasgow, Birmingham and

Wales in their efforts to gain more passenger space and improve conditions.

It was just as well that the General paid attention to improvements, for in 1881 a new operator took to the London streets. The London Road Car Co gained its strength in the same way as the General, by buying over smaller operators, and it was soon a source of many problems to its rivals. The 'road car' name had been chosen because 'omnibus' had foreign connections — as, of course, had London General. The patriotism of the new firm was emphasised further by the fleetname Union Jack, and the small flag carried at the front. A contemporary broadsheet entitled 'No Surrender', welcomed the newcomers as 'Pioneers of all improvements, handsome cars and cheaper fares'.

Road Car was no cheeky upstart, as General was soon to discover. One of the new company's first improvements was the introduction of a new design of horse bus. Passengers boarded by a proper platform and access to the top deck was by a proper staircase. At first the platform and staircase were mounted at the front, behind the driver, but it soon reverted to the rear, setting a basic pattern that was to remain virtually unaltered on double-deck buses for over 80 years. There was one other important improvement: the upper deck seating was on two-seater transversely-mounted seats, the 'garden seat' rather than the 'knifeboard'.

The arrival of Road Car did much to improve the standard of the horse bus as a vehicle, and of the service itself. For the last few decades of their existence, horse buses enjoyed an Indian summer. So much so that in 1898 *The Bus, Tram & Cab Trades Gazette* could write: 'Everyone

4 **Throughout Britain similar buses entered service in the closing years of the 19th century. Young's of Paisley, later to become well known as motor bus operators, operated this garden seat bus, complete with youthful conductor, on a route that was sufficiently demanding to warrant three horsepower traction.**
R. L. Grieves collection

rides in omnibuses in these democratic days. The character of these useful public vehicles has entirely changed during the past few years, and the old lumbering fusty-smelling coach with its manifold drawbacks has given place to a clean, roomy conveyance in which the comfort of the passenger is studied in every way.'

The success of the railways and of horse buses led men to consider some form of street railway. Needless to say, Paris led the way in 1855, and five years later a young American, George Francis Train, came to Britain to sell the idea to anyone who would listen to him. These street railways were the first tramways and the first successful lines in Britain were laid in Birkenhead in 1860. Horse tramways spread through Britain over the next 20 years, often with horse buses providing connections. The initial cost of the permanent way was considered prohibitive in some centres, but by 1880 most towns of any size had tramway networks.

Steam, cable and electricity

There were other rumblings at this time — quite literally in some cases. Legislation had killed the steam coach, but the steam tram encountered fewer obstacles and in the last 30 years of the 19th century a number of tramway systems employed steam power quite successfully, normally using steam locomotives which towed separate passenger trailers. Other systems, fewer in number, adopted cable traction where the trams gripped a continually-moving cable under the road. This was fine as long as the cable was continually moving, powered by steam-driven pulleys. When the cable

broke — and it frequently did — parts of the system simply slowed to a halt. Britain's best-known cable trams were in Edinburgh, where they lasted until 1923. In the United States the famous San Francisco cable cars still operate to this day.

It took two other Victorian discoveries to change all that — in fact they changed the face of the world. First came electricity, and, more particularly, electricity as a motive power. And just as the world was learning how to use electricity, along came the internal combustion engine.

For a change it was the efforts of the Germans, and not the French, that assisted in the birth of the electric tramway. Or rather the efforts of one particular German, Dr Werner von Siemens, whose name is also associated with early trolleybuses. Using a converted horse tram with an underfloor motor Siemens opened a 1½-mile electric street tramway near Berlin in 1881. In Britain, only two years later, Magnus Volk opened an electric tramway on Brighton beach — a tramway that still operates during the summer season. In spite of Volk's pioneering efforts, and other early efforts in Northern Ireland, Blackpool and the Isle of Man, Britain rather lagged behind in its acceptance of electric tramways. The problems of current collection may have contributed to this reticence for the early tramways relied on third rails mounted between the running rails — or even at the side; in the case of Blackpool the conduit system was used with a cable-style slot between the rails, beneath which was the conductor rail.

There was fresh interest in electric tramways when, towards the end of the 1880s, a successful system of overhead wires and spring-mounted trolleys was developed. Britain's first overhead tramway was opened at Leeds in 1891, and this opened the floodgates. The electric tram became a matter of fervent municipal pride and most towns were eager to augment and replace their horse trams with the new-fangled electric trams which proved to be quicker and cheaper than any previous method of urban transport. They were also smoother at a time when many roads left much to be desired; and they were big and undeniably impressive, beautifully constructed by craftsmen and painted in elaborate liveries that echoed the civic pride. The electric trams encouraged white-collar workers to live farther from their places of work and contributed much to the outward sprawl of many British towns and cities.

The electric tramcar enjoyed its heyday in the Victorian and Edwardian eras, before any of the alternative means of transport had really developed.

Between 1892 and 1910, 105 Corporation and 74 company systems were opened. The first electric system closed down as early as 1917, the start of the constant process which continued until the 1950s/1960s, when the last of the real British street tramways gave way to the motor bus. The tramcar is still very much with us, of course. It never achieved the success in Britain that it has enjoyed in recent years on the Continent, with complex and impressive rapid transit systems far removed from the traditional British concept of the tram. The nearest British equivalent is the Tyne & Wear PTE's impressive Metro system, a light electric railway that is a cross between a reserved track tramway and a conventional full-size suburban railway. And of course three of the pioneering tramway systems still survive — the seafront tramways at Blackpool and Brighton, and the Manx Electric Railway, the equivalent of the Interurbans in the United States.

It is ironic that it 1885, the same year that Blackpool opened its first stretch of conduit tramway, developments were taking place in Germany that would ultimately sound the death-knell for Britain's electric tramways. These developments centred round the internal combustion engine.

Two names are irreversibly linked with the earliest successful experiments to produce motor vehicles powered by petroleum spirit. Karl Benz and Gottlieb Daimler were both working independently to harness the petrol engine to drive a road vehicle and in 1885 they each unveiled the results of their endeavours. At one of the Benz's earliest public demonstrations, an observer recorded: 'Without any sign of motive power, such as that generated by steam, and without the aid of any human element, such as is necessary with a velocipede, the vehicle rolled onwards, taking bends in its stride and avoiding all oncoming traffic and pedestrians. It was followed by a crowd of running and breathless youngsters. Those who witnessed this strange spectacle could scarcely believe their eyes. The suprise was as general as it was great.'

The motor car had arrived, and the continentals were quick to recognise its potential; Benz and Daimler each built buses before the end of the century.

German and French names crop up most frequently in the annals of early motoring, and the first successful British enterprise is remembered, appropriately enough, by the pioneering German name of Daimler.

A young and inventive British engineer, Frederick Simms, met Gottlieb Daimler in 1890. Simms was impressed by Daimler's experiments, and negotiated an agreement by which Simms acquired all Daimler engine patent rights for Britain. In 1893 Simms formed a small private company to handle Daimler products, the Daimler Motor Syndicate Ltd. The syndicate was taken over in 1896 and the Daimler Motor Co Ltd was formed, using a former cotton mill in Coventry to produce private motor vehicles, the first built in any quantity in Britain. Daimler was shortly to enter the bus market too, but that belongs to the next chapter.

Far-reaching effects
The year 1896 was an important one for the motor vehicle in Britain. First there was the Highways Act. This was a serious attempt to update outmoded legislation like the Locomotives Act 1865 (the infamous Red Flag Act, which restricted 'road locomotives' to 4mph in the country and 2mph in towns, behind a man carrying a red flag). The 1896 Act removed the most stringent of the early regulations, and eventually a speed limit of 12mph was fixed.

Another event of 1896 which was to have a far-reaching effect on the British motor industry, both in the private and commercial fields, was the founding of the Lancashire Steam Motor Co. This small firm built steam vehicles, including some buses, and might well have disappeared into the mists of time but for the energetic direction of Henry Spurrier and James

Sumner. Many important orders were secured and in 1897 Spurrier told Sumner: 'If we don't make this firm a success now, we deserve to be kicked. We've got the world by the pants and a downhill pull.' The firm was a success, and in 1907 it became Leyland Motors Ltd, notable as probably the first of the pioneering manufacturers to concentrate purely on commercials, and the foundation of what became the British Leyland empire.

Steam and battery electric buses enjoyed a brief spell of popularity in the last years of the 19th century, following the Highways Act. Some years before, as if in anticipation, a battery electric bus was operated experimentally in London. In 1889 Radcliffe Ward obtained a Metropolitan Police licence for his battery bus, described by the *Financial Times* as resembling 'a large and rather cumbrous omnibus'.

The bus was never used in service but Radcliffe Ward was not discouraged. He introduced a 10-seat single-deck battery bus in 1897 which was intended for service in London, but it, too, never ran in public service. Two years later the Motor Omnibus Syndicate Ltd was equally unsuccessful; this syndicate obtained a licence for a 24-seat double-deck Gillett steam bus, but is was never to run in regular service.

It was 1899 before a petrol-engined bus could be seen in service on London's streets, but the rest of the country was quicker off the mark — the strict control exercised by the Metropolitan Police had a strong influence on the development of the

London bus for many years. Outside London, the wagonette was often the first mechanised public service vehicle seen on the streets. The wagonette was rather like a large private car, with an open rear section containing inward-facing benches. The Edinburgh Autocar Co introduced what is regarded as the first *licensed* urban service in May 1898, using Daimler and MMC wagonettes, although the venture failed in 1901. The licensing system was very vague at this time; there had been earlier motor bus experiments, in various parts of Scotland and England in 1897, though these had not been licensed. The wagonette enjoyed a brief success, though by 1905 it had been replaced by vehicles which were more bus-like and less car-like.

Back in London there was a new threat to the established bus and tram services — the underground railway. The first underground railway, the steam-worked Metropolitan, had opened in 1863, but the real threat came in the 1890s/1900s. The first *electric* tube railway was the City & South London opened in 1890, and this was followed by the Waterloo-Bank line in 1898. These early lines had a noticeable

5 The very first licensed urban motor bus service was introduced in May 1898 by the Edinburgh Autocar Company between the city's Post Office and Haymarket. It used this Daimler wagonette, a heavy motor car typical of many used on pioneering bus services, seen here displaying its post-1904 registration number. *Gavin Booth collection*

6 The London Road Car company competed with London General for horse bus business and was equally hesitant about the new-fangled motor bus. This Belgian-built Germaine of 1904 featured a horizontal engine under the driver, and the body was clearly descended from the horse buses, adapted to suit the mechanised chassis. Just out of the top of the photograph is a Union Jack mounted on a flagpole, a symbol intended to draw attention to General's French roots. *Ian Allan Library*

effect on the buses operating on parallel routes, creaming off the longer-distance traffic and leaving the buses to provide a feeder service. With the opening of the Central London line in 1900 — the 'twopenny tube' — the horse bus proprietors realised that something had to be done to combat this new competition. But what?

London's population had doubled in the period 1851-91, and by 1901 had reached a staggering 6,500,000. This combination of factors prompted many of the experiments with mechanical buses, and one of the most important experiments was the operation of two Canstatt Daimlers (built in Germany) with 26-seat former horse bus bodies, between Kennington and Victoria from October 1899 to December 1900. Therefore, as Charles E. Lee observes in *The Early Motor Bus*, 'the twentieth century opened without a single motor bus regularly plying in the Metropolis'.

During the early years of the new century there were many experiments with mechanised road vehicles in all parts of Britain. The records are incomplete as there was no formal vehicle licensing on a national basis. In London the Metropolitan Police kept a close eye on all such developments, and elsewhere it was left to all the diligence of the local Watch Committee. Often there was literally no licensing at all. For this reason we know more about activities in the metropolis than about the developments in the rest of the country.

We do know about two events of 1903 which were to create important precedents. Eastbourne Corporation had rejected the idea of a tramway system and sought and obtained Parliamentary powers to operate buses within the borough; on 12 April it started motor bus services with four Milnes-Daimler 16hp single-deckers. This first municipal enterprise was not without its critics, for only four months later a protest meeting was held in the town 'condemning buses and calling for a proper system of electric trams'.

Farther west, between Helston and Lizard in Cornwall, the Great Western Railway started a bus service. This first ran on 17 August, and again used Milnes-Daimlers, 16hp 22-seat wagonette-type vehicles. These petrol buses had originally been bought to run in conjunction with the Lynton and Barnstaple Railway, but there was such strong local opposition that they were soon sold to the GWR. The Helston-Lizard service was the GWR's answer to demands for a light railway — the bus service was to test the market without incurring too much expense — the estimated cost of the railway was £85,000. This was not the first railway bus service; there had been steam buses operated by the Belfast and Northern Counties Railway in 1902 and, of course, the Lynton and Barnstaple's short-lived experiment, but the GWR service is particularly important as the first step towards the largest of all the railway bus fleets.

The petrol-engined motor vehicle was still very much a novelty at this time, a plaything for the rich, not to be taken too seriously. The traditionalists grumbled that 'a carriage and pair is fast enough for anyone — comfortable, safe, and smart; moreover, it is certain to reach its desired destination'. The Continental manufacturers still led the way, with France and Germany in the lead — it is interesting to note that it was not until 1906 that car production in the United States exceeded that of France.

In Greater London in 1901, 848 million passenger journeys were made. Buses carried 270 million, trams 341 million and local railways carried the rest. In London in 1901 these trams were still mainly horse trams for the metropolis was surprisingly slow to adopt the electric tram which was by then a common sight throughout Britain. The London United Tramways service from Hammersmith to Shepherds Bush which started in 1901 was London's first proper electric service, but the electric tram was never really allowed to develop in London as it had done in many other centres in the country.

Unrealistic legislation

The design and development of the early motor bus was largely hampered by unrealistic legislation. The Government tended to assume that all buses were either mechanised horse buses — admittedly some of them were — or large motor cars like the wagonettes already mentioned. Pressures from bus proprietors and manufacturers prompted the Motor Car Act of 1903 which raised the speed limit for 3-ton vehicles to 20mph, and also introduced vehicle registrations with effect from 1 January 1904. Further legislation,

Early rivals

Throughout the country enterprising men were setting up companies to operate buses. Many of these ventures were destined to be short-lived, but others laid the foundations of firms that are with us today. In the southeast of England, for instance, two companies were formed during 1904 that were later to merge as part of the Southdown undertaking. The Sussex Motor Road Car Co actually started operations that same year, initially with two Clarkson steam buses. The Clarksons were unsuccessful, and were soon sold and replaced by Milnes-Daimlers; but the company was successful. According to *The Southdown Story*, 'there was an enterprising, even, one might say, a faintly swashbuckling air about its doings that is not unattractive'. This was just as well, for a rival company, the Worthing Motor Omnibus Co, was formed towards the end of 1904. Inevitably there was soon competition, particularly for the Worthing-Brighton service, and the more firmly based Worthing company survived the Sussex company which went into liquidation within a few years.

There were many reasons for the early demise of so many motor bus companies. The drivers and mechanics were dealing with unfamiliar machinery, and the buses themselves were still very crude and prone to breakdown.

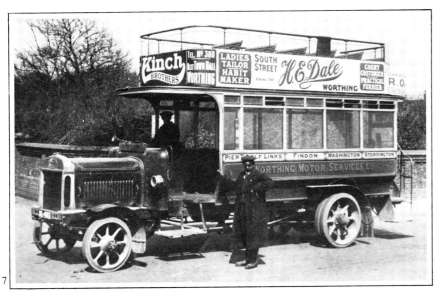

7 **An early Leyland X type double-decker of Worthing Motor Services, with Dodson 39-seat body. It passed with the business to Southdown in 1915.** *H. J. Snook*

the Heavy Motor Car Order of 1904, raised the unladen weight to 5 tons at a top speed of 12mph.

All of this activity at Westminster played a decisive part in the real birth of the bus, and 1905 is widely regarded as the birth date. In 1904, however, the seeds were sown.

The event of 1904 that helped the fledgeling industry develop was the introduction of the Milnes-Daimler 24hp 34-seat double-decker at the Crystal Palace Motor Car Show in February. Daimler patents had been used for many of the earliest petrol engines, and in 1902 the old-established tramcar builders G. F. Milnes & Co Ltd entered an agreement with the German Daimler company to build Daimlers under licence in Britain. Originally 16hp single-deckers were built and these could be fitted with both enclosed single-deck saloon and enlarged wagonette bodies. But the 1904 double-deck model represented an

important landmark in the story of the British bus, the first really practical, purpose-built bus, setting a pattern that was largely unchanged until 1919. The driver sat behind the engine in the open but under a canopy that kept him reasonably dry, if nothing else. The enclosed lower deck had inward-facing seats for 16, with access from the rear platform. The outside staircase led to the 18-seat open upper deck which had forward-facing seats. The high-built wooden body still had many traces of its horse bus origins, but it was to be many years before bodybuilders broke away from this concept.

The Milnes-Daimler double-decker was an instant success, and many of the pioneer motor bus fleets started operations with small fleets of these buses. Two of London's pioneers in 1904 were certainly not new to bus operation. On 30 September Thomas Tilling Ltd, a successful horse bus operator since 1851,

placed three Milnes-Daimlers in service in London; 11 days later another two Milnes-Daimlers started running in London for Birch Bros Ltd. The Birch family were also horse bus owners but their motor bus venture was less successful than Tilling's. J. M. Birch later recalled that 'the roads were very bad, the machines very unreliable, the drivers very inexperienced and the maintenance staff ignorant'. The Birch family pulled out of the motor bus business after only three years and by 1912 had given up their horse buses as well. They were to return, though, as coach proprietors.

Where were London General and London Road Car while Tilling and Birch were introducing regular motor bus services to London's streets? To be honest they were rather slower to appreciate the potential, although at the same time as the Tilling and Birch Milnes-Daimlers started to run both General and Road Car were experimenting with single-deck steam buses. These were 14-seat Chelmsfords, built by Thomas Clarkson, whose name will crop up again in this story, and Road Car had two and General one. Urban single-deck buses enjoyed a brief spell of popularity at this time but relaxed regulations allowed double-deckers to flourish. The London horse bus reached its peak in 1901 — 3,736 buses, of which almost half were owned by General.

Between 1899 and 1904 a total of 92 motor buses had been licensed by the Metropolitan Police in London, 79 single-deckers and 13 double-deckers, and even as 1904 drew to a close there were only 17 motor buses in service in London. Five of these were the Tilling and Birch Milnes-Daimlers already mentioned; London Power Omnibus Co had nine Scott-Stirling single-deckers; London Road Car had one Germaine and one Dürkopp; and London General had one Orion 26-seat double-decker. This was General's very first petrol-engined bus, a horse-bus body on Swiss-built Orion chassis. In spite of General's lack of success with its mechanical experiments it was beginning to realise where the future lay. The company chairman admitted that General had 'studied the causes of their failure', and had 'observed various difficulties gradually surmounted'. He went on: 'We feel the time has now come when services of motor omnibuses can be successfully run by us.' To support this new-found confidence General set aside £20,000 for experiments with motor buses. London Road Car, too, started to move in the same direction with a large order for motor buses. Even so they were still a long way behind the Great Western Railway whose 36-strong motor bus fleet was, ironically enough, the largest in the country in 1904.

But big things were about to happen in 1905 — and that was just the start.

After each chapter the *Checkpoint* page provides a summary of the period covered, with a background of world events; significant dates in the story of passenger transport in Britain; a *Milestone* — a brief portrait of an important bus type; *Profiles* of typical single-deck and double-deck types; and a *Sign of the Times* — a piece of printed material that captures the mood of the time.

Events

1662	Blaise Pascal starts regular horse-drawn service in Paris.
1784	First mail coach service, Bristol-London.
1829	Shillibeer's horse bus service in London.
1851	Great Exhibition in London generates new traffic.
1856	Compagnie Generale des Omnibus de Londres (later London General Omnibus Co) starts operations.
1860	First street tramways in Britain, at Birkenhead.
1883	First municipal tramway, Huddersfield.
1885	Blackpool conduit tramway system opens. First practical motor cars from Daimler and Benz.
1889	Experimental battery bus in London.
1891	First British overhead electric tramway, Leeds.
1896	Daimler Motor Co formed. Lancashire Steam Motor Co formed — later Leyland Motors. Highways Act.
1898	First licensed urban bus service, Edinburgh.
1899	First petrol-engined buses in London.
1901	London's first electric tram (LUT).
1903	First municipal bus services, Eastbourne. Great Western Railway starts Helston-Lizard motor bus service.
1904	Vehicle registration system introduced. Milnes-Daimler double-deck bus introduced.

World Events

1887	Queen Victoria's Golden Jubilee.
1889	Eiffel Tower built.
1890	Forth Bridge opens.
1895	Marconi invents wireless telegraphy.
1889	Start of Boer War. Aspirin invented.
1901	Britain's first submarine launched.
1903	First powered aircraft — Wright brothers.
1905	Automobile Association founded.

Sign of the Times

Electric tramcars were objects of fierce municipal pride at the turn of the century, and many contemporary postcards prominently featured trams. This card of Station Road, Doncaster, shows several typical early open-top trams.

Gavin Booth collection

Milnes-Daimler

It was 1904 before pioneering British bus operators could buy a vehicle that offered an acceptable standard of reliability. This bus was the Milnes-Daimler, a collaboration between G. F. Milnes & Co, the British tramcar builders, and Daimler of Germany. In 1903 early Milnes-Daimlers, 16hp buses, helped inaugurate the municipal bus service at Eastbourne, and the GWR Helston-Lizard service, but the 24hp double-deck model is the version best remembered. The simple layout of the Milnes body set a pattern that others followed; seats were provided for 34 (18/16). The Daimler engine drove through a constant mesh gearbox; final drive was originally by chains, but a differential type back axle was soon adopted.

The Milnes-Daimler became a popular choice with operators like GWR, and London independents Birch, Tilling and Vanguard, and by 1907 represented one-third of the London bus population. A 28hp version appeared in 1907.

The re-formation of London General in 1908, and the combine's decision to develop its own buses, affected Milnes-Daimler's market, and the German connections caused problems during the World War 1. The company was wound up in 1916, but not before its models had done much to set the bus industry on the right course.

Profile

The types covered in the *Profile* feature are based on typical single-deck and double-deck buses of the period. Although they are actual types, they are intended to represent all types, to show in graphic form the development of the motor bus, changes in size, engine position, door position, seating capacity and general layout.

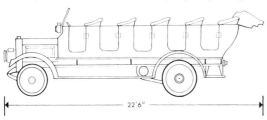

22'6"

Engine at the front, chain-drive to the rear wheels, charabanc body with door to each row of seats; hood folded at back for use in inclement weather; oil lamps; solid-tyred wheels. 18 seats.

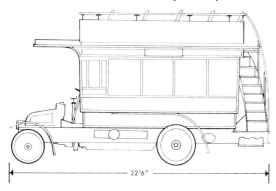

22'6"

Double-deckers used similar chassis to single-deckers; body similar to horse bus style, high-built with rear platform and staircase. 34 seats (18 upstairs/16 downstairs).

The Milnes-Daimler was the first reliable double-deck bus built in quantity, and featured in many pioneering fleets. This was the Lancashire & Yorkshire Railway's first motor bus, a 34-seat Milnes-Daimler new in 1907.
Ian Allan Library

The novelty of our car
1905-18

In the first years of the 20th century the motor bus had taken its first faltering steps towards its serious acceptance as a means of public transport. The first part of the story seems strongly London-biased because that is the way it was; London's requirements for public transport were inevitably the greatest in Britain, but the growing industrial towns and cities were setting their own patterns. The railways still carried the majority of longer-distance travellers with, in country districts, horse or motor buses providing connections from stations to outlying villages. In most towns the electric tram was the predominant mode of transport and again the bus provided feeder services, often linking tram termini with new housing developments or with less accessible spots where the cost of new permanent way would have been prohibitive.

This short-distance role was not adopted voluntarily. The motor bus was still far

from reliable and rural roads did not encourage comfortable long-distance travel. Town roads, though better, were well served by the electric tram, still a fairly recent addition to the urban scene and one that represented heavy civic investment. In any case, the fast and comfortable tram compared favourably with the simple, often unreliable, solid-tyred motor bus.

To be honest, the population was still not motor-minded. Even London General, by far the biggest horse bus operator in Britain, remained vocally pro-horse until about 1910. In 1909, Mr Aubrey Fell forecast that '20 years hence motor buses will be exhibited as curios in museums' — no doubt expressing a personal hope, for he was Chief Officer of London County Council tramways.

The motor bus therefore had to prove itself and establish its role in the overall transport pattern. Some regarded the bus

8 The novelty of early motor buses was such that passengers were prepared to put up with considerable discomfort to sample them. Admittedly, this 1908 Commer featured a Lindley preselective gearbox, but the 'bodywork' was fairly basic — wooden bench seats and rugs for this happy band of 26 pioneer travellers, complete with manually operated horns, front and rear. *Ian Allan Library*

as second-line transport, complementary to trams or underground trains; others with more vision foresaw the days when the flexibility of the motor bus would threaten the future of the tramways — perhaps even the railways. By 1905 some of these men were already active, and although the structure of the bus industry does not really come within the scope of this book, it is useful to look at nine brief case histories in the feature panel to illustrate a trend that was gradually emerging.

Britain catches up

After the Continental domination of the early years, it is interesting to note that most of the new maker's names appearing in the case histories were of British origin. Home manufacturers were at last starting to catch up and between 1905 and 1919 foreign-built buses virtually disappeared; similarly, the British manufacturers who relied on Continental patents evolved designs of their own. The needs of the London motor bus operators and the strict legislation imposed by the Metropolitan Police tended to dictate the fashion for the rest of Britain. London was clearly the biggest potential motor bus market and ambitious manufacturers were naturally anxious to carve themselves a slice.

Names like De Dion, Orion, Lacoste & Battman, Dürkopp and Germaine made way for the home-produced chassis. In spite of the plethora of new British motor bus builders, there was very little difference in the basic layout of their early products. Like the trend-setting Milnes-Daimler of 1904 the typical chassis was essentially straightforward and uncomplicated. The four-cylinder petrol engine was mounted at the extreme front, over the front axle. The size of the engines varied, usually 20-40hp; to transmit the power from these strong, low-speed engines to the solid-tyred rear axles, most manufacturers fitted the differential unit to the chassis and drove each rear wheel by a side chain. The distinctive chain final drive

of early motor buses worked well, if noisily, but gradually the worm-driven differential rear axle was developed and improved, becoming universally fitted.

The manufacturers of the day merely offered a commercial chassis for sale — the customer used it as he wished. Consequently the high-built straight chassis were equally at home with double-deck, single-deck or charabanc bodies and were also used for lorries. Some operators took advantage of this imposed versatility; double-deck and charabanc bodies were often swapped to cater for weekday commuters and weekend excursionists. In fact, many smaller operators fitted a lorry body during the week and a charabanc body at weekends. The only people who did not benefit from the adaptability of early commercial chassis were the passengers, who had a stiff climb into those early buses and a rough ride once they were there — and it was to be many years before these problems were overcome, but great design advances were being made. *Commercial Motor* commented in 1912 that 'the modern motorbus is "noiseless" compared with that of 1906, when it habitually travelled in a series of jumps, partly by reason of clutch deficiencies, partly by reason of gearing deficiences, and partly by reason of ignition deficiences'.

In the last chapter we looked at the Milnes-Daimler double-decker which set a trend which remained largely unchallenged for 15 years. The equivalent single-decker

9 The confident frontage of the Great Eastern company's works and garage in London reflected the mood of these early operators. Posed outside is a 1908 Arrol-Johnston, built in Scotland.
Ian Allan Library

was in most respects a double-decker without the upper deck and staircase, but the charabanc was quite different. A development of the horse-drawn charabanc, the motor charabanc enjoyed tremendous success in the early motor years. Very often it gave Britons their first experience of the motor vehicle and opened up a new market in leisure travel as the charabancs reached out to seaside or countryside which had previously been too far for comfortable day outings.

The driver and the passengers sat together in an open body on full-width seats which were usually reached by side doors, one door on each side to each seat. There was a hood folded at the back for the often-inclement weather, which provided cover at the top, but not at the sides. Some charabancs had permanent top covers with open sides, while some vehicles, not charabancs in the strictest sense, had a raised rear portion, essentially for better vision. The *Worthing Gazette* described the appearance of a Sussex Motor Road Car Thornycroft at Worthing in 1908: 'The new type of vehicle is a sort of wedge-shaped pattern, the several successive rows of seats being placed tier above tier, so that the upper part of the charabanc is raised very considerably above the front section.

It weighs about five tons in all and is licensed to carry 32 passengers.'

Not all of the new British commercial vehicle manufacturers were destined to achieve the success they sought and very few of the names of 1905 are still with us. Some, like Arroll-Johnston, Scott-Stirling and Straker-Squire, lasted for only a few years; others, like Albion, Dennis, Maudslay, Thornycroft and Wolseley were to remain familiar names for very much longer — though not necessarily on buses. Inevitably, many operators favoured local products, and this ensured respectable sales figures. Other makes were more widespread, like the Milnes-Daimler already described.

The Milnes-Daimler and the Straker-Squire, another popular model in the late 1900s, were built in Britain, but Milnes-Daimler used German Daimler designs, while the Straker-Squire used German Bussing patents.

New ideas

The new British designs were not always entirely conventional, though. Among the pioneers were some innovators, and there were lessons to be learned from their original thoughts — although often as not their efforts convinced other manufacturers *not* to follow suit.

There was Thomas Clarkson, who had been trying hard to sell his steam buses for several years. Clarkson built the Chelmsford steam buses which London General and London Road Car used in

10 The pioneering railway bus operator in Scotland was the Great North of Scotland, which operated a sizeable fleet on services feeding from its stations. These well-laden 1913 40hp Maudslay 18-seat buses were operating between Ballater, Balmoral and Braemar, on Deeside. *Ian Allan Library*

11 Bus manufacturers had barely started in business when they were exploring new ideas. The British Daimler company, formed in 1896, built this unusual model, the KPL, in 1910. It had no separate chassis, four-wheel brakes, petrol-electric transmission, two underfloor 12hp engines, and a covered top. This adventurous concept was killed off by a patent infringement action raised by Tilling. *T. W. Moore collection*

1904, and in 1905 Road Car received the first of a number of Clarkson double-deckers. The Clarkson steam bus was a neat and relatively successful design but Clarkson, like so many of his contemporaries, relied on London orders. When London General decided to abandon steam in 1909, Clarkson created work for his buses by founding the National Steam Car Co which built up a fleet of around 180 of these unusual vehicles. National changed over to petrol buses when the Clarksons came up for replacement and Clarkson himself left the company to set up in business outside London, a decision which was to have an important effect on the later development of company buses.

Another unusual model of the time was Daimler KPL, an amazingly advanced double-deck model. Built by the Coventry Daimler firm, the type name was derived from the initials of Knight, Pieper and Lanchester, who designed the engines, transmission and worm drive respectively. The KPL introduced many advanced features: there was no separate chassis, for the underframe and body were constructed as one all-steel unit; there were brakes on all four wheels; it had petrol-electric transmission; and the two 12hp engines were mounted beneath the main structure, each driving a rear wheel. Tilling raised a patent infringement action which effectively killed off both the KPL and Daimler's attempts to form a bus company in London to operate them.

The Tilling objection covered the petrol-electric transmission, for the Tilling management had been interested in the possibilities of petrol-electrics for some time. The consequent lack of gears and a clutch made it easier for horse bus drivers to adapt to motors. Tilling-Stevens was a joint venture between Thomas Tilling and W. A. Stevens of Maidstone, and the company's first TTA1 double-decker entered service in 1911. The Tilling fleet was the main TTA1 operator, but they were sold commercially and Tilling-Stevens achieved reasonable success with successive petrol-electric models over the years. In 1924 Tilling sold its manufacturing interests but Tilling-Stevens continued to build buses for many years, though more often than not these were to conventional designs after the mid-1920s.

Another operator with an interest in developing a reliable bus suited to its needs was SMT, based in Edinburgh. William Thomson, as engineer of the company, was looking for something better than the Maudslays and Ryknields which had helped to put SMT on its feet, and started on his new design in 1910. It was a long process but Thomson knew what he wanted, and, as one of his colleagues recalled later, 'he was a difficult man to argue with'. SMT's first home-made bus,

Case histories

The financial backers who founded the Scottish Motor Traction Co in June 1905 could have had no idea that their optimistically baptised brainchild would, in fact, literally live up to its name, for within 25 years SMT became parent company of the SMT group, basis of today's Scottish Bus Group. One man can take much of the credit for the success of the venture, William J. Thomson, a Caithness man who became the SMT's first engineer. He drew up a stringent set of requirements which he expected his buses to reach. Several different types of motor bus ordered for trial purposes failed to meet his conditions, that a top speed of 12mph should be achieved and that the bus should be able to reach 3mph on a 1 in 3 gradient, fully loaded. Only one make fulfilled his conditions, a 40hp double-deck Maudslay, and nine 35-seat double-deckers were ordered to start SMT's first public services, on 1 January 1906. The local press failed to appreciate the importance of this event as little mention was made in their pages; possibly they pre-judged SMT as yet another over-ambitious upstart. This was not the case of course, and SMT went from strength to strength, initially with Maudslays and Ryknields, and eventually with an advanced home-made vehicle.

Just south of the Scottish border another small bus operator was becoming established, the first steps towards a widespread empire, and carrying a name that is still very familiar today. E. B. Hutchinson's United Automobile Services had actually been formed to take over some Great Eastern Railway routes in East Anglia in 1912, but the next year another branch of the business started operations in County Durham, in the Spennymoor-Bishop Auckland area. Like most of the early motor bus operators, United's development was steady but slow until the end of World War 1. Then in the mushrooming 'bus mania' of the 1920s United expanded at both ends, until it eventually covered a vast area of England, from the Scottish border down to East Anglia. The area was soon split, leaving United to operate mainly in Northumberland, County Durham and parts of Yorkshire.

The British Electric Traction Group was an active product of the 1890s, its purpose being the carriage of passengers and goods and the generation and distribution of electricity. Ironically, it was not only an electric tramway pioneer but also a motor bus pioneer, and its buses were to supersede the trams, laying the foundations for a huge company bus empire which was only absorbed in 1968 by the Tilling group. The Barnsley & District Electric Traction Co was formed by BET in 1902 to operate tramways in and around Barnsley. Only 11 years later the company started a bus service in an area where tramway extension was impossible, using five Brush-bodied Leyland single-deckers costing £822 each. The buses flourished, and the trams floundered, to the extent that the word 'Electric' disappeared from the company name in 1919; a more radical name change in 1928 reflected the expansion which the buses had permitted — the Barnsley-based fleet became the Yorkshire Traction Co.

Another BET venture was the Potteries Electric Traction Co, operating in North Staffordshire. The first PET trams ran in 1899 and only two years later the company was experimenting unsuccessfully with steam buses. In 1905 three Brush-Mutel 25hp double-deckers were bought to provide feeder services for the main tramway routes, but these too were unsuccessful. PET's next bus venture was more significant, when four Daimler single-deckers appeared in 1914; although the buses were impressed for military service in World War 1, they returned to form the basis of a large fleet. The PET trams were finally withdrawn in 1928, killed not only by the company's own buses, but

12   The cameraman and the bus were both novelties in Bellsquarry in the early days of the Scottish Motor Traction company — so much so that this was produced as a commercial postcard. The bus was one of SMT's original batch of 1906 Maudslays, with an 'improved' style of radiator. *George Waugh collection*

by the unrestricted competition of the 1920s which brought a total of 81 bus operators into Stoke on Trent at one stage. The company's old name lasted until 1933 when the familiar and more appropriate title Potteries Motor Traction — PMT — was adopted.

In the thriving city of Birmingham there were several early attempts to promote motor bus services. The Birmingham Motor Express Co started operations in 1903 with three single-deck Napier-engined Mulliners. The company required additional capital the following year and the new Birmingham & Midland Motor Omnibus Co was incorporated to take over the Express company; in 1905 various BET bus interests, motor and horse, were transferred to the new company. The original BMMO company was, rather surprisingly, unsuccessful and motor buses were abandoned in 1907 — in favour of horse buses! With better vehicles the BMMO motor buses bounced back in 1912 and went from strength to strength. Midland Red, as the company became universally known, was at one stage the largest company bus fleet in Britain.

Birmingham also had one of the early municipal bus fleets. The Corporation introduced 10 double-deck Daimler Y types on tramway extension routes in 1913, and in 1914 entered an area agreement with BMMO which included the transfer to Birmingham Corporation of 30 BMMO Tilling-Stevens double-deckers.

The coming of the motor bus to Oxford was quite a different matter. In 1881 the City of Oxford & District Tramway Co started running with four horse trams, and inevitably electrification of the system was soon being actively discussed. The main difference at Oxford was that electric trams never did run in the streets. While various interested bodies were busy talking, Mr W. R. Morris announced that he was to introduce a motor bus service in December 1913. This he did with two Daimler Y type double-deckers which ran in competition with the horse trams; inevitably the trams suffered. Morris's Oxford Motor Omnibus Co bought more Daimlers and operated them equally successfully — so successfully, in fact, that the tramway company offered to run buses instead of the proposed electric trams. Thomas Tilling also wanted to run buses in Oxford, and the three rivals submitted vehicles for inspection late in 1913. Licences were granted to Morris and to the tramway company, but when the tramway buses appeared Morris withdrew to avoid wasteful competition. The Morris name was not destined to disappear; soon he was involved in the lucrative business of building the cars which carried his name, for this was the same William Morris who later became Lord Nuffield, whose factories generated much business for the company which in 1930 had adopted the more familiar name City of Oxford Motor Services.

Bristol, always a busy and go-ahead city, was fortunate in having the Bristol Tramways & Carriage Co as its local operator. The company's horse tram system had been electrified in the last years of the 19th century, and in 1905 it was testing a Thornycroft bus. The outcome of this trial was the first regular bus service, which started on 17 January 1906. Not only did Bristol Tramways quickly appreciate the potential of the motor bus but the company also built its own chassis starting in 1908. The motor side of the business grew rapidly; by 1914 there were over 60 miles of bus routes, served by 44 buses and 29 charabancs. Ultimately both Bristol Omnibus (the operating company) and Bristol Commercial Vehicles (the manufacturers) became notable names in the British bus business.

When BMMO withdrew from motor bus operation in 1908, Sidney Garcke bought six Brush double-deckers and brought them to Deal, in Kent. Using three of the buses — with the other three as spares, Garcke started regular services in April 1908. There had been earlier motor bus experiments in East Kent, but Garcke's Deal & District Motor Services was the most succesful and soon there were other operators chasing the passengers. The shortages and other problems of World War 1 prompted Garcke to engineer a merger between these companies and in 1916 the East Kent Road Car Co was formed to take over the five main competitors. The new fleet inherited 72 buses, a mixture which included Albions, Commers, Daimlers, Leylands, Straker-Squires and Tilling-Stevens.

13 The first motor bus operated by the Bristol Tramways & Carriage company, a Thornycroft Type 80 with United Electric Car body, on its first day of public service, 17 January 1906, in the centre of Clifton. *M. J. Tozer collection*

the appropriately-named Lothian, emerged in 1913. Most novel of the Lothian's many features was the driving position, which was alongside, rather than behind, the engine. This allowed a high seating capacity within the dimensional regulations of the time, and pioneered a layout which rapidly became accepted as standard throughout the country.

Around 90 Lothians were built for SMT between 1913 and 1924, and some even received pneumatic tyres. The Lothians soldiered on in regular service until around 1927, when they were relegated to lighter and duplicate journeys. Even so, a number lasted until 1930, a considerable tribute to their construction in an era of short-lived buses.

Steady growth in London

After its slow start the motor bus really established itself in London during the decade after 1905. From the 17 motor buses licensed in London at the end of 1904, the number grew steadily. There were 230 by the end of 1905, 1,000 by March 1908, and 2,000 by 1913, and not all were owned by General, Road Car or the other former horse bus proprietors like Tilling or Birch. In March 1905 a completely new motor bus operator appeared, the London Motor Omnibus Co trading under the fleetname Vanguard, which was displayed prominently on the sides, starting a new trend.

14 On service between Herne Bay and Canterbury, an East Kent normal-control Daimler (complete with AEC radiator) of 1919. *M.&D. and East Kent Bus Club*

Vanguard started with five Milnes-Daimlers and stole a march on its competitors by obtaining a priority on deliveries from the Milnes-Daimler works. The Vanguard fleet grew rapidly — 36 buses by October 1905, 159 a year later, 366 a year after that. The well-run Vanguard fleet soon represented a serious threat to the longer-established names who were faced with the problems of replacing their horse buses, converting existing garage premises and re-training staff. The Continental manufacturers were quick to cash in on this situation though with varying success. The De Dion chassis was popular with London General and dominated the fleet for a few years.

Paying the penalty

As the fleets grew, so did the rivalry — and inevitably this became wasteful. Things seemed to happen too fast. In 1907 *Tramway & Railway World* said 'The motor bus business in London was rushed. It came before its time. The mechanism of such a vehicle had not been duly perfected, and the pioneers have now to pay the penalties.' After a bad year in 1907, when a fatal combination of low fares and bad weather brought extra problems to London's bus operators, General, Road Car and Vanguard got together to find a satisfactory solution. The outcome was a merger in 1908 and a new, big London General company. The new combine owned 885 of the 1,066 buses in service in London at the time, dominated by 356 Straker-Squires, 312 Milnes-Daimlers, 165 De Dions and 75 Wolseleys. All but 51 were petrol-driven.

15 **Typical of many early motor bus interiors, with upholstered inward-facing seats, necessary because of the restricted width, and a railway-style opening window in the front bulkhead. This is, in fact, a GWR vehicle.** *BR/OPC*

Frank Searle was the new combine's chief motor engineer and faced with such a mixed collection of buses he set about designing an efficient vehicle for fleet replacement. His design was seriously affected by new Metropolitan Police regulations, issued in 1909, which laid down very stringent guidelines for operators in London. Buses had to be no more than 23ft (7.01m) long, 7ft 2in (2.18m) wide, with a maximum of 34 seats (18 up/16 down), and, worst of all, no more than 3½ tons unladen (6 tons laden). Such a low unladen weight was virtually unheard of, and at first it was feared that the regulations would stunt the growth of the motor bus. Undaunted, Searle worked on.

The new General company had inherited a useful factory at Walthamstow which had been used by Vanguard to build and repair vehicles, and here Searle built his first X type, a double-decker which satisfied the Police requirements. It went into service late in 1909 and Searle later wrote: 'In the manufacture of the X type we cribbed shamelessly; any part of the 28 types which had stood up to the gruelling of the London streets were embodied in it.' This caused some critics to describe it as the 'Daimler-Wolseley-Straker' type, but its success was to confound them. Experience with the X type led to Searle's second design for General, one which was certainly a further milestone in the story of the British bus — the famous B type which first entered service in 1910.

Here was the first standard bus — a purpose-built, reliable and efficient vehicle that did a lot to put the General company back on its feet and sounded the final death-knell for the horse bus. The year following the introduction of the B type, the last General horse bus was operated. The last in London was a Tilling bus in 1914, but the last regular horse bus in Britain — between Newcastle and Gateshead — lingered on until 1931. Around 2,900 B types were built, mostly double-deckers, and most had a 30hp four-cylinder engine, a three-speed gearbox and a worm-driven rear axle.

The B type gave London General the firm foundation it required. The motor bus network grew rapidly and early General bus maps proclaimed proudly 'Open Air to Everywhere' as the bus swept onwards and outwards.

The other manufacturers suddenly found themselves with two big problems. There was the effect of the Metropolitan Police regulations, which was gradually overcome by new, lighter designs; then with the B type there was the virtual disappearance of their biggest potential source of business. There was not such an easy answer to this one. Leyland, eager for a foothold in London, invested in the London & Suburban Co, which became London Central, and eventually New Central, with a sizeable fleet of Leyland double-deckers. Thomas Clarkson, as already described, had similar ideas, and so did Daimler with its proposed Premier fleet of advanced KPL buses. Daimler wanted Frank Searle to be general manager of Premier, but when General and Tilling conspired to bring the patent suit against Daimler, the operating plans were dropped and instead Searle was lured away to start Daimler's commercial vehicle department. Not surprisingly the new Daimler 40hp CC double-decker, bearing a strong resemblance to the B type, appeared in 1912 and after a certain amount of wheeling and dealing Searle won an order for 350 buses from the BET Group. These were mainly for a BET subsidary in London, the Tramways (MET) Omnibus Co; this new operator was formed by Metropolitan Electric Tramways to run in association with the MET trams, mainly as a safeguard against the prospect of increased competition from London General.

While all this was happening General was undergoing yet another change in ownership. The Underground Electric Railways Group saw the expanding and improving General as a threat to its underground railways, started buying up General shares and assumed control early in 1912. Under its new masters General bought up some of its competitors and entered into agreements with others. Tramways (MET) was acquired in 1913 and Daimler found that General did not wish to continue the maintenance contract which was part of Searle's deal with BET; instead, Daimler was appointed as sole selling agent for any surplus chassis produced at Walthamstow.

General's bus-building activities at Walthamstow had also been affected by the change of control. The Underground Group felt that sales of Walthamstow products to outside operators was hampered by the connections with General. So the connections were severed and a new Underground subsidiary, the Associated Equipment Co, was formed. Under its more familiar initials, AEC, the new firm soon started to sell to a wider public.

As the motor bus became more reliable it became more widely accepted throughout Britain. Its main function was

16   **Many of the buses requisitioned by the War Office in World War 1 were from London General's huge fleet of B-type double-deckers, the first standard bus, and one that proved its worth in the difficult role of transporting troops to the battlefields of France and Belgium.**
Ian Allan Library

still short-distance urban transport, but there were far-sighted operators exploring longer-distance bus services, and there was the growing charabanc business already mentioned. A development of this which reflected the increasing reliability of the bus was the introduction of extended tours. Surprising as it may seem, Chapman's of Eastbourne offered a six-day North Wales tour as early as 1910, using a Dennis 22-seater. The success of this venture prompted Chapman's to expand the programme and soon passengers were setting off on a 21-day tour to John o'Groats! Other companies followed this lead, like Standerwick of Blackpool and Worthing Motor Services. The Worthing firm adopted the title Sussex Tourist Coaches and ran its first extended tour, to the West Country, in June 1913. A passenger wrote of the large crowd which greeted the tour at Exeter, apparently attracted 'by the novelty of our car'. Clearly, the motor bus was still far from universally accepted and even then there was a new competitor on the scene.

Enter the trackless

The trackless car, or trackless trolley, was the forerunner of the trolleybus, which was to enjoy the peak of its success in the 1930s. Werner von Siemens can take much of the credit for the invention of the trackless car but it took commercial enterprises to bring these new hybrids to Britain. Railless Electric Traction was one of the main firms attempting to interest British operators in trackless cars and these attempts included practical demonstrations, as at Hendon, London for MET in 1909, and visits to inspect systems on the Continent. Dundee, Leeds and Bradford Corporations all sent deputations to Europe in 1908-09, and all showed a keen interest in this new type of urban transport. Leeds and Bradford were sufficiently interested to apply, successfully, for powers to run trackless vehicles. The first parts of the two systems started within days of each other in 1911; Leeds probably won the race to operate Britain's first trolleybus in service, but

Bradford had the more questionable honour of operating Britain's last, over 60 years later. Or so it seemed.

The trolleybus does not strictly belong in this book, except as a rival for the motor bus, but it is interesting to recall just how some of the early systems fared. Most of Britain's trolleybus pioneers were in the northern part of England; where as well as Leeds and Bradford there was Rotherham, Keighley, Ramsbottom, Stockport, Teesside and Mexborough & Swinton; but there were also outposts in Wales, at Aberdare and Rhondda, and in Scotland, at Dundee. The Dundee system was particularly interesting; as early as 1908 a deputation of Corporation officials visited Germany to inspect trackless systems and were suitably impressed. 'The trackless trolley system of traction', they concluded, 'is undoubtedly practicable and well suited for routes where the traffic would not warrant the construction of an ordinary tramway, and the sub-committee are satisfied that there is more likelihood of success with this system than any other.' In this same enthusiastic mood, Dundee Corporation opened its trolleybus system in 1912 — and closed it in 1914. The short life of the Dundee system was attributed more to the Corporation's reluctance to spend enough money on road improvement than to any doubts about its efficiency or its financial performance.

With the demise in Dundee there remained only eight trolleybus systems in Britain when World War 1 broke out in 1914. The war inevitably affected public

transport throughout Britain. There was little material damage to bus, tram or trolleybus systems, but there was a growing shortage of suitable staff and this led to interrupted services and played havoc with regular maintenance. Bus operators suffered from vehicle shortages as the War Office commandeered suitable motor buses for military service. Only the petrol-electric buses were really safe as the War Office chose not to requisition them. London General's large motor bus fleet was a popular source of vehicles for war service; General temporarily lost more than 1,500 buses, mostly B types, and many of these were sent to the battlefields of Belgium and France.

The shortage of petrol brought extra problems to the operators who were still able to maintain bus services — often essential services to military and naval establishments. Many bus companies overcame the fuel problem by running on coal gas carried in cumbersome gas balloons fixed to the bus roofs. These gas buses were crude, but guaranteed a service that could not otherwise have been provided.

World War 1 brought the development of the motor bus grinding to an abrupt stop. By 1918 the buses that were returning from war service were often in poor condition, for at the time the average lifespan of a bus was only five or six years. The setback was only temporary, though; the war had proved the versatility of the motor vehicle, and the next decade was to see a dramatic and exciting renaissance.

Events

1905 First Vanguard services (London Motor Omnibus Co).
1906 First bus services by SMT and Bristol Tramways.
1907 Lancashire Steam Motor Co renamed Leyland Motors.
1908 New London General Omnibus Co formed.
1909 National Steam Car Co founded. Top-covered double-deck buses, Widnes. London General introduces X type bus.
1910 First LGOC B types built.
1911 First British trolleybuses, Leeds and Bradford. Tilling-Stevens TTA1 introduced.
1912 United Automobile Services formed. Underground Electric Railways buy London General. Associated Equipment Co (AEC) formed. Daimler CC model introduced.
1913 First SMT forward control Lothian bus.
1916 East Kent company formed.
1917 First complete electric tramway closure, Sheerness.

World Events
1908 First Model T Ford car.
1909 Bleriot flies Channel.
1912 Sinking of *Titanic*. Scott reaches South Pole.
1914 Outbreak of World War 1.
1918 Armistice signed.

Sign of the Times

The importance of the Great Western Railway as a customer for early motor buses was reflected in contemporary advertising. Maudslay featured this 12-seater in a 1905 trade advert. *Gavin Booth collection*

LGOC B type

Re-formed in 1908, the strengthened London General company decided to develop its own buses, based initially on the best features of its 885-bus fleet. The X type of 1909 was an amalgam of the Milnes-Daimler, Wolseley and Straker-Squire, and from it came the legendary B type of 1910.

A light but sturdy machine, designed to meet the exacting and restrictive legislation of the time, the specification was typical of the time — 25hp engine, cone clutch, chain gearbox, 34-seat body — but if the B type was unadventurous, it was designed for mass production, the first bus built in this way. By 1912 LGOC was turning out about 28 B types a week, and when production ceased in 1919 around 3,000 had been built. Not all were double-deckers, for there were charabancs, single-deck buses, lorries and parcel vans on the same chassis; and not all were for General, for AEC had been formed in 1912 to build and market LGOC's 'home-made' buses, and there were provincial customers.

The development of the motor bus quickly overtook the B type, but its importance in creating the London bus system cannot be underestimated.

Profile

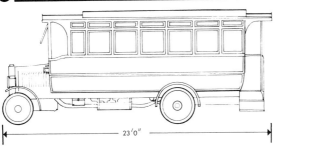

Driver still behind engine (normal control), although protected from elements by windscreen (except in London). High-built body on straight-framed chassis; rear entrance. 22 seats.

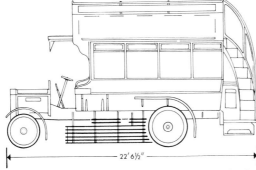

Little apparent difference from pre-1905 vehicle, but constantly improving in terms of reliability. 34 seats (18/16).

London General's B-type bus combined all the best features of its predecessors, and was produced in large numbers on a production-line system. During the General Strike in 1926 General buses were used for the transportation of troops by the military authorities. Two General B-types in Hyde Park. *Ian Allan Library*

Greater comfort and far greater mobility

1919-28

17

Many people might remember the 1920s as a period of unrelieved economic gloom. True, there was severe and prolonged unemployment — during the decade there were never less than one million unemployed in Britain; for others though, living standards rose with the increase in owner-occupied housing and the growth of new council estates.

The bus certainly blossomed in the 10 years following World War 1, but it was not a controlled development — indeed at times the cut-throat competition suggested that the fledgeling motor bus industry had a death-wish. Competition was certainly the keynote of the period, and this competition had several effects. It forced all sections of the bus industry to take stock and resulted in vastly improved vehicles, sensibly-integrated groups of companies and proper all-embracing legislation. Tramways and railways suffered as the motor bus grew in stature, while the bus itself faced new problems from the increasing popularity of the pivate car. In transport, at least, the Twenties were certainly Roaring.

The war played its part in convincing many people that the motor vehicle had a rosy future. The success of the mechanical involvement in the war proved this to the faceless men in authority, while actual experience with motor vehicles persuaded many newly demobilised men to invest their gratuities in transport as a business. And there were many men eager to help former Tommies to realise this ambition by selling them chassis.

Initially these were often vehicles reconditioned after war service, medium-size and simple chassis like the RAF-type Leyland, Daimler Y and Thornycroft J. The new chassis offered by the British builders were little different in 1919. The established bus operators had lost many of their buses during the war and were anxious to restock; for convenience they took chassis types that were basically

17 Generally regarded as the first true daily long-distance motor coach service, the Greyhound Motors service between Bristol and London started in February 1925 and from 1927 used four 'super de luxe buffet coaches', ADC 416As with Strachan & Brown bodies which were fitted out to a particularly high standard. AEC

1914 designs. The keen newcomers to the bus industry were at first forced to follow suit but when a veritable flood of foreign chassis was released on to the British market they had less chauvinistic qualms than their established brothers.

This new invasion force started its attack on Britain in the early 1920s, plugging a glaring gap in the domestically-produced ranges. They came from France, Italy and the United States, and they were cheap, small and fast — on pneumatic tyres. Pneumatics for commercial vehicles were still being developed at this time and could only be used satisfactorily on lighter commercials. Most of the imported chassis were in the 14-26-seat range, and were designed as passenger vehicles; they were not the dual-purpose goods/passenger types normally available in Britain.

The instant success of these imports introduced many new names to Britain's roads, and the best-remembered names sold in reasonable numbers, like the Chevrolets, GMCs and Reos from the United States, and the Fiats and Lancias from Italy.

Competition on the streets

Armed with these fast and attractive little buses, bus operators sprang up all over the country. Some pioneered new routes while others elbowed their way on to existing services. A quick profit was the common denominator throughout and often there was nothing in the way of a formal timetable — buses ran as and when prospective passengers appeared. There were sometimes literally dozens of one-bus operators on some of the best routes and the outcome of such unrestrained rivalry was inevitable. Some busmen fell by the wayside; some went on to consolidate their position by acquiring their less organised contemporaries; others banded together to strengthen their position, and a few of the 'safety in numbers' co-operatives of the 1920s survive to this day. The operators who lacked business acumen often more than made up for this with a brand of low cunning. Buses literally raced each other for passengers; buses turned short to pick up customers; buses happily switched routes if the driver thought there were better pickings elsewhere. But it would be wrong to suggest that these attitudes were universal. Some operators were well organised, with proper timetables and schedules, efficient staff and a proper regard to the provision of a public service. These, it is interesting to add, were the firms which usually survived and which are often still in business today.

The arrival of the foreign chassis added considerably to the number of different makes which British operators could buy. By 1926 there were more than 55 makes of bus chassis on the British market; just over half of these were of British origin, with 12 from the United States, seven from France, two from Italy, two from Switzerland and one from Belgium. Not all of these firms were successful. Far from it. Many were unable to survive in this highly competitive field, while others decided to concentrate on truck chassis. The sales of foreign buses gradually tailed off towards the end of the 1920s as British builders started to catch up. After the slow recovery from the war, the success of the light foreign chassis spurred the main manufacturers into action, and a look at some of the more popular models illustrates the advances. By 1926 there were at least 30 home-produced bus chassis

on the market, with another dozen from the Continent and as many again from the United States. And there were more than 60 builders competing for the bodywork orders.

This was essentially an era of single-deck development for the use of the double-decker was still relatively restricted outside London. The most important new models were, therefore, single-deckers, and the Leyland Lion is probably the best-remembered product of the time. Leyland's five-model L range appeared in 1925, the Leopard, Lion, Lioness, Leveret and Leviathan, all conceived as passenger models and consequently lower-built and more refined than the previous goods-cum-passenger chassis. Of the five new models only the Lion was a real

18

19

18 Municipal operators were largely committed to their electric tramway systems, but increasingly used motor buses for feeder routes and to serve new housing developments. This 1920 Birkenhead Corporation Leyland O-type had Leyland 32-seat bodywork. *Leyland*

19 Many new bus services were started in the 1920s using normal-control buses, although these were typically smaller than this 1926 AEC 414 with 26-seat Strachan & Brown body, used on the service between Burwell and Cambridge operated by the Burwell & District company; this independent outlasted many of its contemporaries, and sold out to Eastern Counties in 1979. *AEC*

success in sales performance. More than 2,500 Lions were sold in four years, and this put Leyland back on its feet after a difficult period immediately after the war.

The Leyland Lion LSC1 — subsequently the PLSC1 — was a forward control model with the driver sitting alongside, rather than behind, the 5.1-litre four-cylinder petrol engine. It had a plate clutch and four-speed sliding-mesh gearbox. Leyland-built bodies were fitted to a good many of the Lions produced, for Leyland had a thriving bodybuilding department for many years.

In the 1920s it was common practice for operators to get local builders to body their bus chassis; the days of the really big national bodybuilders supplying to the whole country were still to come. British bus operators have always indulged in the strange practice of buying chassis at one end of the country, which are then bodied in another part of the country, and possibly then delivered to a third, quite different, part of the country. Only a few of Britain's chassis builders have tried to provide a complete service and Leyland has been most successful. Leyland's functional wooden-framed body style for its Lion chassis was a much-imitated classic of its time.

The rash of important chassis had brought a wider acceptance of forward entrances, immediately behind the front wheels. Other than charabancs, most single-deckers previously had rear entrances, often on platforms double-deck style. Now forward entrances were in vogue, although the rear entrance had its advocates as did the centre entrance — and there were operators who tried to improve passenger flow with two doors, front and rear.

The Leyland Lion is the best-remembered model of its generation, but it was not the first. In 1924 Maudslay introduced its ML range, a comprehensive selection of models of different sizes and layouts; the Maudslay 4.94-litre, four-cylinder petrol engine was most commonly fitted to this steady-selling range. The ML featured four-wheel brakes — previously buses had rear-wheel brakes only — and the combination of four-wheel brakes and pneumatic tyres made motor buses safer and more predictable. Four-wheel brakes rapidly became standard, and solid tyres were rare on new buses by 1925, and non-existent by 1930. As the other manufacturers caught up, a rash of new models hit the market and the most significant were the full-size forward control single-deckers with four-cylinder petrol engines, and suitable for 25ft (7.62m) long, 32-seat bodies; chassis like the Tilling-Stevens Express, the Bristol B, the Dennis E and the Albion PM28.

New fields

Some manufacturers chose to explore new fields and the latter part of the 1920s is often remembered as the heyday of the rigid six-wheel motor bus. The pioneering German builder Bussing was the first large-scale producer of six-wheel buses, and in 1923 had introduced three-axle buses on pneumatic tyres. Guy and Karrier were two of the early advocates of six-wheelers and goods models were soon followed by passenger models, first from Karrier in 1925 and then from Guy in 1926. Karrier's 1925 prototype was a normal control single-decker and an improved version, the WL6, went into production in 1926, and about 160 single- and double-deckers were built until the model was withdrawn in 1930.

Many advantages were claimed for the six-wheeler including greater safety, better riding comfort and improved fuel and tyre economy. Certainly the early six-wheelers hastened the acceptance of pneumatic tyres on heavy passenger vehicles, and the use of single rear wheels increased internal

20 Early buses had few problems with other traffic, and this Bristol Tramways vehicle virtually had the road to itself. The Bristol company had started building its own buses in 1908, and this 4-ton chassis with Bristol 31-seat body dated from 1926. Ian Allan Library

body space. The six-wheel bus was a convenient way around the current Ministry of Transport regulations governing the maximum weight on each individual axle. By spreading the load, longer buses were possible — some were up to about 30ft (9.14m), roughly 5ft (1.52m) longer than the average four-wheel bus of the time. This allowed higher seating capacities, 40 on a single-decker and 66-72 on a double-decker, and in larger towns and cities this extra capacity was very useful.

Guy's first six-wheeler created quite a stir when it was first revealed in 1926; not only was it the firm's first six-wheeler, it was also a double-decker — again Guy's first! The Guy BX was a normal control model with 5.1-litre engine, and was followed by the forward control FBKX in 1927. Sales of this truly massive-looking bus were quite healthy, and improved models stayed in production until 1933. The Guy was involved in intense rivalry between manufacturers shortly after its introduction in 1926, to see which make would first appear on service. Guy won the race in the provinces, at home-town Wolverhampton in July 1926, but another Guy was beaten to the post in London by a London General ADC in June 1927. It is interesting to note that the first General six-wheeler was a 68-seater, twice the seating capacity of the legendary B type of just 17 years before.

The life of the six-wheel motor bus in the provinces was largely confined to the 1920s and 1930s. Some operators continued to buy the double-deck chassis that were

available right until 1939, and the six-wheel single-decker was to enjoy brief spells of popularity in the 1930s and, more surprisingly, in the 1960s. London was the main protagonist of the six-wheeler, though its interest can be traced from the end of the 1920s, first on a large fleet of motor buses and then on its huge trolleybus fleet. These will be examined more closely in a later chapter, but it is appropriate at this point to take a look at London in the 1920s — to go back, in fact, to 1919 to see the war-ravaged and reduced London General fleet struggling to maintain its services.

In the early days of the motor bus London's requirements had set the fashion for the rest of the country, but in the 1920s the absurdly strict limitations imposed by the Metropolitan Police, coupled with General's inability to move with the times, meant that the design of the London bus was generally out of step with developments in the rest of the country.

London General entered the post World War 1 era with a smaller operational fleet than it had in 1914. Many of the buses requisitioned for military service never returned, while others were in poor shape. As a temporary measure around 100 lorries were fitted out as simple buses, and these

lorry buses helped to reduce some of the problems caused by the postwar demands on public transport. A new standard design of London double-decker was quickly produced and the first of 1,132 K type buses appeared in 1919.

The K type was a joint development by AEC and General, both, of course, members of the Underground Group. The AEC chassis had a 28hp four-cylinder engine, a multiplate clutch and a chain gearbox. The open-top General body was flush-sided with wheel arches, permitting extra interior space. For the first time General was able to fit transverse seats on the lower deck, thus increasing the seating capacity to 46 (24/22), 12 more than on the B type. The open rear platform and staircase was similar to the B type, though wider, but the main advance was the adoption of a forward control layout. As *Motor Transport* reported at the time: 'Increased accommodation for passengers is gained through saving the space that the driver at present occupies between the bonnet and the body of the vehicle. The bonnet is built up to the front of the omnibus itself, and the driver sits on the right-hand side in a recess cut in the bonnet and protected by a shield. He sits higher up, and as the exhaust gases escape on the

21 The famous Birmingham & Midland Motor Omnibus Company — Midland Red — built its own buses between 1924 and 1970 and gained an enviable reputation for producing practical and technically-advanced vehicles. This 1924 SOS 31-seat bus represents the first type designed and built by BMMO at Birmingham. The domed roof and domed top to the entrance are unusual features. *Midland Red*

left-hand side, he is much cooler than on the older type.'

The K type was certainly an advance on previous London buses, though the poor driver in his exposed position at the front might not have agreed so readily. Outside London, drivers had been happily and safely enclosed in cabs or behind glass windscreens for at least 10 years — and it was to be another 10 years before buses in service in London would be permitted this 'luxury'. A longer version of the K, the 35hp S type, followed in 1920, with seats for 54 passengers; in all, 928 S types were built.

The K and S types helped London General to rebuild its postwar fleet, but it was not enough to combat the new enemy on the London streets — the independent

busmen, the so-called 'pirates', that appeared in competition from 1922.

Just as the independents could not buy AECs, General's connections with AEC — and probably its innate pride — prevented it from shopping around for more and faster chassis to allow more even competition. General was, however, developing a better double-deck model which was a definite advance on horse bus concepts of the B, K and S, and which proved a transition between these early designs and the sophisticated new models of the late 1920s.

The new model, the NS (standing, apparently, for *Nulli Secundus* — second to none) was designed from the outset as a low-built, pneumatic-tyred, covered-top bus, and no doubt General saw it as the answer to its pirate problems. Unfortunately the Metropolitan Police did not see it quite the same way, and the first NSs of 1923 were open-topped, on solid tyres. Like the K and S before it, the NS was a forward control model but the poor driver was still exposed to the elements. About 2,400 NSs were bought by General between 1923 and 1930 and AEC sold

NS-based chassis on the open market as the 409 and 422 models. The last General NSs were able to appear as the design was originally conceived. They had pneumatic tyres, first introduced in 1928, and they had top covers, from 1925. The driver did not have a windscreen, but special NSs for working through the Blackwall Tunnel did have full enclosed staircases.

Pneumatic tyres were first seen outside London on lightweight single-deckers in the early 1920s and were eventually developed to suit heavier single-deckers from around 1923 and six-wheel double-deckers from 1926. The Metropolitan Police resolutely held out until 1925, and in that year pneumatics were permitted on General's single-deck K types; two years later they were fitted to General's six-wheel LS double-deckers, but they were not allowed on NSs until 1928.

Covered tops had been successfully fitted to double-deckers long before the birth of the NS. Widnes Corporation had four covered-top Commers in 1909, and Liverpool and Birmingham led the way in the 1920s. But the Metropolitan Police insisted that 'no canopy or similar superstructure will be permitted on the roof of an omnibus constructed to carry passengers on the top deck'. The poor passengers found an ally in *Commercial Motor*, which commented in 1919: 'The objection of the police as licensing authorities to any proposals to this end has been the raising of centre of gravity of the vehicle, but the existence of fair grounds for this objection has never been tested, and in any case, it can be met by underhanging the springs, so lowering the centre of gravity materially.' The Metropolitan Police stuck firmly to this view until public opinion, and reports of satisfactory operation outside London, persuaded them to permit top covers from 1925. A press report of the time described the top-covered NS: 'Passengers find them much more comfortable than the old type of bus which is being replaced. There is room for 28 passengers in the padded top-deck seats, handrails up the gangways, sliding plate-glass windows, rubber padded — a real luxury vehicle. They do not appear unwieldy and the public are enjoying the experiment of riding in a covered bus, and during a rainy spell, instead of there being a scramble for the inside seats, the competition is to get to the

Monopoly threatened

On 4 August 1922 London General had a virtual monopoly of bus services in the metropolis. The following day an independently-owned brown-painted Leyland double-decker appeared on the famous route 11 and started a reaction that was to have far-reaching effects on London General and on the design of the motor bus. The full story of the London independents — the pirates, as they became popularly known — does not really belong here, but some background notes will give some idea of the scale of the competition confronting the General.

The Chocolate Express Leyland prompted a slow trickle of other independent operators to venture on to the lucrative General routes. In just over a year this trickle had become a steady stream — and by 1925 there were over 600 independent buses on London's streets. Inevitably, the independents concentrated their efforts on the money-spinning routes, competing not only with General but also among themselves for traffic. Their methods were not always entirely ethical and on many occasions this competition verged on open warfare with buses literally racing each other for custom. It would be wrong to suggest that all the independents adopted these tactics, for there were many responsible and dedicated men among the new London busmen.

These were not only exciting years, they were colourful too, for distinctive liveries and fleetnames were worn by the independents. In addition, their buses were different. The products of General's associate AEC were obviously unavailable, so Leylands, Dennises, Straker-Squires and Thornycrofts flooded the streets. There was, of course, no route licensing at the time and the operators had only to satisfy the Metropolitan Police that their vehicles were roadworthy within London restrictions. The manufacturers, eager to break into the London market, built special buses designed to suit the London regulations.

Leyland's fast and reliable normal control LB chassis was popular with the early independents, as was the Dennis, again a normal control vehicle. Two forward control chassis which could be found in many independent fleets in London were the Straker-Squire and the Thornycroft J. The Straker-Squire was not the most reliable vehicle of its time, as Clem Preece recalls in his book *Wheels to the West*. Early in his long and varied transport career Preece went into partnership as an independent bus operator, and he remembers the A type Straker-Squire as 'mechanically very advanced for its time. The vehicle certainly had a high power/weight ratio and, despite solid tyres, was quite fast — unfortunately it tended to shake itself to pieces as a result. For the cut and thrust of pirate bus work, the quick acceleration and speed were a great advantage, if only the vehicle could have been more reliable'.

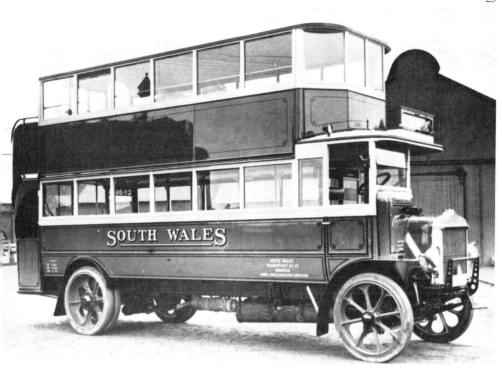

top and look at the unfortunate people on the old buses shrinking under waterproof sheets.'

While London top-deck passengers fared better from 1925, London bus drivers were exposed to all weathers until 1929, when glass windscreens were allowed at last — around 20 years after operators throughout the rest of Britain.

In spite of all these problems, the NS was an important step forward. Its low build made life easier for passengers, and it helped London General to fend off the competition from the independents. A correspondent in *Commercial Motor* in 1925 suggested that General 'would not have been stimulated to build the admittedly excellent NS type but for the new competitors'. There is probably more than a grain of truth in this, but with General, bus replacement was a major exercise. Any new London design has a long gestation period and ideally should be adaptable enough for a long production run. The NS certainly fulfilled this requirement, for the basic design was sound enough to permit the later additions, pneumatic tyres, top covers and driver's windscreens.

The last NSs were, strictly, built by ADC, rather than AEC. In 1926 AEC combined with Daimler's commercial vehicle business to form The Associated Daimler Co, to 'market all standard types of AEC and Daimler omnibus, motor coach and commercial chassis previously manufactured and sold by Associated Equipment Co Ltd and the Daimler Co Ltd.' Both AEC and Daimler-designed chassis were built, normally offered with a choice of AEC or Daimler engines. The alliance was fairly short-lived and in 1928

the two firms returned to their separate ways; in fact they remained quite separate until coming together, more forcibly, under the British Leyland umbrella in 1968.

One purpose of the ADC set-up was to allow AEC to complete the transfer of production from the old Vanguard works at Walthamstow to a new factory at Southall, and when AECs — complete with the familiar triangle badge — started to appear from Southall they were, inevitably, simply developments of ADC designs. AEC's most exciting bus chassis of the 1920s really belong in the next chapter, and so too do the far-reaching developments which led to the restoration of General's monopoly. But in the mid-1920s General was still battling with the so-called pirates, and the situation was rapidly getting out of hand. The official reaction was the 1924 London Traffic Act which restricted the number of buses permitted to operate on certain streets and obliged operators to submit schedules for approval. Operators could not always get permission to run on the routes they chose and they were required to provide all-day services. Deprived of the quick-change traffic-chasing tactics of the early independent days, many of the smaller operators fell by the wayside. Some simply disappeared, while others merged and others sold out to General. Although a few independents held out for five or six more years, by 1928 the pirate threat had all but disappeared.

Competitors all round

So much for competition within the bus industry; what of the competition from

other sources? Just as the 1920s witnessed a dramatic leap forward by the motor bus, the decade was equally important for the motor car.

Between 1919 and 1924 the number of private cars on Britain's roads quadrupled; between 1924 and 1930 this total doubled again, and by 1930 there were over one million cars in Britain. These figures were boosted by models like the Austin 7 of 1922 (selling at £165) and the 1928 Morris Minor (£125). Motorcycles, too, enjoyed a boom in the 1920s — their peak year was 1930, when 724,000 were licensed.

The railways, on the other hand, did not enjoy much prosperity in the decade after World War 1. Run down after the war, the railway companies reorganised in 1923, and no sooner had the four new main line companies emerged under the Grouping than they began to realise that the bus was a serious competitor. From 1925 there was a long and bitter fight between the bus and railway operators as they both sought wider official powers. The railways were actively campaigning for powers to operate bus services; there were still the railway bus services, but the main line companies were thinking on a much grander scale.

The success of the motor bus was also having its effects on tramways, and although there were 14,000 trams in Britain in 1924 — the all-time maximum — the tram was already in decline. During the 1920s 34 smaller electric tramways systems were replaced by motor buses, and in the same period another 11 systems were replaced by trolleybuses, for the trackless tram was still in the ascendant. True, some of the earliest systems had already closed down, but there were some important converts in the 1920s — future strongholds like Wolverhampton, Ipswich, Darlington, Doncaster and Maidstone.

The year 1925 really saw the birth of the express and long-distance network we know today. The actual date can be accurately pinpointed, for on 10 February 1925, Greyhound Motors of Bristol inaugurated an express service to London, the first daily long-distance express coach service in Britain — and probably in the world — and undercutting the parallel GWR train service. Two solid-tyred Dennises started the service, but pneumatic-tyred AECs were soon added. In 1927 four 'super de luxe buffet coaches' were added to the Greyhound fleet,

Coaching for all seasons

Leisure travel by bus continued to spread in the 1920s, firstly in charabancs, and with the introduction of more suitable, lower-built chassis from 1925, in fully-enclosed 'all-weather saloon coaches'.

'The charabanc of the postwar period was a cumbersome monstrosity mounted high on a chassis which swayed dangerously on corners', wrote *Tramway and Railway World* in 1930, adding that 'owing to its solid tyres and inadequate springing, (it) provided little in the way of comfort for its occupants'. The 29 intrepid passengers who set out in July 1920 in 'one of Mr Alexander's handsome and well-appointed motor charabancs' on an extended tour to John o'Groats might well have agreed with these sentiments, but *The Falkirk Herald* reported at the time that it had been 'a delightful tour', and that the passengers had presented Mr and Mrs Alexander with a solid silver set of tea knives. Spurred on by this success, no doubt, Mr Alexander went on to start bus services in the Falkirk area, and Alexanders became one of the main company operators in Scotland.

The new motor coaches prompted operators to consider longer-distance services; soon after World War 1 there were regular trips to the seaside from London, and from 1921 Midland Red was operating seasonal trips from Birmingham to resorts like Llandudno and Weston-super-Mare.

24

24 A happy band of travellers aboard 'one of Mr Alexander's handsome and well-appointed charabancs', a 1923 Tilling-Stevens.
Gavin Booth collection

ADC 416s with Strachan and Brown bodies. A contemporary report describes these amazing vehicles, and emphasises the tremendous advance over the charabanc: 'The latest type of omnibuses put into service on this route are each divided into three main sections, the front and largest of them containing 18 seats, arranged in the conventional manner, the centre having on one side a lavatory, and on the other a small buffet; while the rear part, which is the smoking saloon, contain seats for eight persons. All these seats are padded and covered with red antique leather, and are fitted with head rests. At the back of each seat, for use by the passenger in the seat behind, is a small oval mirror, together with a gusseted pocket for holding newspapers and such-like articles. By pulling a tab a small table is unfolded, which is arranged in a position convenient for holding a lunch tray. Beside each seat is a bell-push for summoning the steward; and a further convenience is found in the electric light switch controlling the roof light installed over each seat.

'Heat from the engine exhaust can be directed and used to provide warmth for the interior. . . . At the back of the driver's compartment there are a clock, barometer, flower vase, an umbrella stand, and a cabinet for cigarettes . . . in the steward's cabin there is a sink and draining board, and large cupboards for food, drink,

25 The charabanc opened up the countryside for many, and new operators appeared in all parts of Britain. J. H. Whitlark & Co Ltd, based at the Royal Forest Hotel at Chingford, Essex, had this smart normal-control AEC with a typical charabanc body — note the side running-boards, the doors for each row of seats, and the folded hood at the rear. The garage in the background sports a fine selection of enamel signs. *AEC*

25

cutlery and china. Water is drawn from a 20-gallon tank on the roof, on which the luggage is also carried. The very latest refinement upon all these carefully thought-out details is the provision made for wireless and loud-speaker.'

The principal firms handling the growing traffic between London and the seaside towns formed London Coastal Coaches Ltd in 1925, and recognised the need for a main coach station in London. In 1928 they started using a fairly basic site in Lupus Street, but the demand for coach travel outgrew the site, and in a few years a more permanent solution had to be sought.

A step forward

Leyland's next new chassis range represented an even greater advance. The Lion and its stablemates of 1925 had taken the design of the motor bus an important

stage further. The new 1927 range was an even more significant development, introducing six-cylinder petrol engines as standard on bus chassis. The two main models, the Tiger and Titan, were for single and double-deck bodies respectively, and were an instant success.

The Titan did more to popularise the double-decker for provincial work than any other chassis. When the TD1 was introduced at the 1927 Commercial Motor Show, it caused a minor sensation, as it was quite unlike anything that had been seen before. As a complete vehicle, with Leyland body, it weighed about 5¾ tons, and the 6.8-litre petrol engine, producing 90bhp at 2,000rpm, proved more than adequate.

The bodywork represented a marked advance, with its distinctive 'piano-front', and it was particularly significant in being the first to successfully employ the

lowbridge arrangement with sunken upper deck gangway, a layout that lasted for 40 years until superseded by the Lodekka and its imitators, and the rear-engined chassis. By 1929 many Titan TD1s were being fitted with enclosed-staircase bodies, but some operators continued to specify open stairs. The lowbridge Titan was the standard

26 **Luggage space on long-distance coaches in the late 1920s was usually on the roof, and roof racks were still a feature on some coaches 20 years later. These Alexanders Leyland Tigers are loading on a wet Glasgow day with passengers and luggage for Aberdeen.**
Gavin Booth collection

26

model until the Hybridge model was introduced in 1930.

One of Leyland's advertising slogans of the late 1920s was 'Bury your tram with a Titan', and there can be no doubt that many municipalities did just that, as the TD1 offered the first serious alternative to the ubiquitous tramcar. The Titan, too, helped many people to overcome their natural suspicion of double-deck buses as the low centre of gravity inspired the confidence needed, particularly when the Titans were widely used on rural and interurban routes.

One-time general manager of the big Southdown company A. F. R. Carling described the Titan TD1 as 'a well-sprung, low-loading double-decker . . . designed from the first for pneumatic tyres, which offered, if not quite the capacity and durability of the tramcar, certainly

something much nearer them than anything available before, and it combined these advantages with the greater comfort and far greater mobility of the bus'.

Without any doubt the 1920s can be regarded as the principal formative period of the bus industry as it is today.

It is remembered as an exciting period, but one whose excesses inevitably led to new controls and an altogether more responsible attitude to public service.

Some statistics dramatically illustrate the rise of the bus in the 1920s. In 1921 there were 48 bus-operating municipalities, with 649 buses carrying 74 million passengers; by 1930 there were 100, with 4,737 buses carrying 823 million passengers. Two company fleets which grew up in the 10 years after the war were United, with a far-flung empire in eastern England, and SMT, operating mainly in central and

27 **The Great North Road between London and Newcastle was a popular route for early long-distance coach operators, and this Gilford CP6 with Strachan & Brown 20-seat body, encountered weather problems on the A1 north of Baldock in March 1927. Owned by Orange Bros of Bedlington, the Gilford was a fast and popular chassis of the time.**
R. L. Grieves collection

southeast Scotland. United had 64 buses in 1919, and 619 in 1928. SMT operated 1,040,000 vehicle miles in 1919, and 10,500,000 in 1928. Dramatic growth indeed.

Events

1919 LGOC introduces K type double-decker.
1920 LGOC S type introduced.
1922 Pirates compete with LGOC services.
1923 LGOC NS type double-decker.
1924 Maudslay ML range appears.
1925 Leyland L range unveiled.
First daily express coach service, Bristol-London.
1926 Karrier WL6 introduced — three axle.
Guy BX introduced — three axle.
AEC and Daimler form Associated Daimler.
Dennis E model with four-wheel braking.
1927 Leyland Tiger and Titan ranges.
Fageol Twin Coach, USA.

World Events

1922 BBC begins broadcasting.
1923 Grouping of main line railway companies.
1925 Baird invents television.
1926 General Strike in Britain.
1927 First talking film, *The Jazz Singer*.
1928 First Mickey Mouse film.

Sign of the Times

Charabanc trips opened up the countryside for many Britons, and this Lancia turned up on several postcards, purporting to be in different parts of the country.
George F. T. Waugh collection

Leyland Titan TD1

The single-deck bus developed fast in the 1920s, while double-deckers were little better than buses of a decade before. London General's NS type of 1923 was lower-built than its predecessors, but it was 1927 before significant mechanical advances were made. The Leyland Titan TD1 was a low-built, modern bus, with a smooth six-cylinder petrol engine. The Leyland body style was decidedly different — the forerunner of a style that was to be developed over the next 40 years. The upper deck structure extended over the driver's cab, and the first TD1s had a novel style of upper deck seating, with an offside sunken gangway; this kept the overall height down to just 13ft (3.96m) — several *feet* lower than previous covered-top double-deckers.

Normal-height bodywork for the TD1, labelled Hybridge by Leyland, was available from 1930, and the TD1 spawned a string of Titan models culminating in the PD3 that went out of production in 1969. Leyland helped to restore confidence in double-deckers with the low-built modern TD1, and other manufacturers were quick to follow with similar models. Indeed the Titan concept was really only challenged by the appearance of the rear-engined Atlantean in the late 1950s — again from Leyland.

Profile

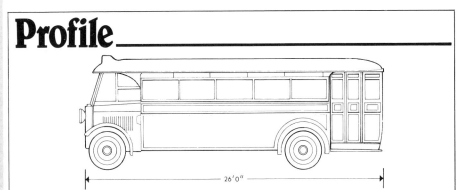

By end of period, driver beside engine (forward control), pneumatic tyres, lower-built chassis; bodies becoming more stylish — some with forward entrances behind front axle, though many still with rear entrances. 32 seats.

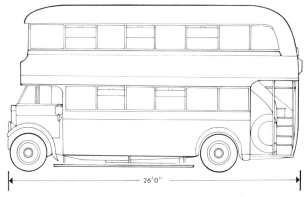

First 'modern' double-deckers appeared in 1927 — low-built, covered tops and, increasingly, totally enclosed staircases; upper deck moved forward over driver's cab. 51 seats (27/24).

The Leyland Titan TD1 heralded the birth of the modern double-decker. This 1930 Southdown example with lowbridge 48-seat Leyland body, was typical of many early examples. *Surfleet*

A boon to many of the public
1929-39

28

If the years to 1918 were the bus industry's rather unsteady childhood and the 1920s its wild and mis-spent youth, then the 1930s must represent its coming-of-age. It is convenient to include 1929 with the 1930s, for many of the events of that year had an important effect on the years that followed. The legislation of the time changed the whole face of the bus industry; it affected the services, tours and vehicles of every operator, large and small, and created a structure that remained basically unchanged for many years. The buses of the late 1930s had reached a particularly high standard and as events turned out this was just as well, for they were called on to render much longer and more strenuous service than could even have been foreseen.

In the last chapter we saw how the railways, in poor condition after World War 1, were ill-equipped to deal with competition from the motor bus, particularly after 1925 when the lower-built proper bus chassis made longer-distance bus and coach travel a truly practical proposition. The railways fought hard and were rewarded in 1928 with the granting to them of road transport powers. Wisely they chose mainly to buy into existing bus companies in preference to competing directly. They purchased shares in companies which belonged to the groups which even then were emerging from the plethora of operators which had appeared in the 1920s.

Sir Josiah Stamp, Chairman of the LMS Railway, wrote at the time: 'The railway companies fully realise the road vehicle has become one of the main factors of transport, especially for short distance travel, and it is not the intention to stifle this convenient form of transport. On the contrary, it is recognised to be a boon to many of the public, and it is the intention of the railway companies further to develop it in its own sphere of usefulness in co-operation with the railway services. To this end the combined experience of the managements of the omnibus concerns and the railway companies should generally prove very beneficial to the public.'

There were inevitable clashes between the bus managers and their new railway

33

29 Double-deck buses like the AEC Regent offered passengers a greater degree of comfort and refinement, and many municipal operators built up their bus fleets in the 1930s. This Regent with 50-seat Short body was one of 10 delivered in 1930 to Chester Corporation. The tramlines are a reminder that these buses were used to replace Chester's trams; in fact Chester was the first municipality to replace all of its trams with motor buses. *AEC*

colleagues. W. J. Crosland-Taylor, one of the founders of the Chester-based Crosville company, recalled that 'individual railway officers were very acceptable, but they had been brought up on tradition, whereas we had been brought up on expediency'. Tradition or no, by the middle of the 1930s, the railway companies owned 15,000 buses.

The important bus fleets of 1929 were the survivors of the cut-throat competition, the firms that had displayed business sense and consolidated their position by acquiring their weaker brothers. There was the British Electric Traction group of companies which had developed bus services in association with its many tramway interests throughout Britain. The BET had also initiated bus services through its associate, British Automobile Traction. Thomas Tilling Ltd, already encountered as a pioneer London bus

operator, had been spreading its wings and in 1928 Tilling & British Automobile Traction was formed, controlling a number of important undertakings. There were other, smaller, groups, like Balfour Beatty and Provincial, and there was National Omnibus & Transport, successor to Thomas Clarkson's London firm. In Scotland there was no real group structure, but there were several larger, responsible firms which were brought together under a reconstituted SMT company.

Things were rather different in Northern Ireland. Unregulated competition continued well into the 1930s, and created serious problems for the bus and railway companies. The solution was the Road and Railways Transport Act, passed in 1935, legislation that gave the country a properly co-ordinated transport system, and the most obvious result was the Northern Ireland Road Transport Board, set up in

1935 to acquire all road passenger and freight operators. In all, 65 bus and coach operators passed into the new Board, including larger firms like the Belfast Omnibus Co, H. M. S. Catherwood Ltd, Great Northern Railway (Ireland), LMS (Northern Counties Committee) and Belfast & County Down Railway Co. A number of these operators obviously had railway roots, for the granting of road transport powers had led to direct

operation by the railway companies and road/rail co-ordination was clearly the intention.

In Eire there were three main bus operators, the Great Southern Railways, Dublin United Tramways and Great Northern Railway (Ireland). GSR was formed in 1924 by merging all the railway companies with rail services wholly in the Free State, and in 1927 GSR reached an agreement with the Irish Omnibus Co whereby IOC ran buses for GSR; in 1934 GSR took over the IOC bus services. Dublin United was originally a tramway company, but became increasingly bus-minded to combat competition from independents. The Great Northern Railway with services on both sides of the border was more of a problem, and continued to go its own way long after the legislation of the 1940s which created the Ulster Transport Authority and Coras Iompair Eireann.

In the re-formed BET, Tilling and SMT groups, strengthened by railway capital, we can see the embryo National Bus Company and Scottish Bus Group of later years. New companies appeared in the 1930s as local firms were merged and the groups embarked on a policy of consolidation, where old rivalries started to disappear and area agreements defined

spheres of operation. All of this allowed the bus companies to get on with the serious business of running buses and the Government made their lives easier with the 1930 Road Traffic Act. The new legislation had no immediate effect on the design of the motor bus. The rationalised vehicle dimensions allowed makers to bring their chassis ranges into line and there was an increased demand from the newly-reconstituted bus companies — often replacements for older vehicles which failed their Certificate of Fitness examination.

Leyland had taken the lead in the 1920s with its trend-setting Lion, Tiger and Titan ranges, and now its competitors were striving to catch up. The man who was largely responsible for Leyland's dominant position was G. J. Rackham, the company's chief engineer. Rackham had started at Walthamstow in Vanguard days and had subsequently been involved in the London General B type. He left AEC in 1916 and in 1922 became chief engineer with the Yellow Coach & Truck company in Chicago. He returned to Britain when he joined Leyland in 1926 and lost no time in evolving the Tiger/Titan range, a fact which had not gone unnoticed by AEC who managed to lure him down to Southall in 1928. The first fruit of this association

30 **Leyland's all-metal bodywork for the Titan TD4 introduced clean lines and a style that was widely regarded as a classic, trend-setting double-deck body design. Lincoln Corporation had 16 of these 1937 TD5 models.**
G. H. F. Atkins

was the 1928 AEC Reliance chassis, based on the ADC 426 model but with a six-cylinder engine. The Reliance was really a stopgap, albeit a successful one, while Rackham developed the first versions of AEC's best-remembered models, the Regal and Regent.

The first examples of the new models used basically the same engine as the Reliance, a six-cylinder overhead-camshaft petrol unit with a swept volume of 6.1 litres. A single-plate clutch was fitted, with a sliding mesh gearbox. The single-deck Regal and double-deck Regent were immediately successful, so much so that by 1942 some 3,500 Regals and 7,000 Regents had been built. Many of these were for London use, as we shall see later, but it is interesting to note that these models were an independent venture by AEC without any involvement by London General.

Legislation and regulation

The Road Traffic Act was an essentially extensive piece of legislation. Introducing it, transport minister Herbert Morrison talked of 'an impossible state of affairs which must be cleared up'. It introduced a national system of route licensing, controlled by Traffic Commissioners each with responsibility for all public service vehicles in newly-created Traffic Areas. Road service licences were required for all PSVs on stage carriage and express carriage services and these vehicles had to carry a current Certificate of Fitness. At the same time the Act laid down new maximum length limits for psvs; 27ft 6in (8.38m) for four-wheel single-deckers, 26ft (7.92m) for four-wheel double-deckers, and 30ft (9.14m) for six-wheel single- and double-deckers; single-deck buses could be 10ft 6in (3.20m) high, double-deckers 15ft (4.57m), and all buses had to be capable of tilting unsupported to 28°. Buses with over 20 seats had to have a conductor, although one-man operated buses were permitted with up to 26 seats if no fare was less than 6d (2½p). This tidied up the varied regulations which applied in different parts of Britain.

It took some time before the Road Traffic Act could take proper effect, particularly when road service licences were concerned. Rival operators fought in the Traffic Courts to convince the Commissioners of their 'right' to hold the licence for certain routes — and it wasn't always a case of first come, first served. For the first few years of the 1930s the battle for passengers transferred from the streets to the Traffic Courts; anyone with an objection to a road service licence could state his case in the Courts.

31

31 **Following the 1930 Road Traffic Act modern designs like the AEC Regal were chosen by many operators to replace outdated vehicles. This Bury Corporation bus, with two-door Brush body, was new in 1930, and was one of three single-deckers bought for evaluation; the others were a Leyland Tiger TS3 and a Crossley Alpha. No more single-deck vehicles were bought until 1938, but this bus lasted until 1948.** *AEC*

Daimler also introduced a new model after the break-up of ADC. Again it was based on an ADC model, the 423, but the new Daimler CF6 introduced a 5.76-litre six-cylinder sleeve valve engine. Daimler had preferred sleeve valve to poppet valve engines since 1909, and had actually introduced a six-cylinder engine in its passenger range in 1926. The CF6 sold well, around 600 between 1929 and 1931, but the finely engineered sleeve valve engines had their shortcomings, as Clem Preece recalled in *Wheels to the West*: 'The special Daimler sleeve valve engine was a wonderful job in theory with white metal-lined steel sleeves, separate cylinder heads, and all sorts of incredible rubber joints and pipe work. The trouble was, that if only one rubber joint were to fail, and the cooling water level dropped, the white metal sleeve lining would melt and the engine quickly become a dead loss. I fear we quickly showed the Daimler engineers that, for our sort of work, robustness came before mechanical perfection.'

Another popular single-deck chassis at the time was Gilford, assembled in High Wycombe. Gilford was not strictly a manufacturer — the firm simply assembled parts built by other companies — but it did produce a number of good passenger models. Most Gilfords were used for coach work, and the combination of light chassis and lively engine was ideal for this. Gilford's 1929 model was the 168, offered in both normal control (168SD) and forward control (168OT) versions, and powered by the American-built Lycoming 6-litre petrol engine. The Gilford company was declared bankrupt in 1936, the combined result of a number of factors; the new company groupings absorbed many of Gilford's old customers, and many of those that survived had bought vehicles on hire purchase and were slow in making repayments. There were also two remarkable front-wheel drive buses, a single-decker and a double-decker, exhibited at the Olympia Show in 1931. The adoption of front wheel drive kept the height of the double-decker down to a phenomenal 12ft 11in (3.94m), but the two buses, which had opposed-piston six-cylinder two-stroke Junkers oil engines, were probably just too advanced for the resources of Gilford, a company which, in spite of its short lifespan — just over a decade — is still fondly remembered today.

During the 1930s, vehicle development was steady, if normally undramatic. There *were* some remarkably advanced models, but none sold in spectacular numbers. It was a period of gradual improvement, and it is interesting to follow one range of chassis through its production life and note the modifications. Leyland's Titan range illustrates these changes most clearly; not only was it built from 1927 right through to 1942, but Leyland also altered the type

designation as each change was introduced, so it is easier to pinpoint the developments. Starting with the 1927 TD1 model as a base, it was succeded by the TD2 (1932) with fully-floating rear axle, triple-servo brakes and a bigger 7.6-litre petrol engine. The TD3 (1933) introduced the choice of petrol or diesel engines and a more compact front end arrangement. There was also the TD3c, with torque convertor; all subsequent models with this transmission also had the 'c' suffix. The replacement TD4 (1935) had vacuum-hydraulic brakes and constant mesh, rather than sliding mesh, gearbox. The TD5 (1937) had worm and nut steering and modifications to the frame. It was succeeded by two models, the TD6c (1938) and the TD7 (1939). The TD6c was peculiar to Birmingham City Transport, with torque converter, but the TD7 which followed it included many common features, like fully-flexible engine mountings and a shorter wheelbase. There was to have been a TD8 model announced late in 1941, but by then Britain was at war and Leyland's resources were employed in other directions.

The Leyland Titan and AEC Regent were by far the most successful of the double-deckers of the 1930s, introducing and in some cases reintroducing double-deck vehicles on routes outside purely urban areas. The Titan and Regent were popular with municipal, company and independent operators, while some of the contemporary models settled into more

specialised slots. Double-deckers based on chassis like the Albion Venturer, Crossley Condor, Dennis Lance and Guy Arab all had their faithful supporters, though they were by no means as widespread as the Leylands and AECs. Two double-deck chassis makers which did become more familiar were Bristol and Daimler. The Bristol Tramways & Carriage Co had actually built some bus chassis as early as 1906, but it was not until 1913 that regular production commenced. Initially chassis were built primarily for the operating company, but soon other operators were buying Bristols. In 1932 Bristol became associated with the Tilling Group and started to supply a good proportion of the group's vehicle requirements, while still competing for outside business. Bristol's first modern double-deck chassis was the G type of 1932, originally with a 7.25-litre petrol engine, and from 1933 with Gardner's 7-litre 5LW engine, and also with a new constant mesh gearbox.

Daimler's best remembered prewar double-deck range also used Gardner diesel engines. The first Daimler COG5s appeared in 1933, but full production really started the next year and in 1935 the first COG6s appeared, using the 6LW unit rather than the 5LW. The Daimler CO series chassis were built as single-deckers and double-deckers, and while all had Wilson preselector gearboxes, most, though not all, were fitted with Gardner engines. The COG5 double-decker was the best seller in the

range, and at one time Birmingham City Transport had around 800 in its fleet.

Breaking new ground
The Leyland body style for the Titan TD1 had broken new ground. It was low-built and sleek with none of the horse bus influence that had previously lingered on, even in designs like the London NS. The concept of a double-deck bus body as a rectangular box for passengers, mounted between the driver and the rear staircase and platform, gradually disappeared. The upper deck crept forward over what was originally the driver's weather canopy, and forward control double-deckers and London's eventual acceptance of glass windscreens, allowed coachbuilders to project the top deck right over the driver's cab. At the back, the staircase and platform were soon enclosed within the body and the 'traditional' British double-decker had taken shape. The low build of the new chassis allowed the designers to evolve sleeker lines, and some

of the most distinguished body styles of all times emerged from the 1930s.

Some builders tried a bit too hard. In an era when streamlining was the rage some designers tried to apply aerodynamic principles to the double-deck bus, but with little success — though they did contribute something towards cleaner lines. Towards the end of the 1930s some significant designs appeared. At the 1937 Commercial Motor Show, the Leeds bodybuilder Roe exhibited an AEC Regent for Leeds City Transport with a four-bay window layout which foreshadowed many designs of 10-15 years later. In 1938 Leyland introduced a modified version of its standard double-deck body, that was probably one of the most pleasing designs of all time.

As the popularity of the double-decker increased, some operators evolved their own distinctive body designs and bodybuilders throughout the country were happy to build them. It was quite possible to find buses based on the same chassis, with bodies by the same builder, looking totally different. The bigger operators, who placed sizeable orders, were the ones with the most distinctive styles; smaller operators could only expect minor

modifications to an otherwise standard design.

Single-deck buses were probably more standardised. There was certainly a wide variety of designs, but these were peculiar to the main operating groups rather than to individual operators. The Tilling, BET and SMT groups all had been evolving body layouts and features suited to their operations and they also had their own favoured bodybuilders. Tilling had Eastern Counties, the former United bodyshops at Lowestoft, which was to become a separate subsidiary of the group in 1936 as Eastern Coach Works. Lowestoft-built bodies became increasingly common in Tilling fleets, usually on Bristol chassis, which again were controlled within the group, but they were not restricted, and many operators with no Tilling connections continued to buy ECW bodies until nationalisation in 1948 prevented them.

Not all of the BET-controlled fleets specified the BET Federation designs which became familiar in the 1930s; some stuck to their own styles, but a faithful group toed the party line. BET fleets did not have the manufacturing ties of the Tilling group; they usually used AEC,

Albion, Daimler, Dennis and Leyland chassis, with bodies — often near-identical — by builders like Brush, Roe, Weymann — and even ECW.

The SMT group had its own body supplier. The Falkirk-based Alexanders fleet had started building bus bodies for its own use in 1924, and the other SMT companies started to use its capacity from the early 1930s. The group's requirements kept the Alexander coachworks busy, and although there were isolated cases of

33 Bedford's entry into the bus and coach market in 1931 was immediately successful, and the company captured a sizeable share of the market for small-size coaches. This 1931 WLB demonstrator with Duple body was photographed on *Modern Transport's* Midlands test route, at Chinley Head near Glossop. *Ian Allan Library*

'outside' bodies being built, the majority of the output was for SMT fleets until Alexander remained independent when the SMT group was nationalised in 1949. In fact, the output was not enough to satisfy all SMT's needs, and other bodybuilders, particularly Leyland, were widely used.

The coach market

The standardised bodywork of the 1930s was mainly to be found on service buses and service coaches. Luxury touring coaches were much more varied, even for the company fleets, and the coachbuilders tended to build bespoke vehicles to suit individual preferences. There was often a basic similarity in the body construction, but the final trim and styling was a matter of individual taste.

At first, coach bodies were based on bus shells, suitably refined with external mouldings and internal decoration, but soon definite 'coach' shapes started to appear. At a time when the railway companies and car manufacturers were 'discovering' streamlining, the coachbuilders kept face by producing some quite remarkable coach bodies, often one-off jobs for Commercial Motor Shows, that were never repeated. It was also a time for gimmickry, and sleeper coaches, radio coaches and observation coaches appeared on the roads; more usefully, some coaches had kitchens, and toilets. Most of the novelty features were fairly short-lived, and gradually more emphasis was placed on passenger comfort, resulting in plushly-finished interiors with quilted roofs, veneered wood facings and discreetly-curtained windows.

We have so far considered the heavy duty vehicles of the 1930s, the often-similar single- and double-deck chassis with their six-cylinder engines, petrol at first, and increasingly diesel as the decade went on. Not everyone needed, or wanted, these chassis. There was a faction which saw a niche for lighter-weight, though full-size, single-deckers, requiring only a small four-cylinder engine, hence designs like the AEC Regal 4 and Leyland Lion.

Farther down the size scale, there was still a steady demand for small-capacity normal control chassis. Albion, Commer, Dennis, Gilford and Guy were just some of the bigger builders that also offered small bus chassis, but a newcomer to the bus business was to change all that — and this new rival was a car manufacturer.

Vauxhall's somewhat late entry into the PSV chassis field in 1931 was undoubtedly influenced by American competition. Since much of this competition was from GMC and Chevrolet which, like Vauxhall, were part of the General Motors empire, it was really only cashing in rather than fighting it. The vehicle which eventually appeared was called Bedford, and the first Bedford WHB bus chassis was completed in July

Important development

Two of the most important technical developments of the 1930s are still very much with us today, for the development and acceptance of the diesel engine and the epicyclic gearbox belong to this decade. The heavy oil engine, offering economy in fuel with a high torque at low speeds, was clearly ideal for passenger work, and several bodies were conducting their own experiments in the later 1920s. The independent bus and coach operator Barton had experimentally fitted an oil engine into a Lancia chassis in 1928, while in Germany the truck and bus builders MAN had introduced a 5-litre oil engine at the 1924 Berlin Motor Show. In Britain the turning-point came in 1928 when Gardner introduced its 4L2 and 6L2 direct injection engines for marine use. Crossley, the Manchester-based private car builder which had only entered the passenger market in 1928, fitted Gardner 6L2 units in experimental Condor double-deckers which were supplied to Leeds and Manchester Corporations in 1930. In the same year Sheffield Corporation introduced a Benz-engined Karrier oiler, and Barton fitted a Gardner 4L2 in one of its buses.

Crossley did much to put the diesel engine on the map, competing with AEC who also saw the benefits. AEC developed its own diesel units, but Crossley, and many other builders over the subsequent years, offered Gardner engines from the 4LW/5LW/6LW range introduced for road vehicles in 1931. Other builders were slower off the mark, but as sales of diesels increased — municipalities were particularly keen customers — they developed their own oil engines or offered proprietary makes. Leyland was slow in introducing its 8.6-litre diesel, which did not appear until 1933, but a large order from SMT group for engines to convert existing petrol vehicles was a welcome shot in the arm, not only for Leyland but for the diesel engine. The SMT group was probably the first wholehearted convert, and others quickly followed suit, so that by 1934 most new heavy-duty PSVs had diesels, except for some coaches for independents and for larger firms like Ribble and Southdown; some of the 'refined' seaside resorts continued to favour the essentially quieter petrol engine. By contrast, Red & White was the first big fleet to go all-diesel, converting its buses between 1933 and 1935.

The preselective Wilson gearbox appeared in 1930, first in Daimler private cars and, almost immediately, in Daimler passenger vehicles. This effective transmission system allowed the driver to select a gear at any time using a hand lever, with a foot pedal to make the actual change. The inherent smoothness together with the fact that the driver's hands could both be on the steering wheel when necessary attracted many operators, particularly those with busy town work. London General was obviously interested, and bought three of Daimler's new CH6 model. The Wilson gearbox clearly impressed London, and although no more Daimlers were bought the transmission system was to be London's standard for many years. Leyland's answer was the Lysholm-Smith torque converter, offered in its chassis from 1933. Buses thus fitted carried the words 'Gearless Bus' on their radiators, for this was almost a fully-automatic system, with no clutch pedal, and a lever that had to be used to engage direct drive above about 20mph. A number of operators specified the 'Gearless' Leylands, but the system was not completely efficient and never achieved the wide acceptance of the Wilson preselector.

34 Daimler standardised on the Wilson preselective gearbox from 1930, and this 1932 CH6 model incorporated this advanced feature. Built for service in Spain, the Weymann body and right-hand driving position give it a very British look — except for the apparent lack of an entrance; this, like the driver, was on the right. *Ian Allan Library*

1931 and delivered to a Bedfordshire operator at the end of August. The WHB was a small, normal control chassis with a six-cylinder 3.18-litre petrol engine, while the WLB, introduced at the same time, was a longer-wheelbase version mechanically similar under the bonnet. The WLB was an instant success and nearly 1,900 were built in its four-year production run. It was succeeded by the WTB in 1935, a more refined approach to the constant demand for a small and economical coach, and this sold over 3,000 chassis in four years. The WTB's successor, the OB, appeared in 1939, but the war prevented production from really getting under way; the OB will reappear in the next two chapters. In the 1930s, however, Bedford really established a strong lead in the small bus and coach market, and statistics dramatically illustrate the company's growth. In 1934, 49% of all vehicles in the 20-seat range

were Bedfords, while in 1936 50% of all registrations in the 15-26 seat class could be claimed; this figure had risen to 70% in 1938.

Not all of the buses of the period could be typecast quite so easily. There were manufacturers less prepared to accept that the motor bus of the 1930s — which admittedly represented a tremendous advance on its 1920s counterpart — had reached the peak of its development. For a number of years as the bus grew in sophistication the engine had stayed firmly at the front. Then AEC and London General started investigating the possibilities of resiting the engine and came up with the AEC Q with its engine mounted on the offside behind the front axle, itself set back from the extreme front to allow, in certain cases, a front entrance ahead of the axle.

The *AEC Gazette* for November 1932 commented: 'Many London readers of this

35

35 **One of the most revolutionary production models of the 1930s was the side-engined AEC Q, which allowed bodybuilders to construct very advanced-looking bodies, complete with entrances ahead of the set-back front axle. Westcliff Motor Services bought this Q with Metropolitan-Cammell bodywork in 1933, seen here with a London-style roof number stencil plate. The lifeguard bar under the front panelling was felt to be an essential safety feature on a front-entrance bus. Passing is a slightly newer AEC Regent with Weymann body.**
Ian Allan Library

journal will probably have seen the Q bus put on the Liverpool Street-Shepherd's Bush service by the London General Omnibus Co Ltd, some few weeks ago. And with those who have so far only seen pictures of this mystery bus, built by AEC at its Southall works, in the daily press and one or two trade papers they will be speculating upon the constructional details of the chassis effectively hidden by the bodywork. It has its engine on the offside immediately behind the driver. So much may be gleaned by any intelligent observer.' London General Q1 was introduced in 1932, and was followed by 233 other single-deckers and five double-deckers delivered to London Transport in the 1934-36 period.

The Q was built mainly in single-deck form, as a basis for both buses and coaches. Royal Blue had four fine AEC Q coaches and Clem Preece recalls them in *Wheels to the West*: 'This Q type was years ahead of its time and could run today against the most modern types without causing comment. However when we tried it out it caused a tremendous sensation — the driver actually sat with the passengers! Added to this it had no bonnet! The engine was on the offside! What is more it rode like a Rolls-Royce. People literally asked to travel on it and were prepared to adjust their times to do so. However, it had certain inherent deficiencies and it died for being ahead of its time.' There were double-deck Qs too, fewer in number, where the engine fitted neatly under the stairs. The Q was relatively successful — considering its then revolutionary layout — and in all some 350 chassis were built, but it went out of production in 1937, presumably while AEC was perfecting a true underfloor-engined chassis. Alan Townsin, the noted transport authority and a dedicated AEC fan, appositely, described the Q as 'a magnificent failure'.

The AEC Q was not the only side-engine chassis to appear in Britain. In 1933 Northern General, operating on Tyneside and in County Durham, introduced its first SE6 chassis, featuring a side-mounted Hercules petrol engine and, unlike the Q, a three-axle layout, the only means at the time to achieve a 30ft vehicle. There had been one six-wheel Q, but the SE6 was produced in fairly large numbers. There was also a more normal two-axle variant, the SE4, built in 1936-38, using an AEC engine.

Oddly, it was operators rather than manufacturers that were setting the pace. Midland Red, by then one of the largest of the English company operators, had started building vehicles, mainly for its own use, in 1923. The company's brilliant and energetic chief engineer L. G. Wyndham Shire, had designed a series of single-deckers which were ideally suited to Midland Red's requirements. Philip Robinson, then chief engineer of the Bristol Omnibus Co, wrote in 1974: 'The SOS vehicles of the 1920s and 1930s were paramount in simplicity and lack of frills — a string bell, the petrol tank doubling up as a driver's seat, and a manually-operated klaxon horn, together with no servo assistance for the brakes. You cannot get much more basic than that. They may not

Sensible moves

The combination of better coaches, railway capital and more paid holidays created a boom in coach touring and particularly in express coach travel, and during the 1930s many significant developments resulted from this. In 1932 London's Victoria coach station was opened, and in its first operational year more than five million passengers used it. In Cheltenham, St Margaret's coach station had become the 'Clapham Junction of the Coachways', an important interchange point for coach travellers from many parts of Britain. Cheltenham was the focal point of Associated Motorways, a voluntary pooling agreement, initially between six of the bigger coach operators — Black & White, Elliott Bros (Royal Blue), Greyhound, Midland Red, Red & White and United Counties. This sensible move was very much to the public's benefit, and simplified licensing procedures for the operators. With a certain justification Royal Blue timetable leaflets at the time included these aims under the heading 'What Royal Blue Service Stands For':

'We have but three axioms, your safety, your comfort and your convenience; to obtain them we spare no effort. Our coaches are the finest we can obtain! They and their drivers are licensed by the Traffic Commissioners through whose areas they pass, and may therefore be taken to be absolutely safe. The work of cleaning and maintaining the coaches never ceases night or day.

'The result we leave to your judgement as an experienced traveller.

'British all through — and proud of it.'

36 **Laying-over at London's Victoria Coach Station in 1935 before starting its express run to Portsmouth, connecting to the Isle of Wight, a new Southdown petrol-engined Leyland Tiger TS7 with stylish 32-seat Harrington bodywork, complete with rear entrance and roof luggage rack. It received an 8.6 litre diesel engine in the late 1940s.** *G. H. F. Atkins*

have been the most comfortable of vehicles, but they must have been among the easiest to maintain.' Large numbers were built for Midland Red and for other fleets in the BET group, and from 1931 Midland Red's SOS range also included double-deck models, the REDD and FEDD types, with rear and forward entrances respectively. Shire was constantly experimenting and a prototype rear-engined vehicle appeared in 1935, followed by three others in 1936; these had transversely-mounted petrol engines coupled to Daimler fluid flywheels and Cotal epicyclic gearboxes. In 1941-44 all four were rebuilt with horizontal underfloor engines, prototypes of a large postwar fleet.

A variation on the front engine theme was the Maudslay SF40, introduced in 1935, with a set-back front axle and front entrance alongside the driver — a layout that only really found favour a quarter of a century later. The SF40 enabled 40 seats to be fitted in a 27ft 6in (8.38m) bus. Initially the four-cylinder Maudslay 5.34-litre petrol engine was standard, but Gardner 4LW and 5LW diesel options were later offered.

Büssing, the German chassis builders, did a great deal of pioneer work developing underfloor-engined buses in the 1930s. Prototypes were unveiled in 1934 and underfloor-engined single-deckers were in full production only two years later. Credit should also be given to the enterprising builders in the United States. Fageol had introduced its advanced Twin Coach in 1927, a transit bus that prioneered a layout that is still familiar today — entrance at the extreme front under the control of the driver, and set-back front axle. This was achieved with twin engines mounted below the floor line, between the axles. In the 1930s White developed a model with a flat 12-cylinder engine — Leyland borrowed a White 'pancake' bus for examination — and Yellow Coach produced an integrally-constructed rear-engined bus; by 1937 Yellow was producing no front-engined buses at all.

In Britain there was similar activity, from predictable and unpredictable sources. Leyland, while enjoying the success of its Tiger and Titan ranges, was busy juggling with engine layouts in 1937. There was a highly experimental single-decker with a transverse rear engine and rear-mounted gearbox, with single tyres all round and a set-back front axle; and there was the Gnu, a twin-steer six wheeler which had a front engine, but could also offer a front entrance.

Less predictable was the development of a rear-engined E-type version of the Shelvoke & Drewry Freighter, the small-wheeled chassis which enjoyed a limited success in the 1920s/1930s, largely in service at seaside resorts. The two rear-engined SDs, ordered for Tram-O-Car service at Worthing, were actually delivered in 1938 to Southdown, which had taken over in the meantime.

The biggest operator of them all, London Transport, apparently shared this dissatisfaction with the reliable if technically unadventurous chassis offered by the commercial builders. London had been the main operator of the AEC Q, in single-deck and double-deck form, and in 1937 there appeared the first TF, a Leyland Tiger FEC with an underfloor-mounted engine. This was followed in 1938 by the CR, a Leyland Cub with longitudinal rear-mounted engine. There were 49 CRs in all, little-used and largely unsuccessful machines, but the 88 TFs were happier vehicles and many lasted well into the postwar period.

It would be misleading to suggest that the main manufacturers were not working on similar projects, and it is fair to say that several of these might have appeared in the early 1940s had it not been for the war. Leyland, for instance, built one Panda chassis in 1940, a twin-steer six-wheeler with an underfloor-engine, and this was supplied to Alexanders in 1941. AEC built an underfloor-engined chassis for Canada in 1939, a direct predecessor of the Regal IV chassis which did not appear until 1950. A more ambitious project was the six-wheel Tilling-Stevens Successor, a 1937 underfloor-engined chassis with an eight-cylinder horizontally-opposed 95hp engine and a seven-speed preselective gearbox; it also featured independent rear suspension and coil springs. It never really left the drawing board.

Between the wars, various firms experimented with producer gas, particularly as the situation darkened in Europe. High Speed Gas (Great Britain) Ltd — a new-sounding title for a company formed in 1933 — was one of these firms. In 1936 the company took over the London factory of the bankrupt Gilford Motor Co, and formed Gilford (HSG) Ltd; the next year the solitary Gilford HSG bus appeared — based on a Gilford CF176 chassis, modified to run on producer gas. The chassis was extensively tested in Scotland and performed impressively enough to convince Highland Transport to buy it. The chassis was modified to run on peat and a Cowieson body was fitted.

Rationalisation in London

While there was all of this activity among the manufacturers, things were happening in London. Three new types all based on chassis in the new AEC range appeared in quick succession in the General fleet. There was the LT class, based on the six-wheel AEC Renown, which eventually ran to over 1,400 buses, making General by far the biggest operator of this model. The LT was built from 1929 until 1932, usually with spacious and well-appointed 56- or 60-seat bodies. At a time of experiment with engines and gearboxes, the LTs had a confusing mixture of petrol and oil engines, crash and preselector gearboxes. Later buses had Lockheed hydraulic brakes in place of the previous vacuum servo type. There were also 35-seat single-deck LTs and private hire coaches, classed LTC.

The code LT meant 'Long T', and the basic T was the single-deck model, based on the AEC Regal chassis. Like the Regal, the London T had a long production run, and the last Ts were built in 1948, 801 buses later. The first Ts were buses built late in 1929 and as the class grew it reflected the changes in regulations, in requirements and in technical matters. Many Ts were built as express coaches for Green Line routes while others were service buses for suburban and country services.

The third T variant was the ST (Short T) double-decker, based on the AEC Regent chassis. The ST was in effect the four-wheel version of the LT, and the two types were complementary to each other to suit varying conditions. The 25ft (7.62m) long ST was introduced in 1929 and usually had seats for 48 passengers; it was built until 1932, when the regulations were altered to permit 26ft double-deckers and higher axle weights. This change largely removed the need for six-wheel double-deckers, and one new longer type, the 26ft (7.92m) STL, replaced both the ST and LT. The STL provided up to 60 seats and was London's standard double-deck model from 1932 to 1939. The first STLs had petrol engines and crash gearboxes, but the oil engine/preselector combination became more familiar. *Tramway and Railway World* described the STL as 'the foremost example of the luxury omnibus in the metropolis'.

On 1 July 1933, little more than six months after STL1 entered service, London's buses underwent a major upheaval.

After many years of discussion a new all-embracing authority was formed to control passenger transport in London, the London Passenger Transport Board. The task of the new Board, according to its Chairman, Lord Ashfield, was 'to take such steps as it considers necessary for avoiding wasteful competitive services and for extending and improving London's passenger transport facilities so as to meet the growing needs of its vast population'. Its nucleus was the London General company and it also took in the services within its area operated by its associated London General Country Services, Green Line and Overground fleets, and those of Tilling, T&BAT and 55 other operators. The new London Transport monopoly also acquired a number of tramway systems including those of London County Council, London United and Metropolitan Electric, and various urban railway services including those of the Underground and Metropolitan Railways.

Here was the first of the giant conurbation authorities, an immense undertaking with a vast responsibility. General's 4,500-strong bus fleet was boosted by the addition of roughly 900 vehicles from its Country and Green Line associates and another 700 buses from a variety of sources. Inevitably, the fleet was a mixed one with more than 30 different chassis makes represented. Not all were in a good condition, but London Transport had to keep as many as possible in running order until replacements could be supplied. Add the 60 trolleybuses and 2,600 trams inherited by the new Board and the sheer size of the undertaking becomes apparent. At its first meeting, the LPTB decided to standardise on diesel engines to effect an annual saving of up to £120 a vehicle. Fleet standardisation was another priority, to eliminate the inheritance of varied makes and models. This started in earnest, and in its first five years LPTB bought nearly 3,000 new buses — 47% of the fleet.

One of the problems of the formation of London Transport was the future of AEC. Lord Ashfield had been chairman of Underground Electric Railways,

controlling General and AEC, and in 1929 he had approached Leyland with a view to an AEC/Leyland merger. A new firm, British Vehicles, would absorb the two firms and increase its strength with other takeovers; Leyland was to be the dominant partner with the incentive of a share of the London bus market. The deal fell through, but in 1931 discussions restarted on a Leyland take-over of AEC. Again the London bus market was the main attraction for Leyland, with a possible guarantee of a 10-year contract to supply 90% of London's buses, but again the talks broke down and AEC and Leyland stayed defiantly separate until 1962 when Leyland eventually acquired AEC. As it turned out, one of the conditions of the Act which created London Transport in 1933 expressly forbade the manufacture of vehicles, so AEC became a separate, independent entity. Its close links with London were not severed, however, and AEC continued to be London Transport's

main chassis supplier for over 30 years, initially with a guaranteed annual purchase of 400 chassis each year for 10 years.

Leyland did get a look in, though, in the 1930s. In addition to the underfloor-engined TFs and the rear-engined CRs already mentioned, there were over 100 Leyland Cubs, medium-sized normal control single-deckers which replaced and augmented the mixed fleet of small buses absorbed in 1933. There were Leyland double-deckers too, 100 Titan TD4s supplied in 1937 with Leyland-built all-metal bodywork that was adapted to resemble the contemporary STL type.

London Transport's crowning vehicle achievement in the 1930s came right at the end of the decade. The prototype of a trend-setting new class made its debut in 1938 rather ignominiously hidden under an old open-staircase body, but the following year a new body was fitted to the chassis, with a big 9.6-litre engine, flexibly

37 **The spread of the trolleybus was spectacular in the 1930s, as municipal and company operators bought them to supplement their fleets and, in some cases, to replace trams. Bradford was an important trolleybus operator for over 60 years, and this 1935 AEC with 60-seat English Electric body was seen in 1936.** *G. H. F. Atkins*

mounted, and an air pressure system to operate both the brakes and the preselective gearbox. An entirely new design of 56-seat body was introduced on the RT, more rounded, well proportioned and better finished. The RT chassis, later to be known as the AEC Regent Mk III, and the more modern body style which it introduced, heralded a new awareness of the need to combine function and aesthetic merit.

Some people might argue that the design of the London bus reached its zenith at the end of the 1930s, but some of the Board's energies were being diverted in other directions. London Transport was not only by far the biggest bus operator in Britain, in a short time it had also built up by far the biggest trolleybus fleet in the country. The Board inherited the 60 London United trolleybuses in 1933, and in 1935 started a major conversion programme, replacing the tramway system. LUT had already reported that its trolleybuses were 15% cheaper than the Twickenham-Teddington trams they replaced. At its height the London trolleybus system operated over 1,800 vehicles in no less than five counties. This was very much the golden age of the trolleybus with 15 new systems growing up between 1930 and 1939, including some important converts like Walsall, Derby, Huddersfield, Bournemouth, Newcastle, Reading, Hull, Manchester and Belfast.

With this spectacular growth, the total number of trolleybuses jumped from around 500 in 1930 to 3,000 in 1938, but there were also some casualties, a few older, smaller systems.

Just as the motor bus and the trolleybus made great advances in the 1930s, so did the motor car. Ford managed to break the magic £100 barrier, offering a fully-equipped 8hp car for this sum; in the United States Ford could justifiably use the slogan 'Count the Fords till the next corner'. As lower prices brought private motoring within the grasp of a wider public, there was need for more legislation to control the spread. The year 1931 saw Britain's first automatic traffic signals, and in 1935 pedestrian crossings and driving tests were introduced, but Britain's roads were becoming increasingly unsuitable for the growth in traffic. Neither Britain nor the United States undertook any major roadbuilding in this depressed decade; not for them the Italian autostrada — built partly to relieve unemployment — or the German autobahns — built with easier troop movement in mind. Germany had 800 miles of autobahns by 1937; it was 1971 before Britain's motorway network reached this figure.

Life in Britain was changing in other

38 **Coach bodywork went through a flamboyant phase as bodybuilders caught the streamline fever and got to terms with techniques to produce more rounded shapes. This 1939 Leyland Tiger TS8 for Mathias of Morriston, Swansea, had full-fronted Duple bodywork that anticipated some of the early postwar designs.** *Duple*

38

Peaks and troughs

Contrasting with the growth of the trolleybus was the continued decline of the tramcar. Over the decade over 70 smaller tramway systems closed, unable to cope with the combination of increasing street traffic and outworn equipment. Typical of the systems was that at West Bromwich, which closed down finally in 1939. Before an earlier route closure, the local press offered this none-too-flattering memorial: 'The coming of the buses on the Bromford Lane and Spon Lane routes, which has been heralded to take place shortly, will be heartily welcomed by the travelling public. The tramcars used on these routes certainly leave a lot to be desired in the way of comfort and speedy travel, while the rails are regarded by other road users as something of a terror. A journey on the antiquated and noisy vehicles which rock and jar at every imperfection in the very imperfect rails is not a pleasant experience by any means. The cars rock in a manner which almost throws one off one's seat, and at the journey's end, one has a feeling that one has just stepped off some weird machine one finds when Mr Pat Collins pays his occasional visits to the West Bromwich fairground. Trams may have been regarded as comfortable and speedy some years ago, but travel has altered with the times and the buses will be a great improvement in these modern times.'

Not everyone would have agreed with these sentiments. Certainly not the tram passengers in Blackpool, Glasgow, Leeds, Liverpool, London, Manchester or Sunderland where fine new trams entered service in the 1930s — big, lightweight and truly modern vehicles providing fast, efficient and comfortable services within the essential inflexibility of the tramway. Some of these operators went on to build new and better trams right through the 1940s into the 1950s — and of course Blackpool has gone on even longer; the new trams were in many cases used on new tramway extensions, some of which were built on reserved private roadways, often giving the tram a slight edge over its motorised rivals.

ways that affected road passenger transport. There was a clear population drift towards the south, while unemployment grew in other areas. In some parts of Yorkshire, Wales and Scotland, for example, unemployment reached over 50% of the working population. And the population was still increasing — it grew by 3% between 1931 and 1938, although in Coventry, with a successful motor industry, it grew by 20%.

Generally, life was improving. Four million new houses were built in the two decades between the wars, and the Holidays With Pay Act in 1938 meant that the number of workers with paid leave increased from 1.5 million in 1937 to 11 million just two years later. All of these changes affected the demand for bus and coach services, and by 1938 the British bus population had reached 53,600.

Britain's railways regained some of their former strength in the 1930s. While on the one hand there was the start of the ongoing process of branch line closure, there was the exciting high-speed streamline era of the 'Silver Jubilee', 'Coronation' and 'Coronation Scot' trains. The railways even got involved with domestic air transport when Railway Air Services was formed in 1934 by the four main line railway companies and Imperial Airways.

The year 1939 represented one of the high points in the story of the British bus. The Road Traffic Act of 1930 had given the industry a respectable foundation, and the technical developments of the decade had helped to evolve a refined and efficient breed of bus. The London RT was probably the best example, but there were others.

In 1939 Coventry Corporation took a number of 60-seat double-deckers into stock, and just as the London RT anticipated the trend towards air-braked, big-engined buses, the Coventry buses were the first double-deckers with high capacity, lightweight all-metal bodies. They were Daimler COA6s with Metro-Cammell bodies, weighing only 6ton 6cwt unladen, and allowing a high seating capacity within the 10½ tons maximum laden weight limit imposed at the time.

Other operators were anxious to obtain higher seating capacities within the length and weight regulations of the time; Northern General had a large fleet of 38-seat AEC Regals with shortened cabs and modified controls, and the SMT group had similarly-altered Regals and Leyland Tiger TS8s with seats for 39 passengers.

The bus industry was well equipped for the problems of the next decade, which imposed a tremendous strain on the resources of the country; all the great advances of the 1930s meant that Britain's buses were in a very healthy state by 1939 as the nation was slowly edged towards war.

39

39 Elderly trams could not always stand comparison with modern motor buses like this Bradford Corporation AEC Regent, with 8.8 litre engine and Weymann 51-seat body, one of 20 delivered in 1935. *Ian Allan Library*

Events

1928 Railways (Road Transport) Act gives railway companies road transport powers
Tilling & BAT formed.
AEC Reliance introduced.
1929 AEC Regal and Regent introduced.
1930 Bus operators experiment with diesel engines.
Road Traffic Act brings regulation to the bus industry.
Wilson preselective gearbox.
1931 Last urban horse bus, Gateshead-Newcastle.
Gilford front-wheel drive buses.
Gardner 5LW and 6LW diesel engines introduced.
First Bedford bus.
1932 Bristol K type double-decker appears.
AEC side-engined Q model.
Victoria coach station opens in London.
LGOC introduces STL double-decker.
1933 Daimler COG range introduced.
Northern General side-engined SE6 model.
London Passenger Transport Board formed.
1934 Bussing (Germany) introduces underfloor-engined bus.
1935 Northern Ireland Road Transport Board formed.
1939 London Transport RT1 in service.

World Events

1929 New York Stock Exchange crash.
1930 Amy Johnson flies from London to Australia.
1933 Hitler becomes German Chancellor.
1934 Cats-eyes invented.
1936 Spanish Civil War.
Edward VIII abdicates.
1937 First Butlin's camp opens.
1938 Chamberlain-Hitler meeting: 'Peace in our time'.
1939 World War 2.

London Transport RT

London General and London Transport had played an important part in the development of the double-deck bus, right from the B type of 1910, and in the 1930s had standardised on the AEC Regent-based STL model. For its next generation double-decker, LPTB specified a Regent with a bigger engine, the 9.6-litre AEC diesel, and air-operated gearbox and brakes. The first chassis appeared in 1938 under an older body, but in 1939 received its new body — a sleek four-bay design with seats for 56 (30/26) passengers. Another 150 RTs appeared between November 1939 and June 1940, and production ceased until after the war.

Although RTs were built for other operators, London built up a massive fleet after the war, initially to replace its tramway system. Around 600 a year were built, taking the class to 4,826 buses; there were also 2,131 Leyland-built RT

Sign of the Times

The growth of passenger transport brought demands for better and faster ticket issue. The Setright, featured in this 1936 advert, offered 143 fare values, and was the predecessor of the Speed model, still in regular use.
Gavin Booth collection

variants, bought to help boost deliveries in the early postwar period.

The RT served London well, its total lifespan covering 40 years from the appearance of RT1 in 1939 to the ceremonial operation of the last RTs in 1979. With the RT, London Transport had anticipated — or helped fashion — the postwar double-decker: big engines, air brakes and epicyclic gearboxes became increasingly familiar, although LT's attention to details of body design was not always apparent in provincial vehicles.

Profile

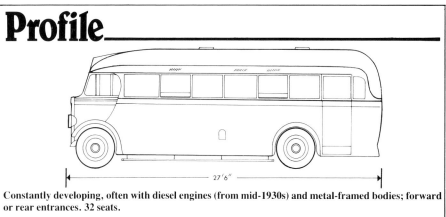

Constantly developing, often with diesel engines (from mid-1930s) and metal-framed bodies; forward or rear entrances. 32 seats.

27'6"

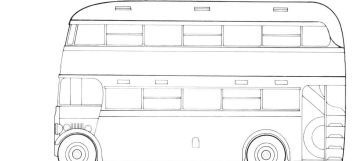

26'0"

Developing in parallel with contemporary single-deckers: diesel engines and metal-framed bodies more popular from mid-1930s. 56 seats (30/26).

A front-end design that was familiar to Londoners for 40 years, although not in this livery or with such an illogical use of the destination boxes. This was one of the 15 RT-type AEC Regents bought in 1950 by St Helens Corporation and built to full London Transport specification; another 25 followed in 1952.
Ian Allan Library

With avidity into battle
1939-45

Some parts of the bus industry were well prepared for the outbreak of World War 2 in September 1939. As early as 1938 the Home Office had approached London Transport to see if vehicles could be made available for ambulance work in the event of the outbreak of the war so many people regarded as inevitable. LT duly obtained kits to convert its coach fleet, and three days before the outbreak of hostilities it withdrew all Green Line services to carry out the conversions. Around 400 vehicles were handed over to Ministry of Health, AEC Regals, Qs and Renowns, and Leyland FEC Tigers. Some filtered back into service, but others continued to do useful war work for the duration.

Hants & Dorset, operating on the equally vulnerable south coast of England, was also well prepared for the war. Sandbags, fire buckets and gummed paper were delivered in large quantities to company premises, and vehicle lighting was adapted to conform with the anticipated blackout regulations.

However well operators prepared for the inevitable war, there was no way that anyone could have anticipated its duration or its intensity. The immediate effects were drastic enough — fuel cuts, severe blackout restrictions and curtailed services, but things were to get very much worse before they got better.

One of the first problems encountered by the bus industry was the mass evacuation of schoolchildren and others from potential danger areas — towns and cities with heavy industry or military and naval installations — to reception areas in the safety of the country. The combined resources of the buses and the railways moved several hundred thousand children in those first, rather uncertain, days of the war. After the first few anti-climatic months of the war more than half the evacuees drifted back to their homes, but after the concentrated bombing on London and the south coast, there was a second blitz evacuation.

Next there were cuts in petrol and oil

40 **Many older buses were pressed into further service during World War 2 in a wide variety of roles. This 1930 former Ribble Leyland Tiger TS2 with Leyland bodywork was converted by Alexanders as a mobile kitchen for the St Andrew's Ambulance Association.**
Gavin Booth collection

supplies, and enforced mileage reductions. Many operators helped to spin out their fuel supplies by cutting down the number of bus stops and often abandoned stops that involved a hill restart; parking buses in town and city centres during off-peak times cut out the dead mileage to and from depots.

In the early part of the war, chassis and body manufacturers continued to complete the orders they had in hand — though for service buses only; no coaches were built, as coach travel, regarded as a 'luxury' soon disappeared from the British scene. Initially there was no obvious relaxation of the high prewar standards in many of the buses that were built in the 1939-41 period,

but production slowed after the fall of France and the Dunkirk evacuations of 1940, and as the situation worsened the Government placed a ban on all new bus building in 1941. Spare parts and partly built buses were 'frozen' by this move, but because of the pressing need for new buses the manufacturers were permitted to complete and release the partly completed buses and buses for which parts were in stock. There were over 500 of these 'unfrozen' buses, including buses destined for export, and they were allocated to operators by the Minister of War Transport, with, if necessary, more regard to pressing needs than to fleet standardisation. The most-quoted example is the Daimler-dominated Edinburgh Corporation fleet, which found itself with a strange mixture of 'unfrozen' AECs, Bristols, Leylands and Tilling-Stevens, with bodywork by Bristol, Northern Counties, Park Royal, Pickering and Willowbrook; Edinburgh's standard suppliers before the war had been Daimler, Metro-Cammell and Weymann.

While the 'unfrozen' buses helped temporarily to fill the gap for some bus operators, longer-term plans were being formulated for a new breed of vehicle — the utility bus. Orders were placed with Guy and Leyland to supply 500 double-deck chassis each, but Leyland's resources were diverted elsewhere, and Guy, with limited double-deck experience, was left to develop the famous utility Guy Arab, using cast iron in place of precious aluminium. The specification was straightforward with a Gardner 5LW engine and a four-speed sliding mesh gearbox, but while most of the first 500 utility Arabs had the 5LW engine, the bigger 6LW unit became available for later deliveries.

A utility body specification was also evolved and was built by many of the leading coachbuilders in their own individual interpretations. The bodies were of composite construction (wood frames), with seating for 56 (30/26) in the highbridge version or 55 (27/28) in the less familiar lowbridge version; seats were

usually of the simple wooden-slatted type. There was to be only one opening window on each side, on each deck, and a single destination indicator at the front. Domed panels were not permitted, and in the early days windows were not permitted in the

42 Unconditionally utility — the interior of a Duple-bodied Bedford OWB, with wooden-slatted seats, hooded lightshades, basic interior panelling and restricted opening windows. *Ian Allan Library*

43 Utility trolleybuses were also built, by Sunbeam, although in some fleets they were badged as Karriers. This Karrier W with Park Royal 56-seat body was one of three delivered to Doncaster Corporation in 1943; note the predominance of servicemen in the bus queue. The bus was rebodied in 1958 with a Roe body which in 1962 was transferred to a new Daimler motorbus chassis. *Ian Allan Library*

43

emergency exit at the rear of the top deck. To add to the appearance of undoubted austerity the buses were often finished in plain grey or brown paint.

The equivalent single-decker was built by Bedford, a utility version of its prewar OB chassis, dubbed OWB. The choice of this normal control petrol-engined chassis was an interesting one, but with a standard utility body seating 32 passengers it provided almost the capacity of heavier single-deckers in a bus that was also suitable for rural operation. The body style on the OWB was built to a standard design by Duple, and by Mulliner, Roe and SMT. The utility Bedfords, over 3,000 in all, were allocated to operators of all sizes, and independent, municipal and company fleets all had OWBs, in some cases squeezing many years of good service out of these useful buses.

The Daimler factories in Coventry were severely damaged by air raids in November 1940, but the company had 44 dispersal factories throughout England and North Wales, and production of aeroplane engines and the famous Daimler four-wheel-drive Scout Car was able to continue. In 1942 Daimler bus production was restarted in Wolverhampton and 100 utility double-deck chassis were allocated to operators in 1943. The Daimler CWG5 was largely based on the successful prewar COG5 chassis, with Gardner 5LW engine and preselector gearbox.

After the first 100 chassis, AEC replaced Gardner as Daimler's wartime bus engine supplier; the AEC 7.7-litre engine was fitted to more than 1,200 Daimler CWA6s.

In all around 1,400 utility Daimlers were built, roughly half the total of utility Guy Arabs. There was one other utility motor bus chassis, when Bristol came back on the scene with a wartime version of the prewar K model. Most were fitted with a version of the AEC 7.7-litre engine and around 250 of the resulting K6A models were built in 1944 and 1945.

There was also a utility trolleybus built by Sunbeam, the W4 model, labelled either Karrier or Sunbeam and built between 1942 and 1945; around 280 were supplied. Sunbeam was an old-established company, building cars and motor buses and, from 1931, trolleybuses. Sunbeam became part of the Rootes empire in 1935 and absorbed the production of Karrier trolleybuses the same year. Sunbeam changed hands again in 1948 when Guy Motors took over, thus completing an ironic circle, for Sydney Guy had left Sunbeam in 1914 to form his own business.

In all, some 6,700 utility buses and trolleybuses were built between 1942 and 1945; naturally enough this was a considerable shortfall on prewar performance, but a creditable performance nonetheless in the difficult circumstances.

This was not the sum total of wartime bus building. There was a certain amount

Intolerable problems

A great deal has been written elsewhere on the intolerable problems which bus operators faced during the war. Although the public was continually asked 'Is Your Journey Really Necessary?', very often it was and bus operators had to try to provide the necessary transport. A few examples serve to recall some of the amazing difficulties which were encountered, and usually overcome, in different parts of Britain.

Inevitably, London was the target for much of the enemy action. London Transport lost many of its vehicles in the air raids of the early war years, and had to borrow buses from other operators. By the end of 1940, 472 provincial buses were working in London. Most were double-deckers — only 83 were single-deck — and they came from 51 operators throughout Britain; the farthest travelled came from the Inverness fleet of Greigs.

The borrowed buses were returned in 1941 when the situation improved and soon London Transport was able to lend buses to provincial towns suffering from vehicle shortages. A total of 334 ST type AEC Regents were loaned in this way.

London Transport received a reasonable allocation of new buses in the war years, though nowhere near the number it would normally expect. In addition to the 150 RTs, ordered in 1939 and delivered in 1939-40, there were 54 unfrozen buses, AEC Regents, Bristol K5Gs and Leyland Titans. From 1942 on, LT took delivery of over 700 utility buses — 435 Arabs, 20 Bristol K6As and 281 Daimler CWA6s. They were a far cry from the high quality vehicles familiar to London bus passengers, but they were serviceable machines at a time when every vehicle was valuable.

London's Green Line coach services were severely affected by the war. Most routes were suspended on 31 August 1939, when the coaches were withdrawn for conversion to ambulances, but replacement bus services were soon introduced on what had previously been coach-only sections and in 1940 Green Line routes trickled back. By September 1942 the war situation had worsened considerably and all Green Line routes were withdrawn — an annual saving of more than 11 million miles. There were no Green Line services until February 1946, but in the meantime LT had carried out a survey to discover what former Green Line passengers were doing instead. Half were simply not travelling; another 20% were using country buses; 10% central buses; under 10% railways; and a negligible number used trams, trolleybuses and tubes.

The Tilling group of companies told the story of its war effort in a 1945 publication *The War That Went on Wheels*. The group brought together 20 bus-operating companies and all were affected to some degree by the hostilities. Some were out of direct danger, like Caledonian, Cumberland, Lincolnshire, Thames Valley, United Auto, United Counties and West Yorkshire — but this did not mean that they had an easy time. Caledonian, for example, found itself with 12 new factories, five aerodromes, a flying-boat station, 12 military camps and a new port; between 1939 and 1945 the fleet increased from 116 buses to 167. United Auto lost 1,400 of 3,600 men to the armed forces, and was heavily involved in evacuating schoolchildren to safer inland spots — 82,000 in two days; United's passenger numbers jumped from 117 million in 1938 to 146 million in 1945.

Tilling fleets on the south and east coasts of England found themselves in a potentially dangerous situation if the expected invasion had come. Previously noisy and colourful seaside resorts became prohibited areas with heavy troop movements, particularly after Dunkirk. Southern Vectis, on the Isle of Wight, found itself in the thick of the Battle of Britain. Salisbury Plain, in Wilts & Dorset territory, became a giant training ground, and aerodromes, transit camps and shadow factories rapidly appeared; at one stage W&D was running 119 buses each day to Blandford Camp alone — more than the entire prewar fleet.

Other Tilling fleets found themselves in target areas for Luftwaffe air-raids. There was a huge influx of workers into the area served by Bristol Tramways for the aeroplane and other factories, and the bus fleet was stretched to the limit. To add to Bristol's problems nearly 2,000 busmen joined the services — and the company was in the midst of a replacement scheme for the Bristol trams. At first the tramway abandonment plans were postponed but early in 1941 one of the tram depots was destroyed, and later the main cable from the company's central power station was damaged, so the end of the tramway system was artificially accelerated.

Crosville, with Merseyside in its operating territory, also had to supply transport for new factories. The Royal Ordnance Factory at Wrexham needed 200 buses alone, and there were 65 aerodromes and camps needing new or augmented services. To meet these needs, 136 buses were borrowed or hired from other Tilling fleets, although only 49 new buses were delivered; normally Crosville would have taken 600 buses into the fleet in the six war years.

Southampton was a major problem for Hants & Dorset during the war, for this important seaport also housed the main Supermarine factory producing Spitfire aircraft. After several false alarms, the factory was eventually destroyed in September 1940, necessitating a high-speed exodus from the area with Hants & Dorset and Southampton Corporation buses evacuating workers to safety.

On another occasion, a dive-bomber attack on Gosport, an H&D driver recalled: 'After the all-clear sounded, I set off again in my "E-type" (a Leyland TD1) and was bowling up to the top of the Rowner Railway Arch when I saw the middle was missing. I just managed to stop in time and reversed back into a field.'

The Royal Blue express services of Western National and Southern National were still in the midst of a typically busy summer when the war broke out. The emphasis then switched from the predominant holiday traffic to traffic of a more essential nature. The Royal Blue services linking London, south central and southwest England were important links, but by November 1942 all services had to be suspended. Replacement bus services were provided over roads not otherwise covered, and it was 1946 before express services re-started.

In BET group companies and municipalities similar problems were encountered. Sussex — Southdown territory — was regarded as a safe area in 1939, and thousands of children were evacuated to its towns and villages; after Dunkirk the south coast came dramatically into the front line and the evacuees were re-evacuated. Many thousands of troops moved into the area, however, and this made great demands on Southdown, already short of vehicles and crews. The company's success in providing essential transport while also saving precious fuel is clearly illustrated by the passenger and mileage comparisons between 1939 and 1944; the total mileage dropped from 22.5 million to less than 16 million in five years; passenger figures rose from 60 million to 90 million in the same period.

Much of Kent was declared a Defence Area, and the East Kent bus company found itself very vulnerable to shelling and bomber fighter aircraft, and to the later flying bombs. The buses themselves were often attacked by German aircraft, and the constant danger faced by the crews around Dover gave rise to the well-deserved nickname the 'Busman's Malta'.

Inevitably East Kent's wartime toll was heavy; many staff were killed or injured, three depots were almost totally destroyed, and many vehicles damaged, but the willing efforts of all staff ensured that the company's important contribution to the war work was a successful one.

Wearside was a centre of shipbuilding and heavy industry, but the recession in the northeast had meant that the Sunderland Corporation tram services did not always serve these areas that were now of vital importance. For this reason, more buses were needed in the tram-predominated fleet, and there was a proportionately high intake of utility buses. The trams played an important part, particularly as crowd-movers; there is at least one reported case of the conductress of a 62-seat tram refusing a passenger because there were already 112 aboard!

Coventry Transport entered the war like every other municipal operator. Bus and tram windows were lacquered in blue, bus roofs were painted grey in place of the normal ivory and frequencies were reduced. There was some slight bombing in August 1940, but three months later the city was the target for a savage air raid which destroyed Coventry Cathedral, reduced much of the city centre to ruins, wrecked or damaged over half the Coventry bus fleet, and forced the immediate withdrawal of the remainder of the tramway system. Luckily there were some hired buses held in reserve, and these were hastily pressed into service, and others borrowed from municipalities, mainly in the northwest of England, and from London Transport.

Faced with more than its fair share of wartime problems, Coventry Transport struggled valiantly on, helped by reasonable supplies of unfrozen and utility buses.

In Scotland the SMT group turned its varied resources to help the war effort. It produced aircraft assemblies, vehicle trailers, heavy tank transporters, ordnance parts, built vehicle bodies, assembled Jeeps and built tank landing craft. Among its vehicle bodies were 481 utility 32-seat bus bodies for Bedford OWB chassis.

SMT's wartime record *Achievement* was published in February 1945, before the end of hostilities, and paid tribute to the group's staff: 'The physical strain of black-out driving of overloaded vehicles, of conducting a bus and collecting fares in a solid jam of people, is obvious and, we believe, appreciated by the passenger. Not so obvious is the mental strain involved in the responsibility of driving 60 to 70 passengers under these conditions, or to appreciate the buoyant mental attitude of the conductress who contrives to squeeze in just two more passengers. Couple these conditions with long working days, and no tribute can be too high for the sheer dogged courage it takes to do it. So, too, with maintenance staffs, lacking even the normal flow of spares, forcing fitness into the bigger vehicles as their mileage piles up, dragging out the service life of vehicles which, to our peace-time standards, are thousands of miles too old. To these men and women must go much of the credit for our war-time achievement.'

of rebodying work on older chassis; in some cases war-damaged buses were given new bodies, and in others single-deck coaches became double-deck buses, providing much-needed extra capacity.

Diversification

One problem of running buses in wartime was peculiar to only a handful of operators. In October 1942, with the object of protecting fuel supplies, the Ministry of War Transport ordered 57 large British bus operators to convert 10% of their fleets for gas operation. The eventual target was 2,500 gas buses — a target that was never reached. London Transport converted 252 ST types and nine Ts, but only 160 ran, and many of these were used in the Country Area. The Tilling group converted 332 buses, which averaged 7.8 million miles a year, saving one million gallons of fuel.

Petrol-engined buses, with their much lower compression ratio, were usually chosen for conversion, using the standard two-wheeled producer gas trailers. These had a firebox, an anthracite hopper, a water tank and a cooler, and produced the gas from activated anthracite and water. The performance of gas buses was good on the flat and sluggish on hills, and operators were delighted to comply with the Government instruction to abandon the use of producer gas in September 1944.

Although bus chassis manufacture was in the hands of only Bedford, Daimler and Guy for the best part of the war, the other bus builders were equally involved in the national effort. AEC built Matador artillery tractor units, armoured cars, mine-sweeping equipment, Marshal lorries and engines for tanks. Bristol, before it returned to bus work, made shells, tank components and aircraft fuselages. Leyland's massive war effort included the production of over 10,000 tank engines, over 3,000 tanks, over 7,500 high explosive bombs, over 11 million incendiary bombs and over 5 million 20mm shells.

Operators too played their parts. SMT, for instance, with a thriving prewar private car business, had useful engineering and production capacity. In various factories throughout central Scotland SMT produced aircraft assemblies and gun parts, assembled motor vehicles, refitted marine engines and built vehicle bodies, including utility buses on Bedford OWB chassis.

London Transport, too, made good use of its vast resources, as a partner in London Aircraft Productions assembling

44

44 Painted in what must have been an attractive combination of East Kent red and wartime grey, a 1936 Leyland Titan TD4 with Park Royal 53-seat lowbridge bodywork; note the air raid shelter sign, a reminder of Kent's vulnerable situation.
M&D and East Kent Bus Club

45 Wartime in London's Piccadilly Circus, with buses, taxis and only a few private cars in evidence. The camouflage markings on the Wolseley in the foreground suggest that it may be on official business. The buses are London Transport STLs and LTs and, in the foreground, one of the 100 STDs, all-Leyland TD4s, complete with reduced destination blind display to save linen. *Ian Allan Library*

46 After its initial shortages, London Transport was able to lend out buses later in the War; this typical ST type AEC Regent found its way to Youngs of Paisley, and is seen in Glasgow. *Ian Allan Library*

47 A small batch of single-deck utility trolleybuses was built, for Darlington Corporation in 1943. These were eight Karrier W types with centre-entrance bodies by Brush. *Ian Allan Library*

48 Heavy wartime loadings necessitated the construction of bus stations in some areas, and this 1943 Nottingham scene shows buses from several fleets using a new facility. On the left are forward-entrance AEC Regents of Midland General; in the centre Leylands of Barton Transport; and on the right a Midland Red SOS. The Barton single-deck Leyland, a 1938 Duple-bodied Lion LT7, was powered by producer gas, hence the rather inelegant gasbag on the roof. *Ian Allan Library*

47

48

53

49 Most gas-driven buses towed a trailer which was the producer unit. The bus, seen in 1942, was a 1931 Midland Red SOS IM6 type, complete with the company's ornate scroll on the emergency door. *Ian Allan Library*

50 June 1940 in Chesterfield, and two Corporation Leylands in wartime garb, with windows partially blacked out, masked headlamps and white-painted mudguards and guardrail. They were new in 1937/38 with all-metal Leyland bodies, a Titan TD5c 51-seater and a Tiger TS8 32-seater. Both buses lasted in Chesterfield only until 1947, and the Titan passed to Alexanders, finally being withdrawn in 1961. *G. H. F. Atkins*

51 Staff shortages meant that many ladies were employed by bus operators, to conduct and in some cases to drive. This lady drove in 1941 for Felix Motors of Hatfield a firm that remained independent until it sold out to South Yorkshire PTE in 1976. The bus was a Roe-bodied AEC Regent. *Ian Allan Library*

50

Halifax bombers. Chrysler built the rear fuselage, Duple the nose shell, Express Motor & Body Works the inner wings and tailplane, and Park Royal the outer wings. LT built the centre section, installed the engine fuselage and front section, completed the erection and test-flew the plane. They used a new building at Aldenham, later to become an important bus overhaul works.

The war effectively cancelled out any problems of competition. As we have seen, bomb damage caused the premature withdrawal of two tramway systems, but some others just managed to struggle on until the end of the war. The hostilities slowed the prewar pace of tramway withdrawal, for trams often came into their own with fuel rationing. The only drawback was the tram's basic inflexibility, particularly where the tracks were damaged in air raids. Some of Coventry's trams were still standing abandoned on isolated sections of track weeks after the system's enforced abandonment.

Trolleybuses had the same advantages and disadvantages. Amazingly, one *new* system opened — the penultimate in Britain — at Cardiff in 1942. The decision to introduce trolleybuses in the Welsh capital had been taken early in 1939, and contracts had been placed.

Private motoring for other than essential purposes came to an abrupt stop early in the war, and it was to be some time before a full return to prewar levels could be made; this wartime cutback forced an extra load on to public transport.

Right in the middle of the war, in 1942, the bus company structure in England and Wales was significantly reorganised. The uneasy partnership between the Tilling and BET empires, Tilling & British Automobile Traction, was wound up, and the territorial companies it controlled were divided between Tilling and BET. Some went to the obvious parent group, while others changed allegiance. Tilling ended up with some of the fleets with the largest operating areas, often predominantly rural in nature; BET fleets were generally in the more densely-populated areas.

As the war situation improved, some of the restrictions affecting bus operators were relaxed; blackout regulations were less stringent, and utility buses were less austere. There was also a certain amount of preparation for a resumption of peacetime production. In 1943-44 Crossley and Midland Red both had built prototypes on which their postwar models were based, and Daimler introduced a completely new bus engine, the 8.6-litre CD6 unit, in 1944.

By VE-Day in May 1945 Britain was counting the cost of six long years of war. The bus industry had kept going in the most difficult circumstances, coping with shortages of staff, of vehicles, of fuel, and in many cases with the wholesale destruction of depots, offices and buses. But the peace had been hard-won and the industry faced a major rebuilding task to re-attain the standards of the late 1930s. Forward planning had been forced into the limbo of an uncertain future; the travelling requirements of peacetime Britain were an unknown quantity; buses that had been bought in the early 1930s with a useful life expectancy of eight or nine years were now running on borrowed time, and were showing their age; while the utility buses provided reliable — if basic — transport, they represented only a small proportion of the normal peacetime vehicle intake for most fleets.

The war had presented a mixed bag of problems for the bus operators, but peace was to present new problems, often with less immediate solutions.

Crosville's contemporary report of its wartime experiences closes with these patriotic words: 'We roared with avidity into battle and like conquerors we step blithely forward into peace. Away with doldrums. Crosville has not time for them.'

SMT's closing words in its *Achievement* booklet reflected its dual role as bus operators and motor car dealers, and they were words that were to be prophetic in their effect on both branches of the business: 'We of SMT are determined that we shall play our part in making the future worth the lives laid down for it. Towards re-creating, and far surpassing, our already high prewar standard of public transport service, we shall re-absorb our men from the fighting forces and draw upon the operational experiences and technical advances of the war years. No hazy dreams of jet-propelled streamlined auto-road projectiles here, but a determined approach to increased technical and operational efficiency, reliability and frequency of service, comfort and safety — on these basic aspects of road transport is industry built, and on them, will be re-built.

'Let us hope, too, that we shall be the means of bringing, to a far larger circle, the enjoyment, convenience, and (often forgotten) the commercial advantages of motoring. There will be new motoring, and better motoring. . . .'

Events

1941 Bus building frozen.
1942 Guy Arab utility double-deck
     introduced.
     Bedford OWB utility single-deck
     introduced.
     Sunbeam/Karrier W utility
     trolleybus introduced.
     Cardiff trolleybus system opens.
     Tilling and BAT groups split.
1943 Daimler CWG5 utility double-deck
     introduced.
1944 Coras Iompair Eireann formed.

World Events

1940 Rationing in Britain.
     France invaded.
1941 Germany invades Russia.
     Pearl Harbour attack brings United
     States into War.
1942 Battle of El Alamein.
1943 Allies invade Italy.
1944 D-day landings.
1945 Germany surrenders.

Guy Arab

The pressing need for new buses during World War 2 forced Guy Motors into unexpected prominence. Guy had been building commercial vehicles since 1914, and although these included full-size buses from the mid-1920s, the company was not in the same league as AEC, Bristol, Daimler or Leyland in terms of

Spartan but rugged, the utility Guy Arab model that played such an important part in maintaining services during and after World War 2. This was the first production example,

built in 1942 with Park Royal body and delivered to Swindon Corporation. It had the Gardner 5LW engine and all-grey 'livery'.
Ian Allan Library

production or customer acceptability.

The 1942 utility Arab was based on Guy's 1933 Arab model, with Gardner 5LW engine and crash gearbox, but using cast iron in place of valuable lighter alloys. Some operators were allowed the bigger 6LW engine where conditions dictated, and utility Arabs quickly appeared throughout Britain, in everything from small independent fleets to the giant London Transport.

The Arab, a rugged, no-nonsense chassis, married to a no-frills utility body, provided bus-hungry operators with vehicles that lacked the smoothness and sophistication of their immediate prewar predecessors, but were welcome just the same.

Around 2,500 utility Arabs were delivered between 1942 and 1945, and supplies trickled on into 1946, to be joined by improved postwar models. The inherent soundness of the chassis meant that many of the utility Arabs survived with new or rebuilt bodies for many years after the war.

Sign of the Times

Profile

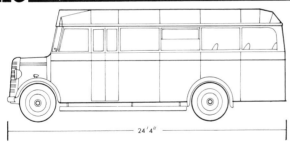

Main single-deck wartime model marked a reversion to an older with semi-normal control, and driver behind engine; petrol engine and forward entrance, though 32 seats (as many as on some bigger buses) in no-frills body.

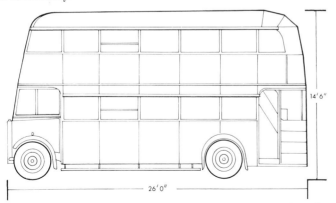

Utility specification was simplified variation of the prewar style; absence of curved metal and opening windows reflected need for basic bus. 56 seats (30/26).

Notice "BUS STOPS"

On and after 12 DEC 1942 picking up and setting down points for passengers will have to be again reduced. We have been instructed to do this by the Ministry of War Transport with a view to saving Petrol and Rubber which is of vital importance to the War Effort. Please make sure you know where the Bus Stops are, lists of same are exhibited in the Buses. Please do not ask the Driver to stop at places not listed and do not blame him if a little inconvenience is caused to you through the new order.

Re WIRELESS ACCUMULATORS.

Wireless Accumulators or other batteries containing Acid are not allowed to be carried in the Buses.

Re CHILDREN

PLEASE NOTE—Children are not allowed to occupy the seats when adults are standing.

Re BUS TICKETS

Used Bus Tickets must be salvaged. Please put them in the receptacle provided and NOT in the Ash Trays.

The problems of wartime prompted operators to make special demands of their passengers.
Gavin Booth collection

56

Morally great, but economically bankrupt 1945-50

An advert for the SMT Group which appeared late in 1946 summed up the feelings of many transport operators in those early postwar days. Under a photograph of a Western SMT driver, newly returned from six years' war service, the copy ran: 'He's back from the Services — back to the same old job — back to the same old bus. He might have had a brand new bus waiting for him — but new ones are needed for export too. We didn't get many replacements during war-time; we can't get many even now, and we are still short of highly skilled maintenance men. So the wartime shortage of 'fit' buses still lingers on. That means we aren't running the kind of bus service we gave you prewar, but we are all out to get enough new buses to give you service and facilities we can boast about once again!'

So the problems of wartime had given way to the new problems of peacetime. In

1945 there was a natural reaction to the strictures of the previous six years — Britain was at peace again and the British people wanted to celebrate. They had money to spend but there was little to spend it on. The BBC Television Service returned in June 1946, but was still available to a very limited audience; the private car industry was still recovering from the pressures of war work, and fuel was still rationed. The result was a tremendous growth in leisure travel, and the bus and coach industry enjoyed an unexpected boom that was to help them through these days of austerity and continued rationing.

Not that things were any easier for bus operators. There were precious few new buses to be had, and most fleets contained an unhappy assortment of time-served veterans, tired after prolonged war service, and vehicles dating from the immediate

52 In 1947 London Transport and the Passenger Vehicle Operators' Association set up a 'relief service' scheme to cope with the demands on London's hard-pressed bus fleet. Nearly 400 coaches were hired in to operate during rush hours, including this Windsorian Bedford OB with Duple Vista body, seen outside Windsor Castle. The semi-normal control OB with Vista body was probably the best known and best loved of the early postwar coaches. *J. M. Aldridge collection*

prewar period, basically sound but often in need of proper overhaul. These were the lucky ones. The less fortunate operators — often those with predominantly coach fleets — had lost some or all of their vehicles to the Services in the early days of the war and were now faced with the problem of rounding them up.

When the first new postwar buses appeared in 1945-46 they were largely similar to their immediate prewar

counterparts. There were of course sound practical reasons for this as the bus builders had been concentrating on everything from Jeeps to planes and new design work was inevitably curtailed. But operators were glad to get hold of anything new. And that meant literally anything. Unfamiliar chassis and body makes appeared in what had once been highly standardised fleets, and there was a great spate of rebuilding and rebodying older vehicles. But all this was aggravated by the desire to re-establish British goods in world markets and priority was given to exports for a while.

Familiar single-deck chassis like the AEC Regal, Bristol L and Leyland Tiger made their reappearance on the British market in 1946, with few major changes to their sturdy and straightforward specifications. Bedford, with the wartime OWB production behind it, bounced quickly back with the OB, which virtually cornered the market for small normal control chassis. Other smaller models appeared in 1946, the normal control Commer Commando and Guy Wolf, and the forward control Guy Vixen. Even Leyland had a stab at the lucrative market for smaller coaches with its normal control Comet range introduced in 1947, but it was most at home competing for the full-size single-deck business where the Tiger had to fight off models like the Daimler CVD6, Dennis Lancet, Guy Arab and Maudslay Marathon. 'Full-size' at the time usually meant 27ft 6in (8.38m) by 7ft 6in (2.29m) (although 8ft [2.44m] wide buses were permitted over routes approved by the Traffic Commissioners, from July 1946), and in spite of the many experiments of the 1930s the engine was still firmly at the front — except in the Midland Red fleet. This Birmingham-based company had managed to get the first British production underfloor-engined buses in service in 1949, with its S6 model designed and built purely for its own use. Next came Sentinel, with the integral STC4 model, and Commer with the petrol-engined Avenger featuring a front-mounted underfloor-engine. These were important

moves, but it took the entry of the big guns and a change in the regulations affecting vehicle dimensions in 1950 to herald the real arrival of the underfloor bus — by which time Midland Red had over 350 underfloor-engined buses in service.

AEC and Leyland, deadly rivals at that time, were both anxious to show their new underfloor models to the world. The first complete AEC Regal IV, with horizontally-mounted 9.6-litre engine, appeared early in 1950, while the first Leyland/MCW Olympic, an integral model with horizontal 9.8-litre engine, was unveiled late in 1949. Early examples of both models were only 27ft 6in (8.38m)

long but the 1950 change in dimensions permitted 30ft (9.14m) by 8ft (2.44m) single-deckers and the new size was eagerly adopted. Britain took a rather conservative line on bus dimensions for some years — in the United States 35ft (10.67m) long buses had been permitted from 1947.

Leyland's Olympic, developed jointly with coachbuilder MCW, enjoyed only a limited success on the home market — but a much more spectacular success overseas — and a separate chassis, the Leyland Royal Tiger, appeared in 1950, opening the floodgates for a veritable rush of similar chassis. By September 1950, when the 15th Commercial Motor Show was

55

56

56

55 This 1935 East Midland all-Leyland Titan TD4, looking slightly the worse for wear, carried a BET group 'British Buses' anti-nationalisation emblem when seen in Nottingham in 1948.
Roy Marshall

56 An AEC Regal I with Burlingham 35-seat body, supplied in 1946 to Howe of Spennymoor, then part of the famous OK Motor Service combine. These basic vehicles helped operators rebuild their businesses after World War 2. It is is seen crossing Newcastle's Tyne Bridge on the main route to Bishop Auckland. AEC

opening, the AEC and Leyland models had been joined by new underfloor models from Atkinson, Dennis and Guy, but their successes and failures really belong in the next chapter as does the undoubted success of another 1950 model, the forward control Bedford SB which replaced the highly successful OB model.

The demand for new buses and coaches attracted many new names to the coachbuilding business. Some were commercial bodybuilders which had turned to coaches — and their efforts were often as mixed as their origins. The magazine *Bus & Coach* for December 1949, for instance, carried adverts from 27 coachbuilders — and that did not include some of the larger firms like Burlingham, Massey, Northern Counties, Plaxton and Roe. Many of the 27 are only vague memories more than 35 years later — names like Crawford Prince-Johnson, Samlesbury, Duffield, All-Weather, Gurney Nutting and Trans-United.

There were crude attempts at streamlining many of the coaches of the period, and often a full-width front disguised the normal exposed radiator, another concession to 'modernity'. But the coaches of the 1940s that weathered best were the simpler designs, often with direct prewar ancestry, which came from the longer-established builders.

Lower and more powerful

The double-decker of the 1940s had a front engine and rear entrance, usually seating 56 in highbridge form, or 53 in side-gangway lowbridge form. It had a

bigger engine than its equivalent of a decade earlier and while Midland Red and Foden — and eventually every builder — fitted tin fronts in place of the traditional exposed radiator, few major mechanical changes had taken place for some years. The Bristol/ECW Lodekka changed all that.

The Lodekka was a revolutionary new design with a low centre of gravity to permit normal-height central gangways in both decks within the 'lowbridge' height of 13ft 4in (4.06m). The prototype appeared in 1949, and the Bristol Lodekka was to prove by far the most successful low-floor double-deck design.

57 As express services re-started after the War, operators bought new coaches to win passengers back. SMT bought this AEC Regal III with fully-fronted Burlingham body in 1948, the company's first vehicle to the new 8ft width, and it is seen attracting much attention in St Andrew Square, Edinburgh, before starting its journey to London. *SBG*

58 Dennis Lancet coaches were popular with independent operators in the late 1940s, and this 1946 Yellow Bus Services coach was based in Dennis's home-town, Guildford. The bodywork was built by Whitson of West Drayton, one of the plethora of small bodybuilders that appeared on the market after the War, but rarely lasted beyond the mid-1950s. *Ian Allan Library*

57

But in 1949 Bristol's front-line double-deck model was still the traditional K type, which reappeared in peacetime form in 1946, joining the postwar models from AEC, Albion, Crossley, Guy and Leyland.

AEC's first postwar model was introduced in 1945, designated Regent Mk II. This straightforward chassis combined the AEC 7.7-litre engine, a sliding mesh gearbox and vacuum brakes — a standardised specification which helped many operators in their urgent demands for new buses. A more refined AEC double-decker, the Regent Mk III, appeared in late 1946 when chassis based on the trend-setting RT type of 1938 were delivered to some provincial customers. The later provincial Regent III model was clearly based on the RT, as originally offered with 9.6-litre engine, preselective gearbox and air brakes, but had a quite different frontal appearance. There were later models with options like the sliding

mesh gearbox, the 7.7-litre engine and vacuum brakes.

Leyland also answered the urgent call for new buses with a fairly basic model, the Titan PD1 which first appeared in 1946. This featured a new 7.4-litre engine, based on units fitted in Leyland-built tanks, and was coupled to a constant-mesh gearbox and vacuum brakes. As with the AEC Regent, the PD1 was soon followed by a more refined chassis which eventually replaced it. The Leyland Titan PD2 first appeared in 1947, with a new 9.8-litre engine and a synchromesh gearbox (the first on a heavy-duty bus), a powerful and smooth combination that guaranteed the PD2 a long and successful lifespan.

The rugged combination of medium-powered engine, constant-mesh gearbox and vacuum brakes was widely favoured in the 1940s and 1950s, and could be found in chassis like the Albion Venturer, Bristol K, Crossley DD42,

Dennis Lance, Foden PVD6 and Guy Arab III. The Gardner 5LW or 6LW engines were available on all except the Albion and Crossley chassis, while Bristol and Dennis also offered their own engines as alternatives. Daimler's postwar CV series gave customers a choice of the two Gardner engines, and Daimler's own 8.6-litre CD6 unit.

By 1950 the chassis manufacturers were offering further refinements in their double-deck models. Operators had found that big engines running below full power were economical and reliable, and even larger engines like the 10.35-litre Meadows 6DC630 and the 10.6-litre Daimler CD650 were introduced. The Meadows engine was available in the Guy Arab, as an alternative to the more normal Gardners, but the CD650 Daimler appeared in an advanced model carrying the same designation, and featuring hydraulic power-assisted operation for steering,

58

59 The first commercially-available underfloor-engined vehicle was the Sentinel STC4, an integral vehicle bodied by Beadle. This Sentinel demonstrator was built in 1950, but although Ribble bought batches in 1949/51, most deliveries were to independent operators. Like other early underfloor buses, this vehicle was built to the 27ft 6in length. *Ian Allan Library*

59

60 A trend-setting coach at the 1950 Commercial Motor Show, a 'Big Bedford' SB with Duple Vega body, the 33-seater that replaced the popular OB model. The price of the complete coach was £2,190 painted in operators colours. *Ian Allan Library*

61 New buses were greatly appreciated in the early postwar years, and East Midland made good use of these lowbridge all-Leyland Titan PD2s, seen in Mansfield in 1948. The East Midland livery at the time was a striking yellow, brown and cream. *G. H. F. Atkins*

62 Birmingham's postwar fleet continued its prewar traditions, with Metropolitan-Cammell-bodied Daimlers like this 1947 CVA6, seen when new. *G. H. F. Atkins*

60
61

62

gearchange and brakes. Neither of these combinations really caught on for home market models, though, as they often proved troublesome, and the Gardner engine continued to find the most favour among operators.

The Midland Red company continued to go its own way as far as new double-deckers were concerned. During and after the war it had been forced to buy AECs, Daimlers, Guys and Leylands, but in 1949 the new BMMO D5 model appeared, based largely on a wartime prototype. The D5 had BMMO's 8-litre engine, a constant-mesh gearbox and hydraulic brakes, and it had a full-width front concealing the radiator. Two hundred D5s were built, the second hundred with doors on the rear platform.

Ultimate standardisation

London Transport suffered from the same postwar problems that dogged every operator — only on a much larger scale. But London Transport ended the war in a much healthier state than the equivalent transport authorities in Berlin and Paris; there was literally no public transport running in Berlin at the end of the war, while in Paris one of the first peacetime tasks was to round up the vehicles which had been dispersed far and wide under the German occupation. London Transport, on the other hand, only lost 166 of its 6,000 buses during the war. Even so one of the first priorities was fleet renewal and LT's prewar standardisation was abandoned in the interests of quick deliveries — but of the 746 new buses ordered for 1946, only 225 were delivered that year. There were AEC Regent IIs and Leyland Titan PD1s and the equivalent single-deck AEC Regals and Leyland Tigers, but London Transport was anxious to take deliveries of its RT model, so huge orders were placed. By the end of 1947 around 4,000 RTs were on order — but only 182 had been taken into stock. The position gradually improved, and between 1947 and 1954 LT received a staggering total of 4,673 RTs; add to this the 1,631 RTLs, Leyland Titans built to London specification, and the 500 RTWs, Titans again but 8ft wide, and the RT family eventually totalled nearly 7,000 buses — standardisation indeed!

The RT, superbly designed and engineered, efficient and reliable, helped London to cope with the unexpected postwar rush of passengers, but deliveries were slow to gain momentum and there were various temporary measures to overcome this. Around 575 coaches — of all shapes, sizes and ages — were hired from private operators for relief work in 1947-49, and there were also 190 brand new Bristol double-deckers intended for Tilling group firms that ran for a while on the London streets. The situation gradually

Rationalisation then nationalisation

The changes in the economic and social climate in Britain following the war forced transport much farther into the political arena. The Labour Government of 1945 inherited a country that has been described as 'morally great, but economically bankrupt', and its solution to many of the problems it faced was nationalisation. In its six-year term of office the Labour Government nationalised mines, electricity, railways, road haulage, gas, iron and steel — and some large segments of the bus industry.

Necessity had largely mothered the fusion of the four mainline railway companies into British Railways in 1948. Forced to work together in the war — with a creditable degree of success — the railways too were suffering from the postwar after-effects. Nationalisation plans had been announced in 1945, and the 1947 Transport Act created the British Transport Commission. The Act came into force on 1 January 1948, and BTC assumed immediate control of British Railways and London Transport. The old London Passenger Transport Board gave way to the new London Transport Executive, and the 1947 Act further affected the bus business in that the railway shareholdings in the many company fleets throughout Britain had automatically passed into the nationalised control of the BTC. The next logical step was the sale of the Tilling group road transport interests to the BTC for just under £25 million. Faced with a similar situation, the SMT Group in Scotland decided that voluntary sale of its bus interests to the BTC was a sensible move, and in 1949 SMT joined Tilling in the nationalised ranks, for a price of £26.8 million. The BTC bus empire was also enlarged with the acquisition of the Red & White group, and of a number of smaller, but important, independent operators which helped them to gain footholds in other parts of Britain, while the nationalisation of electricity brought the Mansfield District, Midland General and Notts & Derby companies into BTC hands.

Another consequence of the Labour Government was the proposal to create Passenger Road Transport Boards which would encompass all bus operators in sizeable parts of the country. The first, a Northern PRTB, was to cover the northeast of England, taking in over 200 operators of all sizes, and over 4,000 buses. Although other area schemes were discussed, a return to Conservative Government in 1951 meant that they were all stillborn.

There were changes too in Northern Ireland, where the Northern Ireland Road Transport Board passed to the Ulster Transport Authority in 1948 along with the Belfast & County Down Railway and the lines formerly operated by the LMS.

63 **London Transport took advantage of its newly-forged links with the British Transport Commission to borrow 180 new Bristol double-deckers from Tilling group fleets to cover a vehicle shortage. This Eastern Counties Bristol K5G had highbridge Eastern Coach Works bodywork.** *Ian Allan Library*

64 Company and municipal trolleybuses in Nottingham in 1949. A new Weymann-bodied BUT 9611T of Notts & Derby Traction alongside a 1931 Brush-bodied Ransomes of Nottingham Corporation. *G. H. F. Atkins*

eased — though at one stage there were more RT bodies than chassis, so the new bodies were mounted on rebuilt prewar STL chassis, and classified SRT; only 160 SRTs were produced, as the chassis problem quickly improved.

There was no complacency in London, however, and plans were already in hand for the RT's successor. In the final years of the war and in the early postwar years LT was also looking at the possibilities of employing a seated conductor on double-deckers, on the pay-as-you-board principle. Several buses, STLs and trolleybuses, were experimentally converted, but without much success. Another conversion was RT97, one of the prewar RTs, which had been damaged by a V1 rocket in 1944, and which reappeared with an air-operated sliding door. The same bus was totally rebuilt to re-emerge as a double-deck coach, RTC1, extensively modernised inside and out. Its sleek lines foreshadowed the RT's replacement introduced five years later, while inside it had an advanced heating and ventilating system, tilted-back seats and fluorescent lighting.

The changes in the bus industry were not confined to the operating side of the bus business. Bristol's bus chassis side, and Eastern Coach Works, had both passed to the BTC with the Tilling sale, and their products were now restricted to nationalised fleets; in practice, the Tilling companies, always staunch Bristol/ECW users, were to buy nothing but Bristol/ECW products for more than 15 years. The Scottish group did buy a proportion of Bristol/ECWs but also retained its normal suppliers, like AEC, Bedford, Guy and Leyland, often with Alexander bodies — although here the situation was rather different. The Alexander coachbuilding activities were severed from the operating company upon nationalisation, and a new private company was formed, handling not only Scottish group work but also an increasing demand from Scottish municipal and independent fleets, and eventually from operators in England and Wales.

A group of leading manufacturers were considering an uncertain future when AEC, Albion, Dennis, Leyland and Thornycroft met in 1945 to discuss a scheme for integration, but it was Leyland — potentially one of the strongest components — which held out against the possibility of monopolies, price maintenance and nationalisation, coming down firmly in favour of competitive enterprise.

AEC and Leyland were the most directly competitive of the heavy commercial vehicle manufacturers. Leyland was jealous of AEC's long links with London Transport which ensured AEC's near-monopoly of London's bus orders. In 1946 Leyland managed to break the monopoly and obtained a 25% share in London's orders, not hugely profitable business, but regular, long-run work. This so pleased Leyland that they proclaimed in their adverts in the trade press that 'chassis and buses are now regularly leaving the Leyland factory for London at the rate of more than three every working day'. Leyland's position was further emphasised by a reminder that 'Leyland is the only single manufacturer of both chassis and bodywork to have supplied London with complete double-deckers'.

In spite of the intensity of their rivalry, AEC and Leyland did pool resources in 1946 to form British United Traction, a combination of their previously separate trolleybus-manufacturing interests. BUT built trolleybus chassis to both AEC and Leyland designs for many years and later

65 London Transport's vast trolleybus fleet was invaluable for moving crowds, like these football supporters leaving the Tottenham Hotspur ground in 1949. The most prominent buses are a 1939 AEC/MCW integral from the L1 class and a 1938 all-Leyland from the K1 class. At this time London Transport passenger carryings had reached a peak at over 4,600 million journeys in a year. *London Transport*

66 Holidaymakers flocked to Britain's resorts by public transport in the postwar years and this July 1950 scene at Wellington Street, Leeds shows Northern General Leylands and AECs bound for Newcastle, and an East Yorkshire Leyland Tiger PS1/Brush on the left, bound for Bridlington; its cantrail message reads 'This is not a nationalised bus', emphasising the independent stand of the BET group. *G. H. F. Atkins*

diversified to supply large quantities of diesel engines for British Railways multiple units.

At the same time AEC was busy looking for ways to expand its empire, and in 1948 it bought over two well-respected manufacturers, Crossley and Maudslay. The enlarged company, Associated Commercial Vehicles, encompassed AEC, Crossley and Maudslay, but the Crossley and Maudslay names survived on for a few years on what were otherwise AEC chassis. There was further empire-building in 1949 when ACV acquired the bodybuilding firms Park Royal and Roe. Guy was also expanding at the time and in 1948 bought over the Sunbeam trolleybus business.

In 1949 Britain's last new trolleybus system was opened, when Glasgow Corporation added trolleybuses to its motor buses, trams and subway trains. The Glasgow trolleybuses played only a small part in the large Glasgow network, during the later part of its comparatively short lifespan.

Glasgow was also demonstrating its faith in electrical traction by continuing its tramway fleet renewal. Between 1948 and 1952 it placed 100 new Cunarder trams in service, and other towns were also investing heavily in the tramcar. Aberdeen, Edinburgh, Leeds and Sheffield all bought new trams in the late 1940s, but they were going against the trend, which was to continue the abandonment process of the prewar period. The total number of trams in service in Britain fell from around 6,000 in 1945 to 4,700 in 1950, following withdrawals at centres like Manchester, Leicester, Southampton, Cardiff, Newcastle and Bradford.

The odds were heavily weighed against the tram in its traditional British role as a method of street transport. A few systems had built tramway extensions on reserved track segregated from other road traffic, following the successful example of many of the Continental tramways, but most British trams had to operate in the middle of roads that were becoming increasingly choked with motor traffic. Add to this the poor state of much trackwork following wartime neglect, and the high cost of a new tramcar — £10,000 as against £4,000 for a new bus — and the era of the British tram was nearing an end.

The postwar Indian summer of the motor bus was also nearing its end. The passengers continued to flock on to the buses, and for many operators 1949 and 1950 were the best-ever years for passenger loadings: Manchester Corporation carried a record 492 million passengers in 1949; Midland Red's peak year was 1950 with 440 million; London Transport's peak year was 1948, Olympic Games year, with 4,675 million passengers. The year 1949 was the all-time peak for new bus and coach registrations in Britain — 10,139, of which nearly half were double-deckers. But then the passenger figures started a slow decline, as private motoring mobilised the masses and television offered an indoor alternative to theatres and cinemas. Fortunately the passenger boom and the change in the structure of the industry had placed the industry in a strong position to face the future.

Not only bus travel was threatened. The coach business too was changing to suit new public preferences in the express and leisure markets. The express coach network had re-started gradually after the war, and initially new coaches had been low on the list of priorities. But as this changed some fine vehicles took to the road, including a fleet of double-deck coaches for Ribble express services. Coach touring got off to an even slower start, but by 1947 some operators were actually running overseas tours — a foretaste of later holiday trends.

Private motoring really got into top gear in 1950 when petrol came off the ration — the same year that London Transport withdrew its last petrol-engined bus, when the Inter-Station Leyland Cubs reached the end of the road with LT.

Events

1945 Postwar bus production resumes.
1946 BMMO introduces S6 underfloor-engined single-decker.
1947 Leyland Titan PD2 introduced.
1948 Sentinel STC — first commercially-available underfloor-engined bus.
Tilling, SMT and London Transport nationalised, British Transport Commission formed.
AEC forms Associated Commercial Vehicles with Crossley and Maudslay.
Ulster Transport Authority takes over from NIRTB.
1949 Leyland/MCW Olympic introduced.
Bristol Lodekka prototype unveiled.
Glasgow trolleybus system opens.
1950 AEC Regal IV and other underfloor-engined single-deckers.
Bedford SB replaces OB.

1949 Gas industry nationalised.
NATO formed.
1950 Petrol rationing ends.

World Events

1945 Atomic bombs on Hiroshima and Nagasaki.
1947 Coal industry nationalised.
1948 British Railways formed from nationalised main line railway companies.
Electricity nationalised.
National Health Service formed.
Ghandi assassinated.

A typical early production Bristol/ECW Lodekka, a 1954 LD6G for Southern Vectis, Tilling's Isle of Wight fleet.
P. R. Gainsbury collection

Bristol Lodekka

Leyland provided one solution to the lowbridge problem in 1927 with the Titan TD1 and its sunken side gangway layout. For many years this was the only way to achieve the 13ft 6in (4.11m) lowbridge height in a double-decker.

Then in 1949 Bristol and ECW, each part of the nationalised British Transport Commission, produced an advanced double-deck model, the Lodekka, which used a dropped-centre rear axle to achieve a low-level downstairs gangway, allowing a normal seating layout on the upper deck.

After testing prototypes, full production started in 1954, though deliveries were restricted to Tilling and Scottish group fleets. Flat-floor Lodekkas followed in 1959, including a 30ft (9.14m) forward entrance version, the FLF.

Other manufacturers emulated the Lodekka for the open market: Dennis produced the Lodekka under licence, the Loline; AEC developed the Bridgemaster and Renown; Leyland offered the Lowlander. None of these enjoyed the Lodekka's success.

All Lodekkas had attractive and sturdily-built ECW bodywork, seating 58 or 60 in the original LD version, and up to 78 in the extended FLFs built for certain operators in 1965-67.

The last of over 5,000 Lodekkas entered service in 1968, replaced by the rear-engined Bristol VRT model.

Sign of the Times

Profile

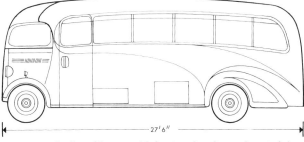

Reversion to prewar standards and layout, with front engine, forward control, increasingly with forward entrance. 35 seats.

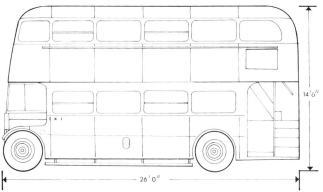

Improving the breed: although basic dimensions unchanged, all-metal body often with four-bay window construction; diesel engine now standard on double-deckers, many with preselect gearbox. 56 seats (30/26).

All-Weather was just one of the many coachbuilders competing for business in the postwar boom years; this 1949 trade advert displays a graphic approach that has dated as much as the body style.

Monstrous masses of shivering tin

1951-60

The bus operators who went into the 1950s confidently expecting the peak loadings of the 1940s were in for a rude awakening. It was certainly an eventful decade, but as the private car and the television set continued to eat into passenger figures, operators had to take an urgent look at the economics of their business. The inevitable outcome was a slow start to the seemingly endless round of fare increases and service reductions and withdrawals.

But there was also a good side to the 1950s. The structure of the bus-operating industry remained fairly static; after the upheaval of nationalisation there was some minor mopping-up to achieve a more neatly-organised industry. There was the nationalised BTC, controlling the Tilling, Scottish and London Transport fleets; the rival BET Group, with the rest of Britain's company buses; roughly 100 municipal bus fleets; and innumerable independents,

ranging from the big ones, like Barton, Lancashire United and West Riding, to one-coach fleets. The main changes in the 1950s really affected the design of the bus, the first positive moves away from the basic concept developed in the late 1920s.

Firstly, though, the threats to the bus industry. In London alone the 300,000 TV sets of 1950 had grown to two million 10 years later. The growth in private motoring was equally dramatic — from 2¼ million cars in 1950 to 5½ million in 1960. The stay-at-home habits encouraged by television, and the spread of the weekend motorist, seriously affected passenger loadings on the buses. The car also became more of a problem in urban areas, creating traffic congestion and hampering the smooth progress of public transport. The bus at least could cope after a fashion, but the essentially less flexible trams and trolleybuses faced new difficulties, and this

67 Wolverhampton Corporation tended to favour local products, like this Guy Arab IV, built in the same town, and Metropolitan-Cammell 60-seat bodywork built in nearby Birmingham. This 1957 example had an Orion-style body, the archetypal 1950s lightweight. The 'new-look' front end structure, covering the radiator, is based on the design first produced for Birmingham Corporation in 1950, and adopted by Daimler and Guy among other builders. *Guy*

was just one of the factors which hastened their demise.

Some of the best-known tramway systems disappeared during the decade, reducing Britain's tramway population from 4,700 to just 400. Notable casualties were London (in 1952), Birmingham and Belfast (1953), Sunderland (1954), Dundee and Edinburgh (1956), Liverpool (1957), Aberdeen (1958), Leeds (1959) and

68 New trolleybuses were still entering service in the 1950s. This Glasgow Corporation BUT 9613T of 1958 with Crossley 71-seat body, was one of 90 similar buses delivered in 1957/58, and was built to the recently-legalised 30ft length on two axles. Opened in 1949, the Glasgow trolleybus system closed in 1967. *Michael Dryhurst*

69 Although most operators quickly turned to underfloor-engined chassis, some still took later versions of the previous front-engined models. David MacBrayne, operating in the Western Highlands and Islands of Scotland, brought two of these AEC Regal III with 35-seat Roe bodywork in 1952. One is seen at Kinlochleven on the Fort William-Tyndrum service on 31 May 1953. Even the local garage had been patriotically decorated in anticipation of the Coronation two days later. *Roy Marshall*

Sheffield (1960). Among the trams consigned so unceremoniously to the scrapyard were relatively new — and expensive — cars with many years of good service in reserve. On the positive side, Blackpool was experimenting with trailer cars, and in 1960 ordered 10 trailer cars for high-capacity motor-and-trailer sets.

68

69

Activity on the trolleybus front was also fairly positive, even though Manchester Corporation reported in 1953 that the trolleybus was 'materially less efficient'. In 1954 Walsall Corporation displayed its faith in the trolleybus by introducing the first of 22 Sunbeam F4A double-deckers with Willowbrook bodies. These were 30ft (9.14m) long on two axles at a time when the maximum permitted length was 27ft (8.23m), and the Walsall Sunbeams anticipated the relaxed legislation of 1956. In 1958 Glasgow Corporation obtained special dispensation to buy 10 34ft 5in (10.49m) long single-deck trolleybuses — 30ft (9.14m) was the legal maximum at the time. These were used for Britain's last tram-trolleybus conversion, in 1958, and the route was the last outpost of the single-deck trolleybus, always a comparative rarity in Britain. Glasgow's experience with buses of this length encouraged the authorities to permit 36ft (11m) buses from 1961.

Infectious optimism

The dawn of the new Elizabethan age boosted British morale, signifying the end of austerity and the start of a new era that was typified by the new Comet airliner and the conquest of Mount Everest. Bus builders seemed to get caught in this mood of infectious optimism, and their new products certainly displayed ingenuity and advanced thinking in the country's best traditions. As we have already seen, the underfloor-engined single-decker really arrived in 1950 when a whole host of new models appeared. This first generation of underfloor models had a mixed reception.

Some, like the AEC, Bristol and Leyland models, sold well; most of the others attracted a small, though regular, clientele. Only the Dennis Dominant, which featured a semi-automatic Hobbs gearbox, could be called a flop (only two were built), but Dennis wisely offered a more familiar package, the Lancet UF, in 1953, and this had a faithful following.

Not all of the significant new models of 1950 had underfloor engines, though. There was the Bedford SB, forward control successor to the highly-successful normal control OB, and destined for a long and fruitful life; and there was the Foden PVR6, which completely defied convention with its transversely rear-mounted engine. Two engines were offered, the Gardner 6LW and Foden's own unusual two-stroke unit. In his book *A Further Look at Buses*, Geoffrey Hilditch described the Foden as 'one of those fascinating near misses', and wondered what would have happened if Foden had decided to develop a rear-engined *double*-deck model with a Gardner engine at the time.

The Foden anticipated fashion by at least 10 years, but made no noticeable impact on the market; nor did another rear-engined model of the 1950s, the Rutland Clipper which was built in small numbers in Surrey from 1956.

All of the new chassis gave body designers much more scope, and the coachbuilders had a brief but extravagant field day. The combination of increased dimensions and plain flat fronts prompted

70 The ultimate version of the Bristol L chassis was the LWL, 8ft wide and 30ft long. This 1952 LWL6B of Western National with attractive ECW 39-seat bodywork, was seen in 1963 at Bodmin General station collecting passengers for St Austell. *A. Moyes*

71 The big Ribble fleet tried examples of two of the very earliest underfloor-engined integrals — the Sentinel STC4 and, as seen here, the Leyland-MCW Olympic. This 1951 example was of the longer HR44 variety, and although the Olympic enjoyed great success in export markets, British operators preferred separate chassis and bodies. *Gavin Booth collection*

some amazing confections; too often the designs attempted to disguise the essentially box-like shape of the underfloor-engined single-decker, and a mass of chrome and other brightwork was equated with passenger appeal, but slowly the designers learned the lesson that a subtle and straightforward approach was the answer.

Coaches in the early 1950s usually had a centre entrance, between the axles, but there were operators who continued to specify a rear entrance. Gradually the bodybuilders perfected the fitment of one-piece coach doors ahead of the front axle and this layout increased in popularity. The underfloor-engined single-deck *bus* had an entrance at the extreme front right from its conception —

but there were operators who still preferred centre and even rear entrances, and some who fitted two doors to improve passenger circulation. Another fad of the time was the standee single-decker, with a relatively low seating capacity and extra room for standing passengers — a successful Continental idea that never really caught on in Britain. Most operators were glad of the extra seating capacity permitted by the new chassis; normally, up to 44/45 seated passengers could be carried, a decided improvement on the 35/39 passengers in the equivalent front-engined models.

Successful as many of the early underfloor buses undoubtedly were, the growing need for economy prompted a widespread movement in favour of

lighter-weight buses. At times in the 1950s this almost became an obsession, but towards the end of the decade reason gradually returned. This desire for more economical chassis spawned a new breed of chassis, spearheaded by Leyland's Tiger Cub and AEC's Reliance in 1952/53. In place of the 9.8/9.6-litre engines of their heavyweight brothers the Tiger Cub and Reliance offered considerably smaller engines. The 5.86-litre O350 engine was standard in the Tiger Cub, while the 7.68-litre AV470 was the larger and more popular of the two Reliance engine options.

There soon followed lighter chassis like the Atkinson Alpha, Dennis Pelican and Guy Arab LUF and later the Albion Aberdonian, although some builders stuck to heavyweights; Daimler never ventured into the lightweight single-deck market. Its underfloor chassis, the Freeline, was introduced in 1951, but never sold in vast numbers, though Daimler's success in the double-deck market probably compensated for this.

72 Atkinson entered the bus chassis market in 1950 with a range of underfloor-engined models, but they never achieved the success of contemporary AEC, Guy and Leyland chassis. Independent operator Lancashire United took several batches of Atkinsons, like this 1952 PM746H with 44-seat Northern Counties bodywork — an all-Lancashire product, with the chassis built near Preston and the body at Wigan. *Ian Allan Library*

73 A prototype Leyland Tiger Cub with lightweight Saro body on test at the MIRA proving ground at Nuneaton. Underfloor-engined vehicles were susceptible to rapid changes of temperature in wet weather, causing problems in the design of an efficient cooling system. The Tiger Cub, often with this style of body, was a popular choice among BET group fleets. *Ian Allan Library*

74 Few manufacturers' photographs capture the unromantic reality of bus operation. On a grey winter morning in industrial Lanarkshire, a new AEC Reliance from the fleet of local independent Baxter of Airdrie picks up work-bound passengers. Bodywork on this 1955 vehicle was built by AEC's associated coachbuilder Park Royal. *AEC*

The AEC Reliance and Leyland Tiger Cub easily dominated the field. Municipalities, independents, and company fleets in the BET and Scottish groups all took large deliveries of both chassis for coach and bus work. They both enjoyed long lives, too — the Tiger Cub lasted on the market until 1970, and the Reliance survived another 10 years, rare for the British PSV chassis.

With notable exceptions, British busmen have been traditionally shy of the advantages of integral construction — until more recent times, at least. The integral bus, a complete structure without a separate chassis, had long been popular on the Continent and most private cars built during the last few decades have been integral. From a safety viewpoint integral construction produces a stronger vehicle, while there are also advantages in weight-saving. The early 1950s saw a veritable spate of new integral single-deckers. There were vehicles like the AEC-Park Royal Monocoach, based on the Reliance chassis, and the Leyland-MCW Olympian, based on the Tiger Cub; they attracted at least a small number of faithful customers. Then there were the models that never really caught on, like the solitary Saro, the various Beadle-Commer types, and the Harrington Contender, which at one stage in its career featured an eight-cylinder Rolls-Royce petrol engine and automatic transmission.

The one integral model which sold well was the Bristol-ECW LS, supplied only to the nationalised Tilling and Scottish fleets. It was, strictly speaking, semi-integral, as Bristol built the running units into an underframe that was capable of being driven to ECW at Lowestoft for bodywork — and even, in a few cases, to Alexander at Stirling. Over 1,400 LSs, in both bus and coach form, were supplied between 1953 and 1957. Bristol's own AVW engine was available in the LS, as were the Gardner 5HLW and 6HLW units. The successor to the LS was the MW, introduced in 1957 and, interestingly, a separate chassis. In its 10-year life over 1,600 were built, again purely for nationalised fleets.

Midland Red had a head-start with the underfloor-engined single-decker; by 1950 its 350-plus had 25 million miles under their belts. Successive home-built BMMO models introduced further improvements, and an interesting prototype appeared in 1953, featuring integral construction, rubber suspension, disc brakes and a fully-automatic Hobbs gearbox; several of its revolutionary features appeared on the production S14 model which followed it, although the S14 had a conventional constant mesh gearbox.

Smaller and simpler buses were still required by many operators, and the manufacturers tackled the problem of providing them in different ways. Bristol and ECW combined to produce the SC for BTC fleets, though only Tilling companies bought any. This simply-designed integral

vehicle featured a front-mounted Gardner 4LK 3.8-litre engine and a 35-seat bus body. In its six-year lifespan only slightly over 300 SCs were built, mainly for the Lincolnshire, Eastern Counties and Crosville fleets.

Albion offered a different solution with its short-length underfloor Nimbus chassis, a rugged little bus which had only a limited success. The underfloor Albion engine also appeared in the Bristol SC's successor, the SU, introduced in 1960.

The full-size lightweight chassis market was really the province of Bedford's SB. First introduced in 1950 with a front-mounted petrol engine, the SB grew to a full 30ft model in 1955; in 1953 the Perkins R6 diesel engine was offered as an alternative, and Bedford's own 300 diesel appeared in 1959. The SB, often as not with coach bodywork by Duple, Plaxton or Burlingham, was the mainstay of many small coach fleets in the 1950s when literally thousands were built.

75 Bedford's near-monopoly in the lightweight coach market was successfully challenged by Ford with its Thames range. This 1959 Trader with Duple bodywork made an overland trip from London to Moscow to prove its durability. The body styling, with rounded lines and a curved waistrail, was typical of the products of the time. *Ian Allan Library*

75

The SB's main competitor in the early 1950s was the Commer Avenger, a chassis that had first appeared in 1949. It was unusual with its front-mounted underfloor petrol engine, but otherwise carried bodies similar to those fitted to Bedfords. In 1954 the Avenger was fitted with Commer's unusual TS3 (two-stroke, three-cylinder) diesel engine, and in this guise continued in production for some years. The arrival of a new model from Ford in 1957, the Thames Trader coach chassis, largely narrowed the choice to Bedford and Ford.

The trend towards weight-saving and fuel economy had left a serious gap in the model lists — there was nothing really suitable for AEC and Leyland customers looking for a big-engined single-decker; the Regal and Royal Tiger underfloor models were by the mid-1950s aimed mainly at export customers. Leyland introduced a further export model in 1954, the Royal Tiger Worldmaster with the new 11.1-litre 680 engine and a semi-automatic pneumocyclic gearbox. From 1956 a few of these were supplied to British customers, but in 1959 Leyland unveiled a new big-engined underfloor chassis, the Leopard, which combined the lighter chassis structure of the Tiger Cub with the 9.8-litre 0600 engine of the Royal Tiger

range. The new Leopard was an instant success, but the story of its success really belongs to the next chapter.

AEC answered the call for a larger engine with the 9.6-litre AV590 engine, offered in the Reliance as an alternative to the 7.68-litre AV470.

London Transport took deliveries of two very different single-deck models in the 1950s. The AEC Regal had been a popular model with LT for many years and it was logical that the underfloor Regal IV should continue the tradition. London's first Regal IVs, classified RF, apeared in 1951, and over the next two years 700 were delivered. The first 25 RFs were 27ft 6in (8.38m)×7ft 6in (2.29m) private hire coaches, while the remainder, although 30ft long, were still only 7ft 6in wide. There were also 15 8ft (2.44m) wide Regal IVs built for London Transport, the ECW-bodied RFW class coaches.

But the main most significant RFs were the 700 Metro-Cammell bodied vehicles delivered initially as 25 private hire coaches, 263 Green Line coaches, 225 Central Area (red) buses and 187 Country Area (green) buses.

Other Regal IVs in London were the 65 attractive BEA airport coaches built for the services between central London and

76 Just six years after the end of World War 2 London Transport sent two buses to Berlin to create interest in the British Industries Fair. These were RTWs, London's first 8ft wide motor buses, Leyland Titan 6RTs with London-styled Leyland bodywork. *Ian Allan Library*

77 Smaller buses were still required for some rural areas. London Transport opted for special Guys, while Aldershot & District took eight Dennis Falcons with Strachans 30-seat bodywork in 1956, like this one — complete with conductress — on service between Alton and Haslemere. *Ian Allan Library*

the expanding Heathrow Airport. They followed an earlier tradition of deck-and-a-half coaches, with half the passengers in a raised rear portion above a large luggage compartment. The Park Royal-bodied Regal IVs for BEA brought the roof line of the rear compartment forward at the same level.

London Transport experimented with demonstration vehicles from the manufacturers during the 1950s, and at various times tried an AEC Reliance, Bristol LS and Leyland Tiger Cub. Three AEC Reliances with Willowbrook bodies, class RW, were bought in 1960 but were

78

79

78 Although many independent operators sold out to company fleets around this time, others continued — and, indeed, continue. South Notts of Gotham was using this 1951 all-Leyland Titan PD2/12 on its Nottingham-Loughborough main road service in 1952. The Leyland Farington body, here in lowbridge form, was the ultimate version of the 1936 design seen on a Lincoln bus on an earlier page. *G. H. F. Atkins*

79 The East Kent company bought 30 of these Guy Arab IV with attractive Park Royal bodywork in 1953, and this one was still in operation in 1967 on a Canterbury-Folkestone service. *A. Moyes*

80 Glasgow Corporation operated buses, trolleybuses and trams — occasionally together, as the wiring demonstrates — but replaced its trams during the 1950s and 1960s, and then replaced its trolleybuses. It built up a large fleet of buses from various builders; this 1957 Leyland Titan PD2/24 had Alexander bodywork. Glasgow was an early user of fully-automatic gearboxes, as fitted to this bus. The Leyland 'new-look' front was based on a design produced for Midland Red. *Robert F. Mack*

80

8
OLD MARSTON

974 CWL

short-lived. The only other single-deckers bought at the time were replacements for the ageing Leyland Cubs on the lighter-loading Country routes. There was no proprietary chassis which suited LT's needs, so a special version of the normal-control Guy Vixen was bought and fitted with 26-seat bodywork by Eastern Coach Works. There were 84 of these 25ft (7.62m) long buses, fitted with Perkins P6 diesel engines, and they proved useful machines on one-man rural routes.

London's bus of the future

Throughout the world, though, the double-decker is synonymous with London, and LT was still receiving large batches of RT variants in the early 1950s. The massive intake of new buses in the first postwar decade gave LT a really modern fleet and gave its vehicle designers a chance to catch their breath and to consider the London bus of the next decade. For a start, trolleybus replacement was in the offing, following the final tramway withdrawal in 1952, so a new double-deck design had to provide something like the 70 seats in LT's 30ft (9.14m) trolleybuses. Two-axle motor buses were still restricted to the 27ft (8.23m) length, but some coachbuilders were already managing to squeeze up to 66 passengers within the box dimensions of the time. The Routemaster, 'London's Bus of the Future' was unveiled in August 1954, a chassisless vehicle with the AEC 9.6-litre engine, and a 64-seat light alloy body; the whole bus weighed 6.75 tons — considerably less than an RT. Prototype RM1 had a LT-built sub-frame, fitted with fully-automatic transmission and featuring independent front suspension and rear coil springs. Other prototype Routemasters followed, RM2 initially with a smaller engine for Country work, RM3 with Leyland engine and Weymann body, and CRL4 a coach version with Leyland engine and ECW body.

Four years after RM1's debut, the first production Routemaster was introduced, incorporating many improvements and alterations like power-assisted steering and warm-air heating. Although there had been a dramatic new development in double-deck bus design in the Routemaster's long gestation period, the compact, manoeuvrable and nippy RM, with its open rear platform, was the ideal bus for work in central London.

If London Transport seemed to pursue rather individual policies, it was simply because it was so different from any other British transport undertaking. The sheer

82 Some of the first 30ft long double-deck models were simply lengthened versions of the previous 27ft buses, with rear entrances. This 1957 City of Oxford AEC Regent V with well-proportioned 65-seat Park Royal bodywork is typical of this trend, although the seating capacity was lower than normal; 65 was possible on a 27ft bus, and 72-74 was possible with the extra length. *AEC*

83 Some operators still specified traditional exposed radiators and rear entrances on 30ft double-deckers. Bury Corporation bought a batch of these Leyland Titan PD3/6 in 1958 with 73-seat MCW Orion bodies built at the Weymann coachworks at Addlestone. The use of rear hub covers and platform doors was unusual on a municipal bus. *Ian Allan Library*

immensity of the LT area and the vast fleet needed to serve it put it in a very special position. At the end of 1953, for instance, the LT fleet of over 10,000 vehicles comprised 7,201 double-deckers, 893 single-deck buses, 372 coaches and 1,797 trolleybuses. The huge London fleet was particularly valuable when crowds of visitors thronged the metropolis for the Festival of Britain in 1951 and the Coronation in 1953.

Central London's unique traffic problems required unique solutions. Britain's first parking meters appeared on London streets in 1958 in an attempt to control the stream of private transport which seemed in danger of swamping the city. One of London Transport's solutions was BESI, the Bus Electronic Scanning Indicator, which allowed staff at a central control point to pinpoint individual buses on a small selection of routes, and to deal with abnormal service intervals and potential traffic jams.

If BESI was a sign of the times, so were bus strikes. The six-week strike by London Transport crews in the summer of 1958 was just another step in the steady erosion. Already, between 1950 and 1955, there had been a 10% drop in passenger figures. An interesting side-effect of the 1958 strike was the reappearance of 'pirates'; an odd assortment of buses appeared on some London streets, firstly illegally, but eventually with a certain amount of official blessing.

The design of the double-decker underwent dramatic changes in the 1950s. The Bristol/ECW Lodekka went into production in 1953 and sold in large numbers to Tilling and Scottish fleets. The production Lodekka had a dropped centre double-reduction rear axle to keep the overall height down to 13ft 5in (4.09m), and was offered with Gardner 5LW or 6LW or Bristol AVW engines. As regulations and requirements changed, so the Lodekka changed. After the change in dimensions in 1956 which permitted two-axle 30ft (9.14m) long double-deckers, Bristol built six prototypes to the new length, and in 1958 a new flat-floor version appeared. From 1960 the flat-floor Lodekka became standard, offering 27ft (8.23m) or 30ft (9.14m) rear or forward entrance models. There were fresh engine options too when the Bristol BVW and Gardner 6LX units became available. By 1957, 1,000 Lodekkas had been built; the number had doubled by 1961.

Bristol continued to build its traditional K range in diminishing numbers for Tilling fleets until 1957. Improved, widened and lengthened versions of other well-proven double-deck chassis continued in production, but gradually the slower-selling chassis like the Albion Venturer, Crossley DD42, Dennis Lance and Foden PVD6 disappeared from the lists.

Coaching improvements

If the 1950s saw the start of the slow decline in passenger figures and the start of the fare rise spiral, it also saw steady improvement on the coaching side. Bigger and (sometimes) better coaches gave operators an incentive to develop new long-distance and express services. In Scotland, for instance, Northern Roadways obtained licences to operate from Edinburgh and Glasgow to London, traditionally the territory of Scottish Omnibuses and Western SMT. The fare for the Northern Roadways overnight 'Pullman De Luxe Sleeper Night Coach' was £2, when the established operators still charged 30s (£1.50), but Northern Roadways offered hostesses and snacks. The Northern Roadways venture was comparatively short-lived, but their competition at least prompted the Scottish Group fleets to re-equip their services with coaches which featured reclining seats, individual reading lights and toilet accommodation. Competition of a similar nature reappeared 30 years later.

The competition between coach operators of all sizes was emphasised in 1955 when the first British Coach Rally was held at Clacton, an opportunity for friendly rivalry between firms and a chance for the general public to see an impressive array of hardware.

Coach design took an important step forward when Plaxton announced its Panorama body in 1958. Its main features were the unusually long side windows which were of obvious benefit to coach passengers, and which started a fashion that caught on very quickly.

The opening of the Preston bypass in 1958 was another significant event in the development of coach travel, for this was Britain's first stretch of motorway. The next year 73 miles of the M1 motorway were opened and coach operators throughout the country were quick to realise its potential. Midland Red introduced a

84 The Scottish Bus Group's express services to London were worked by heavyweight coaches with 30-seat bodies fitted with toilets. These Western SMT Leyland Leopards with Alexander bodywork, preparing to leave Victoria Coach Station for Glasgow, were among the first of the new Leopard model, and were reportedly returning an average of 16.89mpg at 50mph cruising speed. *Leyland*

Birmingham-London motorway service in November 1959 which cut nearly two hours from the established coach service timings, and at one stage it was responsible for a staggering 900% increase in through passengers between the two cities. The fast timings and the low fares won the day — the coach fare of 21s 3d (£1.06) compared well with the rail fare of 42s (£2.10). The coaches used on the Midland Red services were BMMO-built CM5Ts, capable of sustained 80mph running.

Ribble had different ideas about motorway coaches; its Gay Hostess coaches were *double*-deckers. The double-deck coach had never been really successful in Britain; even in the 1920s there were double-deck coaches, but then and subsequently the idea never became widespread. Ribble had always supported this layout and in the late 1940s had introduced its famous White Ladies, Leyland Titan coaches. The Gay Hostesses were something rather different and were not simply double-deck buses with fancy trimmings and coach seats.

They were Leyland Atlanteans, then a fairly new model, with MCW bodies seating 50 (34/16) and featuring an impressive list of coach features; there were reclining seats, individual reading lights, parcel racks, and toilet and kitchen accommodation. Ribble and subsidary Standerwick were justly proud of these impressive vehicles and introduced the prototype in 1959 in a characteristic blaze of glory. In a booklet welcoming passengers aboard 'this fabulous and luxurious vehicle' Ribble enthused: 'May we tell you what is our aim in providing a magnificent vehicle of the kind in which you are now riding? It is to give you, the passenger, greater comfort and added amenities at our current low fares'.

The Gay Hostess carried a steward or hostess who sold light refreshments during the journey and who 'will be pleased to help you in every way possible and at intervals will make announcements of interest over the excellent public address system'. The Gay Hostess prototype was joined by a fleet of production coaches and by some less-luxurious versions, the second generation of White Ladies, but the Ribble Group was the only big operator to support double-deck coaches at that time.

The main competition in the first half of the decade was between AEC's Regent and Leyland's Titan, particularly for the lucrative municipal tram-replacement business. AEC and Leyland were also, favoured by the BET company fleets, but the main market for the Daimler CV and Guy Arab models was among the municipalities.

The so-called 'new-look' tin fronts which Midland Red and Foden had pioneered were adopted by the main builders. Daimler, Dennis and Guy (and occasionally AEC) used a style that had first appeared early in 1950 on Crossleys for Birmingham, and it is suggested that Birmingham's action was prompted by the 'new-look' fronts on Midland Red's buses operating in the same city. Leyland adopted a design developed for Midland Red, while AEC at least chose a front-end structure that bore some resemblance to its distinctive traditional exposed radiator.

Cutting down weight and increasing passenger capacity became the preoccupations of the early 1950s, all in the interests of supposed economy. Double-deckers seating 66 passengers were not uncommon, and it was often possible to reduce unladen weight to a little over 6.5 tons, at a time when 7.5-8 tons was more normal. The chassis makers built better and lighter variations of the existing models and some operators favoured smaller engines as a possible aid to economy. Symbolic of this trend was the Daimler CLG5 unveiled in 1952, a 58-seat double-deck bus weighing only 6.10 tons; the CLG5 was a lightweight version of the CVG5, and the body was a new design by MCW, the Orion — weighing only 1.80 tons. The Orion was to become the most famous, perhaps the most notorious, of the lightweight designs, lacking interior lining panels and other refinements; Edinburgh bought 300 on Leyland Titan PD2/20 chassis, and these prompted an Edinburgh Bailie to describe them as 'monstrous masses of shivering tin' — in spite of which they went on to give 15-20 years' good service. The bigger engine usually won the day, and as buses have become larger the power/weight ratio has become more important.

Most manufacturers gave double-deck operators the choice — Bristol, Daimler and Guy, for example, all offered either the 7-litre Gardner 5LW or 8.4-litre 6LW units. AEC offerd a choice too, between its 7.7-litre and 9.6-litre engines, but Leyland stuck to the one engine, the 9.8-litre 0600. It was surprising, then, when a revolutionary new Leyland double-decker appeared in 1954, fitted with the 5.76-litre 0350 unit — admittedly turbocharged. What was even more surprising was the position of the engine, which was transversely mounted on the rear platform. This prototype, the Low-Loader, was used by several operators and the data

85

86

85 One of the most dramatic of the early 1950s coach designs on underfloor-engined chassis was the Windover Kingsway, seen here on an AEC Regal IV chassis for the Sheffield United Tours fleet. The attractive side elevation, with almost straight waistline and slim window pillars, was perhaps marred by the heavy frontal treatment. Few operators would name a coach 'Gay Adventure' in the 1980s. *AEC*

86 The Burlingham Seagull was widely regarded as the most successful of the early coach bodies on underfloor chassis. This 39-seat 1952 example, arriving at Wembley Stadium with a private party for 'Sleeping Beauty on Ice', was on Leyland Royal Tiger PSU1/13 chassis for Westcliff-on-Sea. *Ian Allan Library*

Previous experience may have discouraged Midland Red from building front-engined forward entrance double-deckers in the 1950s, but the company was still looking to the future. While Leyland and Daimler were developing their rear-engined models, Midland Red was trying to adapt the underfloor layout for double-deckers. AEC had dabbled with an experimental underfloor chassis, but the essentially high floor level was always a problem. The two Midland Red D10 models which were built in 1960-61 overcame many of the problems, and was an advanced design with many of the features of the D9. In the event, Midland Red opted for a proprietary chassis, the Daimler Fleetline, as a successor to the D9, and no more of its home-made double-deckers were built. It was to be more than 20 years before production underfloor-engined double-deckers would be seen in Britain.

But the pride of place must go to the Atlantean, introducing a style of bus that is still very familiar today. The setback front axle allowed an entrance alongside the driver, and the engine — the big 0600 unit after all — was mounted transversely across the *rear*. The prototype Atlantean was integrally-built, a layout that was soon abandoned in favour of a separate chassis, but it was recognisably the forerunner of the standard double-decker of today, with its flat-fronted Metro-Cammell 78-seat body.

The Atlantean was not the first rear-engined double-deck bus model. Yellow Coach, in the United States, had built 71-seat one-man operated buses to this layout in 1936 for service in New York and Chicago. But to Leyland must go the credit for an ambitious step, and for popularising a layout that has become the accepted norm.

Production Atlantean chassis appeared in 1958 and Daimler followed with its Fleetline in 1960, initially with a Daimler CD6 engine, but the Gardner 6LX soon became standard. Gardner engines had been favourites with British bus operators since the first diesel engines appeared, and

assembled was incorporated in the first Leyland Atlantean, which appeared in 1956.

The year 1956 was an important one for the double-decker. Two-axle 30ft (9.14m) deckers were at last legalised and most builders announced lengthened versions of their existing 27ft (8.23m) models. In addition to longer Regent Vs, AEC introduced the Bridgemaster, an integral low-floor model with Park Royal body, and Dennis announced the Loline, a version of the popular Bristol Lodekka built under licence, and therefore available to non-nationalised firms.

Midland Red, of course, went its own way. Its main double-deck model in the early 1950s was the D7, a fairly orthodox

vehicle with the BMMO 8-litre engine and a constant mesh gearbox. Its 30ft (9.14m) successor appeared in 1958, the integral D9, with BMMO's 10.5-litre engine, a semi-automatic gearbox, disc front brakes and rubber suspension. The 72-seat body had a traditional rear entrance, although many operators were turning towards forward entrances, behind the front axle; Midland Red had in fact featured a forward entrance on its immediate prewar FEDD model, and there had been a brief interest in this layout in the late 1930s. The arrival of the 30ft (9.14m) double-decker prompted a revival of the forward entrance, though the designs were sometimes clumsy, and often restricted passenger space.

87

88

87 A stylish coach body that still owed much to
the designs of the 1930s and 1940s with its curved
waistrail and centre entrance: this Willowbrook
37-seat body on Guy Arab LUF chassis, was from
the immaculate fleet of Black & White, and was
taking part in the Clacton Coach Rally in 1955,
the first event of its kind, and predecessor of
today's Brighton rally. *Ian Allan Library*

88 The well-finished interior of the Black &
White Guy/Willowbrook was also fairly
traditional, with a host of fixtures and fittings
that had changed little over the years.
Ian Allan Library

the addition of the 10.45-litre 6LX in 1958
widened their appeal.

The 6LX engine was fitted in a last-ditch
stand on behalf of the front-engined
double-decker, the Wulfrunian, which
helped bankrupt Guy and did very little
else in the process. This revolutionary
chassis first appeared in 1959, permitting
bodies with the entrance ahead of the front
axle and the staircase over the nearside
front wheel. It featured air suspension and
disc brakes, and the 6LX engine was
sandwiched between the driver and the
front platform. As a design it seemed
sound — spoilt perhaps by operators'
reluctance to accept this degree of
sophistication. It was a spectacular failure,
and only 137 were built.

Transmission systems also advanced
during the 1950s. The traditional friction
clutch and constant mesh gearbox was
favoured by Bristol, Dennis and Guy
customers, while Daimler stuck to its fluid
flywheel/preselective gearbox, and
Leyland offered a synchromesh gearbox.
AEC offered both preselector and
synchromesh boxes, but in the middle of
the decade development of semi-automatic
and fully-automatic epicyclic gearboxes
was sufficiently advanced to persuade some
of the major manufacturers to offer them
as options. Normally the semi-automatic
box was favoured, permitting direct gear
selection without the need for a clutch
pedal, but some operators, notably
London Transport, specified

fully-automatic boxes. The rear-engined
double-deck Atlantean and Fleetline
models were only available with the new
epicyclic transmission systems.

Ironically, Daimler, with over 20 years'
experience of preselectors, introduced a
synchromesh gearbox option in 1958, and
five years later replaced this with a Guy
constant mesh box.

Among the manufacturers there was
little activity. Leyland acquired Albion,
the long-established Scottish bus and truck
builder, in 1951, an early stage in its
empire-building that was to gain
momentum in the 1960s. One possible
liaison that never materialised was a
proposed merger between Leyland and
Rolls-Royce in 1959, but Leyland was
more interested in arch-enemy AEC,
which was suffering at the time from its
price-cutting war with Leyland. Leyland
and AEC were to remain defiantly
independent for a few more years, but one
merger that anticipated the dramatic
changes of the next decade was Jaguar's
acquisition of Daimler in 1960. And the
next decade was certainly to prove one of
the most significant in the story of the
motor bus.

Events

World Events

Leyland Atlantean

What is now accepted as the normal British double-decker had its roots in a revolutionary Leyland model of 1956. The Atlantean had its engine mounted transversely at the rear, and with the entrance ahead of the front axle resulted in a shape that was dramatically different at the time. The original Atlantean was an integral bus with MCW 78-seat body, but it went into production from 1958 as a separate chassis.

Leyland and other builders continued to offer front-engined double-deckers for another decade, and some operators stuck to these, but the rear-engined bus gradually increased in popularity, particularly after Daimler introduced its competing Fleetline model. This had a drop-centre rear axle, allowing low height bodywork, and while Leyland produced models to compete, Daimler cornered this part of the market. For normal-height buses, though, Leyland and Daimler battled it out, each with its supporters. Leyland lost some ground to Daimler until the improved AN68 Atlantean appeared in 1972, outlasting the Fleetline and other 'first generation' rear-engined double-deckers.

Around 15,000 Atlanteans were built, and the model remains available for export customers requiring a reliable and well-tried vehicle.

Leyland's decision to produce the Atlantean was a courageous one, and helped to change the shape of the British double-decker quite conclusively.

Sign of the Times

The introduction of Ribble's Gay Hostess double-deck coaches in 1959 was accompanied by this descriptive leaflet introducing passengers to the novel concept. *Gavin Booth collection*

Profile

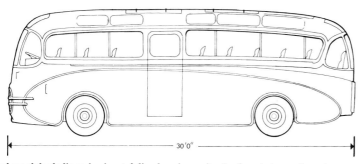

Rounded coach body lines, horizontal diesel engine under the floor between the axles, manual or epicyclic gearbox; at first, centre entrances favoured, then front entrances ahead of front axle. 37 seats.

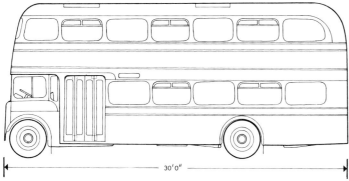

1956 change allowed longer double-deckers; many had forward entrances behind front axle; low-height models (as here) used drop-centre rear axles to give normal seating layout on both decks. 72 seats (40/32).

Wallasey Corporation 1, one of the first Leyland Atlanteans, is exhibited to local dignitaries and press late in 1958; the Metropolitan-Cammell bodywork was typical of many early Atlanteans. *Ian Allan Library*

Does it work?

1961-68

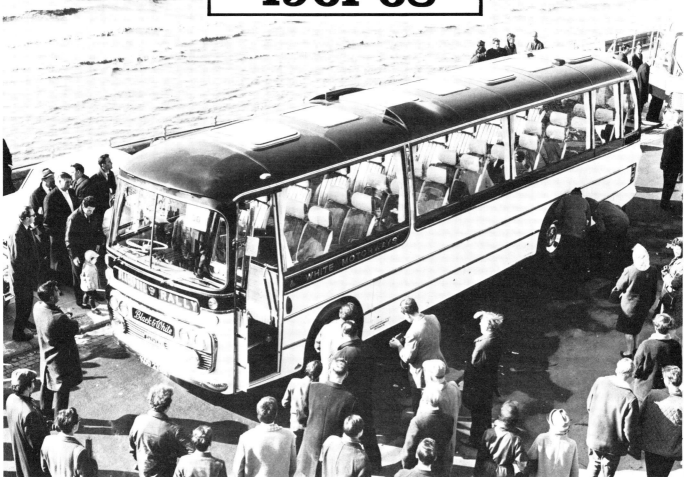

The 1960s were unsettled years for the bus business. There were changes in all sectors of the industry, but the major changes came after much-needed new legislation altered the whole face of road passenger transport in Britain; the far-reaching effects of the 1968 Transport Act will be considered in the next chapter.

In the early 1960s the continuing decline in passengers and the continuing lack of suitable staff forced the bus industry to take a long hard look at itself. While some operators adopted a defeatist attitude, dismissing these factors as inevitable, others set out to salvage the healthy part of their operations and took steps to stop the rot that was setting in to the rest. Many saw one-man operation as an answer and set about converting existing vehicles; sometimes this was enough to give the kiss-of-life to ailing rural routes — but often it had been left too late.

One-man operation has always been around, but many large operators shied clear of it until it was almost too late. Some urban fleets tried ambitious schemes on a fairly large scale; Sunderland Corporation designed two-door single-deckers to accept special pre-purchased tokens, but the scheme was a failure. London Transport, as we shall see, also placed its faith in two-door single-deckers with sophisticated equipment and these enjoyed a relative degree of success. But even one-man operation failed to save many services and time and time again operators found it quite impossible to retain some routes. In some cases independent operators stepped in to keep services going, but some only confirmed the findings of their bigger brothers.

After a long fight, one-man *double*-deckers were legalised from July 1966, a change that was to have

89 Daimler's Roadliner rear-engined chassis was one of the notable failures of the 1960s, but this Plaxton Panorama coach example from the Black & White fleet was attracting much attention at the Blackpool coach rally in 1967. At the Brighton rally that same year it was Coach of the Year, and a similar vehicle was runner-up. The Panorama body pioneered the use of large-size windows in Britain. *Daimler*

far-reaching effects, particularly in urban fleets. After a few tentative experiments at places like Brighton and Great Yarmouth, one-man double-deckers were soon appearing throughout Britain, helping to alleviate some of the more serious staffing problems.

Another important consequence of this development was its effect on double-deck bus design. The traditional double-decker of the 1950s, a front-engined 27ft (8.23m) bus with open rear platform, was still in favour, as was its 30ft (9.14m) counterpart. By the 1960s many were being built with forward entrances behind the front axle. Challenging these, Leyland's rear-engined Atlantean was selling steadily, to be joined by Daimler's Fleetline when production got under way in 1962. But the front-engined designs still had life in them, and new models were still appearing, though the manufacturers were concentrating on the low-floor chassis which only Bristol with its restricted Lodekka model had successfully explored. Leyland's attempt was the Lowlander, a

low-floor model based on the Titan, but built at the Albion plant in Glasgow. Its main support came from fleets in the Scottish Bus Group, where it succeeded late-model lowbridge Titans — the last large-scale stronghold of the old side-gangway layout. Dennis introduced the Mk III version of its Loline model in 1961, featuring a different clutch and constant mesh gearbox, and it was built fitfully for a few more years. The integral AEC/Park Royal Bridgemaster was phased out in 1963 after a none-too-successful life; its replacement, the Renown, first appeared in 1962, a low-floor model available as a separate chassis. Its suspension layout was more conventional than that on the Bridgemaster, and a semi-automatic gearbox was offered as an

option. Guy had a stab at this market with the Arab V, first built in 1962, but this was not a true low-height model, permitting bodies to be built to the height of around 14ft (4.72m) between the 'lowbridge' and 'highbridge' heights.

None of these models really caught on, though much of this reluctance was due to the alternatives offered by the new

90 BET group companies bought the new rear-engined double-deck models in sizeable quantities. Western Welsh was one of several opting for the unusual lowheight Atlantean with its semi-side gangway layout at the rear of the upper deck. This 1960 Western Welsh example, at Cardiff bus station in 1963, was bodied by Weymann to the bland style of the time.
Michael Dryhurst

91 Only a couple of dozen independent operators were still buying new double-deckers in the 1960s; Delaine of Bourne bought this Leyland Atlantean PDR1/2 in 1966 with Willowbrook 76-seat bodywork ornamented in the style of this immaculate fleet. *Geoff Coxon*

rear-engined models. Here was the basis for a modern-looking bus, with seats for up to 78 passengers, and the dropped-centre rear axle of the Daimler Fleetline permitted 13ft 6in (4.11m) high double-deckers with normal seating on both decks; the early low-height Atlantean PDR1/1s had needed a semi-lowbridge side-gangway upper deck. Although a true

low-height Atlantean, the PDR1/2, appeared in 1964, it never achieved the success of the Fleetline. Once production of the Fleetline really got into full swing, the movement towards rear-engined buses really gained momentum. Municipalities, BET company fleets, and even independents all bought Atlanteans or Fleetlines — sometimes both — with

92 Daimler's Fleetline with its drop-centre rear axle offered a genuine lowheight layout on both decks, and North Western chose Alexander bodywork for batches bought in 1964-67. The Alexander body styling, with its rounded lines and extensive use of plastics and curved glass, was one of the trend-setters of the time.
R. L. Wilson

93 The Walsall Corporation fleet was noted for its original ideas and its eccentric collection of buses. Its Daimler Fleetlines were special short-length chassis, with a reduced wheelbase and front-overhang, and 99 similar buses were bought in 1962-69. Two-door bodywork, one folding, one sliding, was built by Northern Counties, and featured translucent panels on the upper deck. Walsall Corporation disappeared into the new West Midlands PTE in 1969.
T. W. Moore

amazingly uninspired bodies by the main coachbuilders. Gradually, often at the instigation of the operator, more attractive body designs appeared; notable among these were the styles supplied to municipalities like Bolton, Glasgow, Liverpool, Manchester, Nottingham, Oldham and Sheffield. But, as Geoffrey Hilditch commented in his book *Looking at Buses:* 'the big question for any fleet engineer was "Does it work?" '

Not every operator went overboard for rear-engined buses. The Tilling Group stuck to the well-tried Bristol/ECW Lodekka as its double-deck model, and the 70-seat forward-entrance FLF variant was supplied in increasing numbers; there was even a 31ft (9.45m) model with seats for up to 78 passengers. The Scottish Bus Group bought both Lodekkas and Albion Lowlanders for several years, but moved on to Daimler Fleetlines in due course. Some municipal operators stuck faithfully to the traditional 27ft (8.23m) rear open platform double-decker, though as things turned out they were not to have a lot of choice in the matter.

Various changes in the manufacturing industry hastened the demise of the front-engined double-decker. Jaguar Cars had bought over Daimler in 1960 and rescued the ailing Guy business the following year, bringing two old rivals under the same management. Two even deadlier rivals came together in 1962 when Leyland bought out AEC, joining Standard-Triumph in what was to become the Leyland Motor Corporation. A share exchange with Bristol gave Leyland another useful foothold and brought Bristol chassis and ECW bodies on to the open market for the first time in 17 years. The Leyland empire-building continued in 1966 when Rover was acquired — the same year that Jaguar's parallel expansion had brought about a merger with the British Motor Corporation to produce British Motor Holdings. The biggest merger of all, between Leyland and BMH, was very much on the cards from this time, but in the end Leyland took over the sickly BMH in May 1968 to form the British Leyland Motor Corporation. Under the British Leyland umbrella on the bus-side were chassis-makers AEC, Albion, Daimler and Guy, and bodybuilders Park Royal and Roe, plus the interests in Bristol and ECW.

London reshapes

While the Routemaster family was satisfying immediate needs, LT was looking ahead to the next generation of London bus and ordered several batches of experimental vehicles. The first to enter service in 1965 were eight Daimler Fleetlines for the Country Area, followed by 50 Leyland Atlanteans for the Central Area and 14 AEC Reliance coaches for the Green Line fleet. The most significant of the new orders, though, were the six AEC Merlins with bodies seating 25 and with standing room for a further 48 passengers 'for experiments in handling big surges of rush-hour passengers in Central London, for example between main line termini and business centres'. When these buses did enter service, in April 1966, they were the first of the famous Red Arrows, and as such merit closer examination.

Boarding at the wide front entrance, passengers were confronted by two turnstiles, released only when a 6d (2½p) coin was placed in the slot. All 25 seats were in the rear portion of the bus behind the central exit doors, while the front part of the bus was for standing passengers only. The first Red Arrow service was between Victoria station and Marble Arch, and operated only during the Monday-Friday working hours of 07.30 and 19.15. The fast flat-fare Red Arrows were very different from normal London concepts, but caught on quickly and were joined by a small network of similar services.

The Red Arrows were a glimpse of future trends, for a few months after they first appeared an important report *Reshaping London's Bus Services* was published detailing many of LT's forward plans. It was drawn up as a result of the continuing decline after passenger totals reached their peak in 1948, and the problems that followed. There were the growing difficulties of congestion caused by the private car, particularly acute in Central London, and the shortage of suitable staff to man the buses. To overcome these difficulties LT plumped for radically different techniques. The plan proposed that routes should be shortened, that one-man operation should be extended, that more standing accommodation should be provided on shorter routes and that new methods of fare collection should be worked out. The ideas were good on paper but time showed that not all worked in practice.

The basic network of trunk routes using two-man double-deckers was to be supplemented by Red Arrow type buses in the West End and the City and fed by suburban satellite routes operated by one-man single-deckers. 'Experience with the Red Arrow buses shows that a high proportion of standing accommodation is acceptable to short-distance passengers, who are the great majority on Central Area's buses', commented London Transport, and it seemed that LT had turned against the double-decker. Certainly the high-capacity double-deckers favoured by other operators found little support in London where the official feeling was 'little more can be done to increase the effective capacity of the two-man double-decker. If the bus is so big that the conductor cannot get round it in time to collect all the fares, it is not efficient. In London, where many passengers ride for short distances only, the 72-seater is the largest vehicle of the present type that can be operated practically'.

In any case, large orders for AEC Merlin single-deckers were placed and in 1968-69 a total of 650 Merlins were bought, a mixture of Red Arrows and one-door and two-door buses with different ratios of seated/standing passengers for Central and Country routes. Many of the new Merlins entered service in September 1968 when a massive revision of LT services was undertaken, incorporating many of the proposals in the *Reshaping* plan. There were seven new Red Arrow routes, and rail-linked suburban schemes at Walthamstow connecting with the new underground Victoria Line, and at Wood Green. For a multitude of reasons not all of these services were a complete success, and the Merlins were never the happiest buses in London service. More rear-engined AECs were bought, but these were the shorter Swift model, generally a more successful design, and with the very last Routemaster double-deckers entering service in 1968, the next breed of London bus was to be very different to its predecessors.

94 London Transport's 50 Leyland Atlanteans had Park Royal bodywork, and gave LT experience of operating rear-engined double-deckers. *R. L. Wilson*

Double-deck changes

All of these changes affected the bus chassis built by the manufacturers involved. The long-running AEC Regent, Bristol Lodekka, Daimler CV, Guy Arab and Leyland Titan models were all gradually phased out by the end of the 1960s, leaving only the rear-engined Atlantean and Fleetline models to meet the demand for double-deckers. They were, however, joined by a third model, the Bristol VRL, which was first introduced in 1966. The VRL was another rear-engined design, but featured a Gardner 6LX engine mounted longitudinally in the rear offside corner, rather than in the more common transverse position. The prototype VRLs were 33ft

(10.06m) long, and were among the first double-deckers to take real advantage of the 1961 change in dimensions which permitted PSVs of up to 36ft×8ft 2½in (11m×2.5m). Double-deckers of around 31ft (9.45m) were found in many areas, but Daimler and Leyland only introduced 33ft (10.06m) versions of their Fleetline and Atlantean models in 1966. Several operators were quick to specify the longer chassis, sometimes with up to 86 seats, but many reverted to the more manageable 31ft buses. To cater for the longer chassis and for a widespread demand for more powerful buses, bigger engines became available in 1966; Gardner's beefier 6LXB was soon appearing in Daimler Fleetlines; Leyland introduced the 11.1-litre 680

95 City of Oxford surprised many with its decision to add five Dennis Lolines to its predominantly AEC fleet in 1961. They had 63-seat East Lancs bodies and, admittedly, AEC engines, but no more were built for Oxford; the requirement for lowheight buses was subsequently met by AEC Bridgemasters and Renowns and Daimler Fleetlines. The Lolines were short-length buses with forward entrances. *Ian Allan Library*

engine as an alternative to the popular 9.8-litre 600; AEC replaced the AV590 unit in the Regent V with the 11.3-litre AV691.

96

96   AEC's lowheight Bridgemaster model was developed with in-house coachbuilder Park Royal. Leicester City Transport was a Bridgemaster customer, buying two in 1959. Leicester was one of the first municipal operators to change to a brighter livery layout. *AEC*

A transverse-engined version of the Bristol VRL, designated VRT, appeared in 1967, and very few VRLs were built. The VRT became the standard Tilling Group double-decker and the Lodekka was no longer listed, although the model did feature for the last time in the 1968 Tilling bus order. The early VRT was not a complete success, suffering perhaps from a rush to get it into service — not for the VRT the old Tilling tradition of building a handful of prototypes for extensive proving trials before production started. A most unusual version of the longitudinal-engined VRL appeared at the 1968 Commercial Motor Show, a 36ft (11m) 60-seat double-deck coach for Standerwick. The Leyland 680 engine shared the rear portion of the lower deck with toilet and luggage accommodation, for only 18 of the seats were downstairs. Another 36ft (11m) double-decker was on show at Earls Court in 1968 and it too had a longitudinal rear engine. It was a Daimler CR36 for Walsall Corporation, with an offside-mounted Cummins engine and an 86-seat Northern Counties body. The engine position allowed a doorway to be fitted behind the rear axle and there was also a door in the more traditional front position. Two staircases were fitted, for the entrance was at the front with stairs behind the driver, and the rear stairs were over the engine, leading to the rear exit — and supervised by a television camera. Neither of these 36ft (11m) designs was really successful. The Standerwick Bristol VRL was joined by a production batch and they did some useful work on motorway services; but the Walsall Daimler was to remain unique and had a short life for such an advanced and expensive design.

With arrival of one-man double-deckers,

the final death-knell of the familiar front-engined designs was really sounding, and by the end of the 1960s the last examples of the AEC Regent, Daimler CV and Leyland Titan had been delivered. In their place, operators were taking increasing numbers of two-door double-deckers, with a front-entrance for one-man operation, and a central exit, usually immediately behind the front axle. Some really crisp designs were coming from British coachworks, like the classically simple standard design from Park Royal and the trend-setting Mancunian style for Manchester Corporation. These marked a final break from the long-running designs which many builders insisted on producing, and which made no concessions for the totally

different lines on the rear-engined double-decker.

While all this was going on in the double-deck market, the single-deck world was far from quiet. The immediate effects of the 1961 legislation which permitted 36ft (11m) buses were merely longer versions of AEC's Reliance and Leyland's Leopard, though by 1962 the manufacturers were beginning to catch their breath and a veritable rash of new designs appeared that year. There was Bedford's 36ft (11m) model, the VAL, with a front-mounted engine, but with an entrance at the extreme front ahead of twin-steering axles, for the VAL was a six-wheeler, a unique solution to the length problem. Bristol's model was equally unconventional for the time, as the RE featured a

horizontally-mounted rear engine; this was a layout that soon became familiar throughout Britain, but the RE was certainly the first — and probably the best — of the 1960s rear-engined designs. Daimler showed an experimental rear-engined chassis at the 1962 Commercial Show, but it was two more

97 Guy's remarkable Wulfrunian model, with front engine, air suspension and disc brakes, never realised its potential and contributed to the company's eventual bankruptcy. There was great operator interest in the concept, though, and two demonstrators toured the country in the early 1960s. *Guy*

years before the production version appeared. The front engine retained a wide circle of admirers, particularly where front entrances could be offered. The Bedford VAL spearheaded the resurrection of interest, supported by the Thames 36 and less successful models from Albion and Dodge. The Thames 36, later called the Ford R226 and eventually to become the R1114, was joined by a 32ft (9.75m) model in 1965, the Ford R192, later the R1014, Bedford's 32ft (9.75m) equivalent was the VAM, and with the six-wheel VAL and the two Ford models, represented the mainstay of many a coach operator in the 1960s.

Bristol's clear lead with the rear-engined RE chassis was followed up by several new models first seen in 1964. There were AEC's Swift and Merlin, Daimler's Roadliner and Leyland's Panther and Panther Cub.

The 36ft (11m) AEC Swift featured a horizontal AH505 8.2-litre engine mounted at the rear of a low-frame or high-frame chassis. The low-frame Swift was intended for urban work, where an easier front entrance and interior floor height would be useful; the high-frame version, for tour and express work, permitted underfloor lockers in place of the normal rear luggage boot. Constant mesh and semi-automatic gearboxes were offered, and the bigger 11.3-litre AH691 engine was also offered, though in this form the chassis was strictly designated Merlin. A 33ft Swift was a further option. With the Swift, according to contemporary publicity, AEC put 'the sting in the tail'.

Leyland's Panther family was similar. Low-frame and high-frame versions of the 36ft (11m) Panther were introduced, and the 9.8-litre 600 engine was mounted horizontally, coupled to a semi-automatic pneumocyclic gearbox. The low-frame Panther Cub with the 6.54-litre 400 engine,

98 Leeds City Transport was one of the operators choosing longer double-deckers when these were legalised. These allowed an increased seating capacity of up to 86, but Leeds opted for a two-door layout and 78 seats on these Roe-bodied Daimler Fleetlines delivered between 1966-70.
Leeds City Transport

99 The growth of the motorway network and the relaxation of length regulations in 1961 meant that bigger and better coaches appeared on British roads. On one of the new motorways, an AEC Reliance, with the popular Harrington Cavalier body from the fleet of Yelloway, the famous Rochdale-based independent. *AEC*

was intended for buses around 33ft (10.06m) long.

Daimler tackled the rear-engined problem rather differently. Its Roadliner featured a vertically-mounted vee-form engine, the compact 9.63-litre Cummins V6-200, and full air suspension as standard. Only a low-frame 36ft (11m) model was offered.

None of the new chassis was a complete success. A few were bought for coach work but the majority were used for close-frequency urban work in a variety of centres. London Transport, as we shall see, bought a large fleet of Merlins and Swifts but suffered from the same problems as its provincial brothers.

A different type of rear-engined chassis appeared in 1965 when Albion introduced its VK43L Viking model. The Viking name had reappeared in 1963 on the front-engined VK41L model, a 32ft (9.75m) lightweight chassis with a Leyland 400 engine mounted at the front; now the VK43 placed this engine vertically at the rear. The result was a fairly rugged lightweight chassis which proved successful with fleets in the Scottish Bus Group, although it was not widely bought outside Scotland. Other activity in the rear-engined market was Daimler's single-deck version of the Fleetline, following a batch of single-deck Fleetlines which were supplied in 1965 to Birmingham City Transport, and a few single-deck Atlanteans.

100 **Plaxtons Panorama body in its 36ft version on an AEC Reliance for Sheffield United Tours, seen in 1963 near Brighton on the British Coach Rally. The side panelling was finished in wood-style laminate, a novelty that, perhaps thankfully, did not catch on.** *AEC*

100

One of the more successful 1960s single-deckers was the Bristol LH, replacing the rear SU. With Bristols back on the open market, a lightweight underfloor-engined chassis was called for, available in various lengths up to 36ft (11m). Two engines were available, the Leyland 400 and Perkins 6.354, and the LH proved a reliable and useful machine both as a rural bus for Tilling fleets and as a coach model for nationalised and independent fleets.

Greater standardisation

In the single-deck bus field the 1960s saw a much more positive move towards vehicle standardisation, and by the middle of the decade several clearly identified patterns were evolving. The independent busman buying a new bus would often as not choose a Bedford or Ford with coachwork by Plaxton, Strachans or Willowbrook; some chose heavier chassis like the AEC Reliance or Leyland Leopard, but still patronised the same coachbuilders. The Tilling fleets had the Bristol RELL, with attractive ECW body, while the Scottish Group favoured the Alexander Y-type body on AEC Reliance, Bristol RE or Leyland Leopard for heavyweights, or Albion Viking and Bedford VAM for lightweights. The company fleets

controlled by BET had a wider range of suppliers, though as always AECs and Leylands were predominant. A few bought Daimler's Roadliner, while the wider availability of Bristol's RE brought it into a number of fleets. Several builders were required to supply the needs of BET fleets, but a functional standardised design was evolved in the early 1960s and built by a number of coachbuilders throughout the country. This neat design with its wrap-round front and rear windscreens was adopted by several builders as a standard single-deck style, and this guaranteed it a long life even after BET had withdrawn from the British bus business.

With fewer builders and fewer models the luxury coach market lost much of its variety at this time. In the main the independents stuck to Bedford and Ford for chassis, and Duple and Plaxton for bodies, though an increasing number bought Reliances and Leopards. Duple and Plaxton reigned supreme in the heavyweight coach market too, particularly when Harrington withdrew from the field in 1965.

In London, where standardisation had always been essential, the 1960s were typified by the lack of it. The Routemaster was entering service in large numbers — number 1,000 was delivered in 1961,

101 **The most unusual 36ft coach chassis of the 1960s was Bedford's VAL, with its twin-steering layout and small-diameter wheels. This early VAL was fitted with Plaxtons 52-seat coach bodywork.** *Bedford*

London's 21,669th AEC. But the design had been conceived some years before, and had been overtaken by changes in fashion and regulation. A 30ft (9.14m) Routemaster was designed in 1961 by inserting a short extra bay into the standard RM shell, and many of the later Routemasters were 30ft (9.14m) RMLs. A variation was RMF1254, a forward-entrance 30ft (9.14m) Routemaster, but although it was demonstrated to various operators in Britain this bus never entered LT service and was sold to Northern General where it joined 50 similar vehicles which had been bought direct after the Routemaster went on to the open market. The only other Routemasters built were short forward-entrance vehicles supplied to BEA, and ironically some of these were bought by London in 1975 to alleviate a vehicle shortage; the problems of operating RMF1254 were conveniently forgotten.

102 Modern materials meant that service bus interiors became fresher, brighter and easier to clean. This is the inside of a Hants & Dorset Bristol RELL with dual-purpose ECW bodywork. *ICI*

103 Birmingham City Transport surprised many by buying 12 Ford R192 buses in 1967, fitted with Strachans 46-seat bodies. Lightweight single-deck buses were popular with independents and some company fleets, but rarely joined the fleets of municipal operators, particularly one as large as Birmingham. *Ford*

The adaptability of the basic Routemaster design was further illustrated when 68 RMCs were delivered in 1962 for the Green Line fleet, 57-seat coaches with rear air suspension and platform doors. The last Routemasters were built in 1967-68, 30ft (9.14m) buses and coaches, to bring the class to 2,760 vehicles. There was also a very advanced rear-engined bus, FRM1, which used more than 60% RM parts, but in spite of its sophisticated specification and apparent potential — many regard it as one of the finest double-deckers built in recent years — the project was abandoned.

104

105

104 An interesting variant of the London Transport Routemaster model was produced for British European Airways for services to Heathrow Airport. A fleet of 65 forward-entrance Routemasters was bought in 1966/67, designed to tow luggage trailers. These replaced attractive deck-and-a-half AEC Regal IVs like those in the background, bought in 1952/53. London Transport bought the Routemasters from British Airways in 1975, mainly for training and crew transfer duties. *Ian Allan Library*

105 London Transport continued to place its Routemaster fleet in service until 1968, and this 1964 example is seen in Silver Jubilee livery in 1977. The Routemaster, first seen in 1954, and still in active service over 30 years later, represents the ultimate development of the British front-engined/rear entrance double-decker. *Robert F. Mack*

106 Midland Red emphasised its anti-PTA stance with these advertisements; ironically, most of Midland Red's Birmingham area operations were sold to West Midlands PTE in 1973, reducing this great fleet in size and influence. The bus is an Alexander-bodied Daimler Fleetline, a type chosen to succeed BMMO's own in-house double-deck types. *Stewart J. Brown collection*

Electrification and preservation

But London Transport was not the only transport undertaking with problems in the 1960s. Far from it. The same factors that were making life difficult in London were affecting transport fleets large and small throughout Britain. And it was not only road passenger transport that was suffering. British Railways incurred severe losses and clearly drastic action was required to prevent this situation worsening. One outcome was the Beeching Report of 1963 which proposed axing 5,000 miles of unprofitable lines from the total route mileage of 17,000 miles. The effects of the Beeching cuts were drastic, but proved only to be a holding action in the face of a deteriorating economic situation. One bright spot on the railway horizon was the onward spread of electrification. In 1960 the first stage of the West Coast electrification was completed, from Crewe to Manchester and in 1966 the section from London Euston to Crewe was complete, bringing dramatically improved journey times and a more reliable service.

While the railways regarded electrification as a solution for the future, municipal operators were abandoning electric traction as fast as they could. Glasgow, the last bastion of real street tramways, fell in 1962, while the trolleybus conversion of the 1960s left only a handful of faithfuls at the end of the decade. London, Ipswich, Hull, Rotherham, Manchester, Newcastle, Nottingham, Derby, Glasgow, Maidstone and Belfast were just some of the fleets which went completely over to motor buses at the time. Britain's last new trolleybus was delivered in 1962 to Bournemouth Corporation, one of only a handful of survivors by 1968.

On an encouraging note, the efforts of the Tramway Museum Society were beginning to bear fruit. Formed in 1955 to establish a working tramway museum, the Society had bought a site in 1959, a disused quarry at Crich in Derbyshire, and by 1964 members of the public were able to relive the pleasures of electric tramcar rides. Since that time the Tramway Museum at Crich has grown to become a deservedly popular tourist attraction, and houses an impressive collection of trams from British and overseas systems, ranging from 19th century examples through to trams built after World War 2, which never had the chance to live their full lives on their parent tramways.

The bus preservation movement was making impressive advances, too. Only a few of the old buses had been set aside for preservation, some by private individuals, but most notably by London General/London Transport which had saved examples of its most significant bus models, though for many years these were not on public exhibition. The conversion of LT's former Clapham depot to the Museum of British Transport gave the public the first opportunity of examining these priceless vehicles properly. The first portion of Clapham, with small exhibits only, opened in 1961, and in 1963 the Museum proper was opened with a fine collection of railway relics and sections devoted to buses, trams and trolleybuses, mainly the London Transport vehicles, augmented by various other museum-pieces acquired by the BTC. Another important collection was placed on show when the Glasgow Museum of Transport opened in 1964, using the Glasgow Corporation tramcar collection as the centrepiece, and containing many examples of Scottish-built cars and commercials, including a Glasgow Albion bus. A further section was later added, containing a number of Scottish railway locomotives.

Private preservation was becoming very popular at the same time and an increasing number of rallies were being organised to allow the proud owners to exhibit their vehicles. The first of the Historic Commercial Vehicle Club's famous Brighton Runs was held in 1962, and the situation has really mushroomed since that time with scores of rallies each season attended by some of the thousands of preserved buses and coaches.

While the preservationists were looking fondly back, the bus industry was viewing the future with growing concern. If the problems of the 1960s were to be faced and overcome, changes would be necessary to the structure of the industry and to the legislation that controlled it. The first public intimation of the changes that were to follow were contained in a White Paper presented in 1966, and followed the next year by a more detailed document which contained several far-reaching proposals. A new Transport Act was promised, and this would help establish a more efficient transport structure. In four important areas, Birmingham, Manchester, Liverpool and Newcastle, new conurbation authorities would be set up using the existing municipal bus operators as a base. The Transport Holding Company bus interests in England and Wales would be replaced by a new body, the National Bus Company, which was to control not only the Tilling fleets but also those of the rival BET Group, which, only months before the White Paper was published in 1967 had agreed to sell out to THC for £35 million.

The Scottish Bus Group was to pass into the control of a new body, the Scottish Transport Group, which would also take over the road and sea services of David MacBrayne and the railway-owned Caledonian Steam Packet shipping fleet.

At the same time it was announced that a major reorganisation of London Transport was also on the cards, for LT's Central Area operations were to pass into the direct control of the Greater London Council, and a new company, London Country Bus Services Ltd would operate the Country Area and Green Line services under the control of the new National Bus Company.

Late in 1968 the Transport Act became law, and in 1969 things really started to change.

Events

1961 Jaguar acquires Guy.
   36ft long buses legalised.
1962 Leyland merges with AEC.
   Bristol RE rear-engined single-decker introduced.
   Last new British trolleybus, Bournemouth.
1963 Beeching Report on British Railways.
   Transport Holding Co takes over from BTC.
1965 Leyland acquires 25% share in Bristol and ECW.
1966 One-man operated double-deckers legalised.
   Bristol VR double-decker introduced.
1967 Ulsterbus takes over from UTA.
1968 BET group sells out to THC.
   First postbus service, East Lothian.
   Leyland takes over BMH to form British Leyland.

World Events

1960 Last British Railways steam locomotive built (*Evening Star*).
1961 First manned space flight.
1963 Great Train Robbery.
   President Kennedy assassinated, Dallas.
1965 Death penalty abolished in Britain.
   Rhodesia declares UDI.

1966 Aberfan disaster, 144 children die.
1967 *Torrey Canyon* oil disaster.
1968 Robert Kennedy, Martin Luther King assassinated.
   Russia invades Czechoslovakia.

The share exchange with Leyland in 1965 allowed Bristol to sell its chassis on the open market again, and former BET group Potteries fleet bought RESL6Ls with ECW 44-seat bodywork in 1971. *A. Moyes*

Bristol RE

The single-deck bus enjoyed a resurgence of interest in the 1960s, resulting from the increased legal length permitted from 1961, and the fact that one-man *double*-deckers were not permitted until 1966. With seats for up to 54 passengers, a 36ft (11m) single-deck bus, one-man operated, was an attractively economical proposition.

The first rear-engined single-deck chassis to appear was the Bristol RE, available only to state-owned fleets. With horizontal Gardner 6HLX engine longitudinally-mounted behind the rear axle, and a constant mesh gearbox, it used familiar units, and soon appeared in both bus and coach form. The engine position allowed a low step height and saloon floor, an advantage over the normal mid-underfloor-chassis of the time.

When Bristol chassis appeared on the open market, the RE range was broadened to include Leyland 600 and 680 engines, and semi-automatic transmission. Other operators, now able to buy REs, did so, with a variety of body makes and styles. Most were buses, although coach models were normally only chosen by the state-owned fleets.

Other chassis builders produced rear-engined single-deckers, but none achieved the success of the RE, which remained in production only until 1975 for home customers, and for some years more for Ulsterbus.

Profile

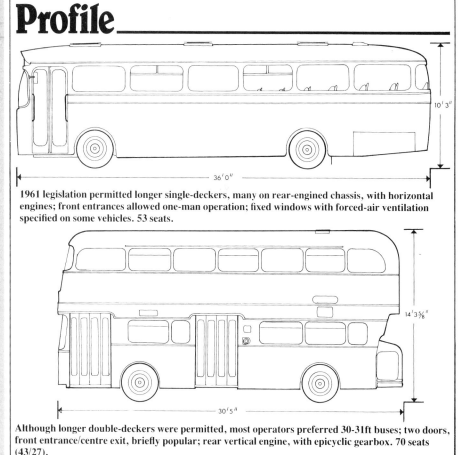

1961 legislation permitted longer single-deckers, many on rear-engined chassis, with horizontal engines; front entrances allowed one-man operation; fixed windows with forced-air ventilation specified on some vehicles. 53 seats.

Although longer double-deckers were permitted, most operators preferred 30-31ft buses; two doors, front entrance/centre exit, briefly popular; rear vertical engine, with epicyclic gearbox. 70 seats (43/27).

Sign of the Times

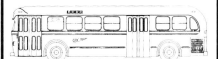

SWEDISH BUSES

available September 1967 when Sweden changes to right-hand traffic.
E.g.

"CAPITOL" 35ft. (200 buses) 28000 Sw. kr. (£1940) FOB Swedish Port, AND thousands of buses of VOLVO and SCANIA VABIS manufacture from £695 to £1350
   SOLD by The Swedish National Defence Industries
THROUGH C. Björnemark, 10 Harrowby Court, Harrowby Street, London, W.1. PADdington 4457.

When Sweden changed the rule of the road in 1967 it placed this advert in the British trade press in its search for customers for displaced right-hand drive buses. Ulster Transport Authority inspected one, but no further interest was shown. *Gavin Booth collection*

Low-tech, local and people-oriented 1969-79

107

107 **Seddon developed the Pennine VII for Scottish Bus Group as a Gardner-engined alternative to the Leyland Leopard, a response to Leyland's unwillingness to build a Gardner Leopard. Two SBG fleets received these Seddons between 1973 and 1982 and a Western SMT example, with the apparently timeless Alexander Y-type body, is seen on a busway in Irvine new town.** *SBG*

The first of January 1969 was an important day in the story of road passenger transport in Great Britain. On that date two new authorities assumed control of Britain's company buses — the Scottish Transport Group in Scotland, and the National Bus Company in England and Wales. The Scottish body was given wider-ranging powers, for the new STG controlled not only the Scottish Bus Group but also shipping services in the Clyde and Western Isles. The STG inherited 4,862 buses and a bus-operating staff of 18,125.

National Bus, with the rest of the THC fleets, brought the newly merged Tilling and BET companies under common management with a total fleet of 20,637 buses and a staff of 80,344.

The formation of STG and NBC were just two results of the 1968 Transport Act, comprehensive and far-reaching legislation which altered the whole structure of the bus industry. One of its best-known provisions, Section 34, allowed Local Authorities to make grants towards the bus

services where retention of a loss-making facility was considered essential; Section 34 was to affect the pattern of bus services provided in many rural areas.

Another grant which had important repercussions was the Bus Grant which initially provided 25% towards the cost of new buses which complied with a set of specifications designed to encourage the introduction of more up-to-date vehicles and the spread of one-man operation.

Grant-eligible single-deckers could be high-floor vehicles, in 9m, 10m or 11m lengths, or low-floor buses in 10m or 11m lengths (9m, 29ft 6in; 10m, 32ft 10in; 11m, 36ft). In effect this meant that most current models, whether front, underfloor or rear-engined, were eligible. Manual, semi-automatic or fully-automatic transmission could be fitted, as could either manual or power steering. It was assumed that high-floor models would be single-doored, although centre exit doors were optional on low-floor chassis.

For ease of passenger flow, acceptable

floor heights and door widths were detailed, and a minimum power/weight ratio was laid down to ensure adequate performance.

The double-deck Grant specifications were rather more restrictive, for only transverse rear-engined models were included, presumably on the basis that front engined double-deckers were not normally suitable for one-manning. Normal-height double-deckers in both 9.5m and 10m lengths were eligible for the Grant, as were 9.5m low-height models. The most familiar variant, the 9.5m (31ft 2in) normal-height double-decker, could have one or two doors, semi- or fully-automatic transmission, powered or manual steering; the 10m version had to have two doors, and power steering. The low-height specification assumed only a single, front, door.

The Bus Grants were immediately welcomed as a means of re-equipping and standardising fleets, and a chance to expand one-man operation. The specifications were in the main well thought out, and covered the most familiar types of vehicle entering service in Britain at that time, allowing for local prejudices and preferences. There was room, too, for less orthodox vehicles to suit peculiar operating conditions, and special approval could normally be obtained to secure a grant in these cases. The Bus Grant was later increased to 50%, and the grant specifications were subsequently amended and relaxed.

The main critics of the Bus Grant specifications were the operators who wanted to continue buying front-engined double-deckers — though there were fewer of these by then. The last AEC Regents, Guy Arabs and Leyland Titans for the British market were delivered in 1969; the previous year Northampton Corporation had received the last batch of Daimler CVG6s, the last truly traditional British double-deckers of the once familiar front engine/rear entrance type. Interestingly, these Roe-bodied CVG6s joined a fleet composed entirely of Roe-bodied CVG6s of varying ages.

The last British front-engined double-deckers were all for municipal operators, and this was the main market. The British Lodekka had last figured in Tilling Group orders for 1968, and the BET fleets had turned to rear-engined models or high-capacity single-deckers. The Scottish Bus Group had bought its last Lodekkas in 1967, and was ordering Bristol VRTs and Daimler Fleetlines to meet its double-deck requirements. SBG was a constant and vocal critic of rear-engined double-deckers — its Bristol VRTs were exchanged for National Bus Lodekkas by 1974 — but it was to play its part in an unexpected latter-day resurrection of the front-engine layout.

One other factor which undoubtedly played its part in the death of the front-engined double-decker was the formation of British Leyland, which faced many problems as it tried to weld together manufacturers that had been deadly rivals. Its main problems were on the private car

side, and much of BLMC's investment went towards improving this situation. The commercial vehicles were left rather to fend for themselves, and it was hardly surprising that Leyland decided to rationalise its complex bus range and cancel out some of the inevitable duplication — hence the hasty demise of the front-engined double-deckers, and the general acceptance, however reluctant, of the grant-preferred rear-engined types.

Effective organisation and planning

But if the Bus Grants were an important short-term result of the Transport Act, the emergence of the Passenger Transport Authorities, as the new conurbation bodies were designated, were of greater long-term significance. The first four PTAs were in busy urban areas where history had blurred formerly clear-cut boundaries, and where several municipal transport undertakings were serving large centres of population, sometimes on a joint basis, sometimes quite independently. The 1966 White Paper suggested that these new authorities should be created in those areas where it was felt necessary 'for the effective organisation and planning of public transport'. In practice, the first four PTAs were to be in the Birmingham, Manchester, Liverpool and Newcastle conurbations.

The PTAs were to be the policy-forming bodies, comprising local authority representatives and other local people. The day-to-day management was to be controlled by Passenger Transport Executives, each controlled by a Director General and a small group of specialist Directors.

On four month-apart vesting dates the new PTEs took over the existing municipal bus undertakings in their areas. The first, on 1 October 1969, was West Midlands PTE, combining the Birmingham, Walsall, West Bromwich and Wolverhampton municipalities; next was Selnec (South East Lancashire, North East Cheshire), combining Manchester with Ashton, Bolton, Bury, Leigh, Oldham, Ramsbottom, Rochdale, SHMD, Salford and Stockport; then came Merseyside PTE, an amalgam of the Liverpool, Birkenhead and Wallasey fleets; last of the first four PTEs was Tyneside, consisting only of the physically separate Newcastle and South Shields undertakings.

Under the Transport Act the PTEs were charged to 'secure or promote the provision of a properly integrated and efficient system of public passenger transport', and this involved liaison with other operators in the area, including British Rail. At first, though, it meant integrating municipal bus operators with very different backgrounds, very different outlooks and very different fleet sizes —

including some of the largest fleets in the country. Selnec, the largest of the PTEs, inherited some 2,500 buses of many different makes; the municipalities it encompassed all had highly individual views about the ideal vehicle. Inevitably in Lancashire, Leylands were predominant, but there were many Daimlers, and even some representatives from AEC, Albion, Atkinson, Bedford, Bristol, Dennis and Guy. With such a mixed inheritance, Selnec started to develop standard vehicle types which would suit its conditions. Several of the former municipal fleets which passed to Selnec, notably Manchester, Bolton and Oldham, had worked hard to design really modern and well-considered double-deckers for their services, and some of the best points were incorporated into the prototype Selnec standard types which first appeared in 1971, and continued in production on Leyland Atlantean chassis until 1984.

The four original PTEs grew as they became established. Selnec acquired from NBC the services of North Western which ran within the Greater Manchester area, while the rest of this famous company was split between Crosville, Trent and National Travel. The unusual Selnec name was becoming increasingly familiar when on Local Government reorganisation in April 1974, the PTE became the Greater Manchester PTE; the new Greater Manchester County included Wigan, and the municipal buses there passed into GMT control.

The West Midlands PTE acquired a large part of the Midland Red operation in 1973, the local services within the PTE area, while the boundary reshuffle in 1974 added the Coventry municipal fleet.

At Merseyside the boundary changes brought the Southport and St Helens undertakings under PTE control. On Tyneside, the Sunderland Corporation bus fleet was acquired in 1974, when the PTE was named Tyne & Wear PTE. Here as in other PTEs local agreements have been reached with NBC and other operators; Northern General and United buses operating within Tyne & Wear County, for instance, wear a yellow livery based on that of the PTE, and there have been major service revisions.

Three new PTEs were added to the original four in 1973-74. The first, Greater Glasgow, which took over the former Glasgow Corporation Transport operation on 1 June 1973, was unique for several reasons; it was the only PTE in Scotland, the only PTE based on just one undertaking, and the only PTE with an underground railway, the vintage Subway system. The huge Strathclyde Region then assumed the co-ordinating role and in 1980 the PTE adopted the Strathclyde name. The subway was modernised and reopened in 1980. In April 1974 the South Yorkshire and West Yorkshire PTEs were

established. The South Yorkshire body took over the Doncaster, Rotherham and Sheffield municipalities, while West Yorkshire PTE took over Bradford, Halifax (with the related Calderdale JOC), Huddersfield and Leeds undertakings.

Big changes
The whole face of British municipal bus operation changed in the years from 1969 and 1975. With the formation of the PTEs, and Local Government reorganisation, the total number of British municipalities dropped from 91 to 51 in these six years. There were mergers and name-changes in April 1974 in England and Wales, while in May 1975 the three remaining Scottish municipalities passed into the control of the Regional Councils, the top-tier authorities, equivalent to the counties south of the border.

Many familiar names disappeared during this period, as fleets merged as famous

independent operators were acquired to help PTEs and NBC fleets to consolidate their position.

But the biggest upheaval was undoubtedly caused by the formation of National Bus Company, faced with the fusion of two very different groups of bus fleets. Both Tilling and BET went about things in their own highly individualistic ways. In some areas the BET and Tilling companies overlapped; in others fleets of one or other group reigned supreme. With their tramway origins, the BET companies could be found in many industrial areas, while Tilling fleets tended to serve the more rural parts of England and Wales. Inevitably there were exceptions, like the BET fleets in the predominantly rural southeast corner of England, but the pattern was there. The Tilling fleets held the less-populated areas — the extreme north of England, both on the east and west, the whole of East Anglia, north

108 Selnec PTE continued the traditions of two of its principal constituents, Manchester and Bolton Corporations, and designed attractive standard buses. On the left of this 1981 scene in Manchester's Piccadilly is a Mancunian, an example of the trend-setting body built for the Corporation by Park Royal and subsequently by other builders. On the extreme right is a Selnec standard, an early example of a type that grew to over 1,800 buses on Leyland Atlantean and Daimler Fleetline chassis; Park Royal built this body, although Northern Counties bodywork was more common. Selnec's 1974 successor, Greater Manchester PTE, continued this tradition. *T. W. Moore*

Wales, and the more distant parts of the West Country. The BET fleets were on Tyneside, around Manchester, Birmingham and the Potteries, in industrial Yorkshire and the South Wales valleys.

The 20,000-plus buses inherited by NBC were a mixed bunch, too. There was a wide selection of makes, layouts and styles from the BET fleets, intermixed with the orderly Bristol/ECW monopoly in the Tilling strongholds. Although BET had ideas about vehicle design, they were by no means as rigidly enforced as in the rival camp, where the existence of tame chassis and body builders was the most important factor.

Starting with 44 operating units, the organisation of NBC was of prime importance, and the group underwent various structural changes in the 1970s. Fleets were grouped into Regions; fleets merged; Regions changed. Familiar names disappeared into history, and familiar liveries were soon submerged into an efficient, if slightly soulless, corporate identity. The multitude of liveries dating back to Tilling and BET days — and beyond — were replaced by two standard shades, poppy red and leaf green, sometimes with a white relief band. Dual-purpose vehicles received the local coach livery, with the fleet colour on the lower half and a white top. In all cases fleetnames were applied in a standard style with a new double-N logo.

NBC's long distance coaches received a rather bland all-white livery in 1972 with prominent National fleetnames in blue and red. Although the corporate identity scheme was slavishly, if sometimes reluctantly, followed in the 1970s, by the end of the decade cracks were appearing in the corporate facade, and a degree of individuality returned.

Scottish Bus Group, on the other hand, has jealously maintained the separate identities of its seven operating companies, though its one concession to a corporate identity was the introduction in 1976 of a standard blue/white livery for the Scotland-London express coaches of four of its subsidiary fleets, featuring a prominent SCOTTISH fleetname.

The changes of January 1969 were only a start. Exactly one year later the giant

109 The National Bus Company's standard double-deck model in the 1970s was the Bristol VRT with ECW bodywork, a type that became familiar throughout much of England and Wales. NBC's most northerly VRTs were United's examples, and one is here operating out of Berwick-on-Tweed bus station in 1980. *A. Moyes*

110 National's corporate all-white coach livery speeded the demise of many familiar liveries. This 1972 Tillings Bristol RELH6G with ECW coach body was on extended tour duties in Inverness in 1973. *Gavin Booth*

London Transport empire was split into two — corresponding with the old Central and Country Areas. On that day the London Transport Board was replaced by the new London Transport Executive, responsible to the Greater London Council, which assumed control for an area of about 630sq miles, mostly within a radius of 15 miles from Charing Cross, and roughly corresponding to the GLC area. The green Country and Green Line fleets passed to a new subsidiary of NBC, London Country Bus Services Ltd.

London Country inherited its fair share of problems. After several years as a poor relation to the red Central Area buses, the green Country Area fleet had become an elderly collection — RTs and RFs in the main, but with newer vehicles including Routemaster buses and coaches, and a growing fleet of Merlin/Swift variants. Fleet renewal was an obvious priority, and the first new buses received after the split were LT-style AEC Swifts. Leyland Atlantean double-deckers and AEC Reliance coaches were quickly ordered, and vehicles were diverted from other NBC subsidiaries — Daimler Fleetlines, Leyland Atlanteans and AEC Swifts. The Atlanteans spearheaded a large fleet, most with Park Royal or Roe bodies, and from 1977 Duple and Plaxton bodied Reliances allowed much-needed upgrading of the Green Line express fleet.

The LT image was quickly abandoned, and London Country soon adopted the guise of a typical NBC fleet — though this was far from the case. London Country and its problems were treated as a special case by NBC, not least because of the unusual shape of its area — John Aldridge appositely described it as 'a network that looked like the mint with the hole'. Special buses were bought for the experimental Superbus services in Stevenage, Metro-Scanias and Leyland Nationals; the Nationals were the first of a large fleet for London Country, buses and Green Line coaches. London Country and London Transport each chose ECW-bodied Bristol LHs for RF replacement, an interesting example of similar thinking.

Even without a large part of its less remunerative services, London Transport's remit was a difficult one. The traffic conditions in the heart of London were steadily deteriorating, and LT's resources were stretched to the limit. The problems with the large intake of single-deckers had disrupted the fleet replacement programme. A shorter variation of the unhappy Merlins had been ordered, a 33ft 5in (10.19m) bus based on the AEC Swift chassis, with the rear-mounted 8.2-litre AH505 engine. The first 50 were one-door 42-seat buses classified SM, but the rest, 650 SMS buses, were two-door vehicles. All were delivered between 1970

and 1972, and proved more successful than their longer brothers — indeed in 1973 it was announced that the 36ft (11m) MB family would be sold prematurely. The Merlins and Swifts did allow LT to expand one-man operated services, and after experiments with the Leyland Atlanteans, one-man double-deckers came to London.

When large orders were placed for new double-deckers, LT chose the Daimler Fleetline model, and the first, with two-door Park Royal 68-seat bodywork, appeared in 1970. The new Fleetlines were fitted for one-man operation, and were classified DMS. The first DMSs entered service early in 1971, and were followed by large quantities of similar vehicles, some with Metro-Cammell bodies.

With the DMSs, LT appeared to prove what it had been saying all along — that operating conditions in London are uniquely arduous. Although supposedly bought 'off the peg', the Fleetlines were

111 **The Anglo-Swedish Metro-Scania single-deck citybus was tried by several fleets, including Selnec PTE, the authority covering the Manchester conurbation. These powerful buses were easily distinguished by their asymmetrical windscreens.** *G. R. Mills*

heavily Londonised, but it transpired that LT's maintenance system, geared to Routemasters, could not always cope with buses that were perfectly acceptable in equally arduous conditions in Birmingham and Manchester.

The DMS fleet, supplied between 1970 and 1978, totalled 2,646 buses, roughly 40% of the total Fleetline production in this period. In 1976, before all its Fleetlines had been delivered, LT admitted that the model was not totally successful in London service. Withdrawals started in 1979, and by late 1984 there were only the later B20 type left; these 400 buses had extra sound-deadening at the rear end.

The London Fleetlines were quickly snapped up by other operators — NBC, SBG, PTEs, municipalities and independents all found the DMS family a cut above the average second-hand double-decker, and even the notoriously difficult operating conditions in Hong Kong posed no problem for examples exported for China Motor Bus.

The 1970s were not London Transport's happiest years, with problems affecting its management structure, its vehicles and its engineering practices. Dr David Quarmby, LT's bus managing director until 1984, described the LT of that time as a railway organisation trying to run buses. 'Railways are systematic, hi-tech organisations which need a strong centralised and functionalised management', he told Alan Millar of *Commercial Motor*. 'Buses, on

the other hand, are low-tech, local and people-orientated.' He spoke of LT's DMS problems: 'Although the Fleetlines did have some problems with us, it was our inability to respond to different maintenance needs which caused most trouble.'

London had also bought Fleetlines equipped for conventional two-man operation, classified DM, and the next new type of double-deck bus for LT was also designed for crew operation. This was an order for 164 of the Anglo-Swedish Metropolitan model, described later in this chapter. This was the double-deck equivalent of the Metro-Scania city bus, six of which were bought by LT in 1973 for experimental operation alongside six Leyland Nationals. These 12 buses represented modern thinking in city bus design, with fully-automatic transmission, air suspension, power-assisted steering and extra soundproofing.

One London innovation around this time was the appearance of the first overall advertising bus, for Silexene Paints, in 1969. This brightly-painted Routemaster was the first of many advert buses to appear in London, and eventually in many other parts of Britain. Advertisers and designers had a field-day faced with this novel form of mobile hoarding, and some really bizarre confections resulted.

Although LT had its large fleet of Merlins and Swifts, many had been bought as double-deck replacements, and there

was a pressing need for a shorter, smaller-capacity model to replace the dwindling fleet of RFs, AEC Regals IVs dating from 1952-54. The eventual choice was the Bristol LH model, with ECW body, and deliveries started in 1976. Even smaller vehicles were the Ford Transits delivered in 1972-73 at the request of the GLC, for one-man operated minibus routes in London suburbs — often on roads not previously served by buses.

The single-deck bus reborn?

While London was experiencing single-deck problems, manufacturers and operators in the rest of Britain were anticipating the decline of the double-decker, and an increasing demand for high-capacity single-deck buses. A forecast that was mistaken, as it turned out. In 1969 British Leyland and National Bus got together to form a new company, the Leyland National Co Ltd, to manufacture a completely new integral city bus at a new purpose-built plant at Workington. The project was inaugurated early in 1970, and later that year, at the

112 **NBC fleets bought local coaches for inter-urban work, usually Leyland Leopards with bodywork by various builders. Willowbrook 53-seat bodies were fitted to these 1979 Midland Red vehicles, one of which is seen on an Expressway service between Coventry and Leamington in 1982.** *T. W. Moore*

113 Volvo achieved success in the British
market with the B58 underfloor-engined chassis,
and Western SMT specified it for eight coaches
for its Glasgow-London services in 1976.
Alexander M-type bodywork was fitted, a style
designed for SBG, with small double-glazed
windows, reclining seats and toilet. The extra
length of the 12-metre coach is apparent.   *Volvo*

114 The Halifax municipal fleet survived until
1971 when, with the Todmorden municipal fleet
and Hebble local services, it became the
Calderdale undertaking; Calderdale passed into
the West Yorkshire PTE in 1974. This lowheight
Daimler Fleetline was delivered to Halifax in
1970 with Northern Counties 74-seat bodywork.
T. W. Moore

London Commercial Show, the prototype
National was unveiled. As introduced, the
bus was available in 10.3m (33ft 9in) or
11.3m (37ft) lengths, as a one-door or
two-door bus, and in right- or left-hand
drive versions. The rigid specification
reflected the high degree of automation at
the Workington plant, for the National was
built on production line techniques learned
from Leyland's experience in the private
car industry.

The low-floor National, with
rear-mounted Leyland 8.2-litre 510
turbocharged engine, quickly became a
familiar sight in many parts of Britain;

115 This style of Park Royal body was developed for NBC fleets, but also went to Plymouth Corporation on Leyland Atlantean AN68/1R chassis in 1975. The window spacing was pioneered by Park Royal and was adopted by several other bodybuilders including MCW, Northern Counties, Roe and Willowbrook. *M. S. Curtis*

116 The Irish state transport company Coras Iompair Eireann bought British-built chassis for many years, but these Leyland Atlantean AN68/1 were among the last. They had angular Van Hool McArdle bodies, built in Ireland by a subsidiary of the Belgian Van Hool company. *R. L. Wilson*

National Bus, inevitably, was the main customer, but demand never built up to the 40 buses a week figure for which the factory was designed.

The concept of rigid standardisation was relaxed to a certain extent as Leyland produced customised Nationals to help boost sales. These included a Business Commuter version, a flat floor Suburban Express, a casualty clearing unit and mobile banks.

After a troublesome start, with more than its fair share of teething troubles, the National settled down to become a familiar part of British bus operation, in service with a wide range of operators. London Country and London Transport were among the largest users, each with over 500 examples supplied over a 9-10-year span.

The arrival of the National prompted a certain amount of activity among other builders. One side-effect was Leyland's

decision to discontinue production of competing chassis in its own range, hence the relatively early demise of the Leyland Panther and more sadly missed, Bristol RE ranges. This in turn affected the independent bodybuilders who saw the source of separate chassis drying up in favour of the integral National. Some counteracted this by specialising in double-deckers — though a similar situation was due to affect the double-deck market. Metro-Cammell entered an agreement with the Swedish bus and truck builders Scania, to build a model for the British single-deck market, the Metro-Scania, based on the Scania BR111 model, but assembled in Birmingham.

The first Metro-Scanias appeared in 1969, integral city buses available in 10m (32ft 10in) and 11m (36ft) lengths, with rear-mounted Scania 11-litre engines and fully-automatic transmission. This

sophisticated model enjoyed a certain success, entering service with a number of municipal and PTE fleets, and even with London Country, London Transport and the one-time Winchester independent King Alfred. With National Bus heavily committed to the National, though, Metro-Cammell found the single-deck market restricted, and chose to concentrate on a double-decker with Scania units. There was one coach aimed at the British market, based on the Scania CR145 model, but its advanced specification — with 14.2-litre V8 engine, air suspension and power assisted steering — meant a high price-tag, and it created little interest.

Seddon introduced a rear-engined bus chassis in 1969, the RU model with Gardner 6HLX engine, and although it enjoyed a certain success, it had a relatively short life on the British market. Seddon became more involved in the bus market at this time, and offered several variations on its Pennine chassis range, with front, rear and underfloor-mounted engines. The most novel was the Seddon Midi, a 6.5m (21ft 3in) bus with Pennine Coachcraft body built on a Pennine IV 236 chassis. This useful little 25-seat bus was fitted with the 3.86-litre Perkins 4.236 engine, driving through a five-speed synchromesh gearbox — though later versions for Greater Manchester PTE had Allison fully-automatic transmission.

A bigger Seddon, the Pennine VII, appeared in 1973, and was developed in conjunction with the Scottish Bus Group. It was a traditional heavy-duty underfloor-engined model, suitable for 11m (36ft) or 12m (39ft 4in) bodies, and combined a number of well-tried components like the Gardner 6HLXB engine and ZF four-speed gearbox. The Scottish Group companies bought this chassis in large quantities, and some other operators have specified it for coach work.

During the early 1970s, imported cars and trucks were taking an increasingly large slice of the British market, and it was inevitable that bus builders should attempt to follow suit. Scania's involvement with Metro-Cammell has already been described, and Swedish rival Volvo made the most concentrated attack, picking up some useful sales in Britain for its 11m (36ft) and 12m (39ft 4in) B58 coach chassis. This model was first imported in 1972, and featured an underfloor-mounted 9.6-litre engine. At the same time the B59 rear-engined city bus chassis was introduced to Britain, but although this highly-sophisticated bus was enthusiastically received — a *Motor Transport* tester described it as 'one of the most impressive public service vehicles I have ever handled'; no sales were made. More successful, but only just, was another sophisticated European model, the Mercedes-Benz 0305. Selnec PTE took two with Northern Counties bodies in 1973, but no more followed in British service.

Volvo was the first importer to dip more than a tentative toe in the UK market. Mercedes-Benz had previously attempted to sell its complete 0302 coach in Britain, but there was no market at the time for this high-specification vehicle. The Volvo B58 could be fitted with Duple or Plaxton bodywork, and was more acceptable on the domestic market; Volvo has consistently outsold other imported chassis. DAF chassis appeared on the scene later in the decade and started to attract increasing orders from independents.

But the British manufacturers continued to dominate the home market, with a well-tried range of models. British Leyland had the steadily-selling underfloor-engined chassis, the AEC Reliance, Bristol LH and Leyland Leopard. The LH, favoured by NBC and London Transport as a lightweight 9.5m (31ft 2in) service bus, also found a market in its LHS form as the basis for short-length bus and coach bodies.

The Reliance, and particularly the Leopard, continued to sell steadily as heavyweight coach chassis. National Travel and Scottish Bus Group, and

Bending the rules

The double-decker has always been the British answer to the demand for high-capacity buses, but in many parts of Europe the articulated bus achieves similar results. Although double-deck buses are not unknown in mainland Europe — West Berlin and Vienna have been particularly enthusiastic users — the artic with space for 150 or more passengers, mostly standing, is more common. Although legislation prevented their use in Britain, an 18m (59ft) left-hand drive DAB, built by Leyland's Danish subsidiary, was brought into Britain in 1977 under special dispensation, and visited several operators. South Yorkshire PTE had helped to set up this evaluation programme, and used the bus on a free service in Sheffield for a three-day test. A right-hand drive MAN artic followed in 1978, as did a Stockholm Volvo B58, but the main thrust still came from South Yorkshire, which obtained permission to operate artics. Five MAN and five Leyland-DAB artics were delivered and in 1979 started a free city centre circular service in Sheffield. In 1980 the use of artics on fare-paying services was authorised, but in 1981 staff problems forced the PTE to abandon this pioneering experiment. The buses subsequently entered service with other operators, notably the MANs with Midland Red (North) and two of the Leylands with McGills of Barrhead.

Mercedes-Benz sent a pusher (rear-engined) 0305G artic to Britain in 1979, but few other operators showed much interest. British Airways bought seven Leyland-DAB buses for airside use, and Luton Airport operates three Mercedes 0305G with bodywork built to the French Heuliez design by Lex Vehicle Engineering.

117

117 **The South Yorkshire PTE Leyland-DAB articulated buses were useful at absorbing Sheffield queues. The bodywork was built around Leyland National components. The Cityliner service was a free circular route, so passengers could board speedily using any of the three doors.** *T. W. Moore*

important independents like Barton, Grey Green and Wallace Arnold, chose the Leopard as a standard coach model, while the Scottish fleets, among others, also specified Leopard buses. The Leopard was beginning to show its age by the late 1970s, and was starting to lose sales to the imported chassis.

In 1968 the regulations governing length had been relaxed to 12m (39ft 4in), and an increasing number of longer coaches were specified, allowing up to 57 seats.

Bedford and Ford retained their dominant position in the lightweight coach market, and increasingly they were specified for rural bus duties by independents, municipalities and nationalised fleets. Bedford replaced its 10m VAM model in 1970 with the YRQ, with a centrally-mounted vertical underfloor engine, and this was followed by the 11m (36ft) YRT in 1972; these were replaced by the bigger-engined YLQ and YMT chassis in 1975. Ford, on the other hand, stuck to the front-engined R1014 and R1114 models, improved versions of chassis that had first appeared in the mid-1960s.

Coach bodywork was normally in the familiar hands of Duple and Plaxton, who traditionally split the market needs fairly evenly between themselves. Duple's main 1970s range was the Dominant, introduced in 1972, and augmented by the deep-screen Dominant II in 1976. Plaxton's Elite range was replaced by the Supreme in 1974-75, and the first home-produced high-floor coach body was the Plaxton Viewmaster of 1976. The high-floor designs, permitting additional underfloor luggage space, were popular in mainland Europe, but it would be some years before British operators specified these designs in large numbers.

The growth of special services requiring smaller buses created a market for mini and midi size vehicles. In addition to the van-based minibuses like the Bedford CF, Commer PB and Ford Transit, and the bigger Ford A, Leyland Terrier and Mercedes L406D, there were specially developed integral midibuses from coachbuilders like Alexander and Marshall.

But the midibus market proved to be a limited one. Seddon's Midi sold less than 100 in its three-year production run. Alexander introduced the S type in 1974, a 7m integral vehicle based on Ford A series components; fewer than 30 were built. Marshall's offering was the Camuter with Perkins rear engine, and in 1976 the design was adopted by Vauxhall as the Bedford JJL, with Bedford 330 engine and Allison fully-automatic transmission. The widely-admired JJL, a 7.5m (24ft 7in) 24-seat bus, never went into production.

There was very little choice where double-deckers were concerned. For some time only British Leyland's three-model range, Bristol VR/Daimler Fleetline/Leyland Atlantean, was available — and there were complaints from operators that they were not available enough. While BLMC poured its investment cash into the private car divisions, the normally profitable commercial vehicle side was struggling to maintain deliveries of new chassis and

118 Volvo's Scottish-built Ailsa front-engined double-decker was particularly popular with Scottish operators. Tayside Regional Transport, successor to the Dundee municipal fleet, bought several batches; this was one of its 1976 deliveries, with two-door Alexander body. *R. L. Wilson*

119 The double-deck Metro-Scania, named Metropolitan, was chosen by several important operators at a time when Leyland's previous monopoly of the double-deck market was widely criticised. Customers included PTEs and larger municipalities, and the biggest fleet, surprisingly, was London Transport's, with 164 delivered in 1975-77. In London, as in most cities, they had short lives. *T. W. Moore*

spare parts. And there was an increasing undercurrent of dissatisfaction with the reliability of the rear-engined designs compared with the now-discontinued front-engined models.

Leyland struggled on, though. The Leyland 680 engine was offered in the Daimler Fleetline — a particularly valuable option for a period when Gardner engines were in short supply. Then there was the AN68 Atlantean, a vastly improved version of the 14-year-old PDR series, introduced in 1972, which greatly helped Leyland's double-deck fortunes and restored the Atlantean's rather tarnished image.

These efforts did not please every operator. In 1972 Northern General unveiled two remarkable confections — the Tynesider and the Wearsider. With a successful fleet of Routemasters, Northern was looking for a way of converting these for one-man operation. The Tynesider was the first step towards this, a Leyland PD3 Titan heavily rebuilt as a normal control vehicle, with the driver alongside the forward entrance, behind a Routemaster-type 'snout'. The next stage

was the conversion of an accident-damaged Routemaster in a similar fashion — the Wearsider, but there were no more of these bizarre rebuilds.

Apart from Northern General's efforts, double-deckers started to look much more similar around this time, mainly following the introduction of a crisp new standard design from Park Royal-Roe in 1968. This was quickly adopted by most of the PTEs, by NBC for Atlantean chassis, and even by London Transport — probably the first time that most of the major operators in England have operated similar-looking buses. The design was produced, with modifications, by Park Royal and Roe, and by Metro-Cammell, Northern Counties and Willowbrook, all in the interests of standardisation.

The industrial unrest of the 1973/74 winter, and the three-day working week, meant that bus chassis and body production got badly out of step for some years. By late 1974, 5,000 buses were on order for local authority fleets, many were up to two years late. More than half were Fleetlines, representing four years normal production. This situation caused growing

frustration and resentment amongst operators, and the market was ripe for competition.

The Scottish Bus Group had continued to favour the front-engined double-decker, and acted in an advisory capacity in the development of a new model, the Ailsa. The Scottish-based Ailsa Trucks group had successfully imported Volvo trucks for some years, and the Ailsa bus featured a Volvo engine. This was the 6.7-litre TD70 unit, a compact turbocharged engine which fitted neatly beside the driving position to allow a normal entrance on the front overhang.

121 The Dennis Dominator, like the Foden, was designed to fill the gap created by the ending of Fleetline production, and certainly achieved greater success. It proved popular with municipal operators like City of Cardiff, as shown with East Lancs body, and with PTE, SBG and independent fleets. *M. S. Curtis*

122 Dennis built a single-deck version of the Dominator, and the first examples were eight for Darlington Corporation in 1980, with Marshall 46-seat Camair bodywork. The principle of common chassis for single-deck and double-deck buses goes back over half a century, but the Darlington buses joined an all-single-deck fleet. *M. S. Curtis*

The Volvo Ailsa was supplied as an underframe, and Alexander built an integrated body structure on many of the early examples, following its introduction in 1973.

Leyland's monopoly was further challenged the same year by the appearance of yet another British/Swedish collaboration, the Metropolitan. This was essentially a double-deck version of the Metro-Scania city bus, and like the Ailsa was ordered in reasonable numbers by PTE and municipal fleets, often as a protest against Leyland's monopoly, though there were signs of a falling-off in demand as Leyland's future plans became clearer. It was known that an advanced double-deck model was in development, and that it would eventually replace the VR/Fleetline/Atlantean trio.

The replacement was to be a gradual one, though, with the Fleetline disappearing first. Fleetline production had transferred after 7,000-plus chassis from Coventry to Leyland, and in 1976 even adopted the Leyland name. The demand for a Gardner-engined successor prompted Dennis and Foden to re-enter the double-deck market with new rear-engined models in 1976 and 1977.

Foden had built double-deckers before, but not for many years, and was best known as a truck maker. Its 1976 model was initially produced in conjunction with Northern Counties, resulting in the designation Foden/NC. Only seven were bodied.

The last Dennis double-deck model had been the Loline of 1967, and 10 years later Hestair Dennis (renamed following take-over by the Hestair Group in 1972) produced the first Dominator with Gardner 6LXB engine and Voith automatic transmission. There was an initial flurry of interest among municipal operators, and Leicester was an enthusiastic early customer. The Dominator also sold as a single-deck bus from 1978.

The latter-day success of the AN68 Atlantean guaranteed it a stay of execution, while improvements to the Bristol VRT model in 1974 gave it a further lease of life. The Mk 3 version of the VRT featured a Leyland 510 engine as an option to the Gardner units normally fitted, but then in short supply.

The bus that Leyland hoped would eventually replace these chassis appeared late in 1975 when details of the B15 project were revealed. Like the existing Leyland double-deckers it was rear-engined — in Leyland's words 'the location of the mechanical units takes second place to the needs of the fare-paying passengers and driver'. The engine was the TL11, a turbocharged version of the Leyland 680 series, and the Gardner 6LXB was also offered. The production version of the B15, introduced in 1977, revived the well-loved type-name Titan.

The new Titan was an advanced, sophisticated and highly-standardised design, available only in one body size, 9.5m×2.5m (31ft 2in×8ft 2½in), and only as a 4.4m (14ft 5in) normal height bus. Leyland intended the Bristol VRT to satisfy the decreasing demand for low-height vehicles.

The Titan's integral construction allowed a low entrance step height, and saloon heights on both decks were more generous than normal. One-door and two-door buses were available, and extensive Leyland research into human factors was reflected in the design and layout of the entrance and exit areas.

Initial reaction to the Titan was enthusiastic, and Leyland showed a commendable degree of care in the introduction of the model. The Bristol VR and Leyland National had demonstrated the folly of rushing designs into production without adequate service proving, and their early reputation lingered on.

A prototype B15 entered service with London Transport in 1976, on an experimental basis, and the degree of sophistication was such that London became Titan's most enthusiastic customer. There were other buyers, but these were insignificant compared with London's eventual fleet of 1,125, supplied between 1978 and 1984. London's first Titans were built at the Park Royal works, but poor productivity forced the closure of this famous plant, and transfer of production to Workington, alongside the National.

The gradual acceptance of integral vehicles caused problems for the old-established bodybuilders outside the Leyland empire. The situation had been further aggravated by the success of the Leyland National, which virtually killed the single-deck bus body market.

Some builders diversified, and formed alliances with other chassis builders. Alexander bodied many of the Ailsas, and produced the S type midibus; East Lancs worked closely with Dennis on the Dominator, and even built coach bodies; Metro-Cammell linked with Scania to build the Metropolitan model, and was set to develop this concept and follow an even more independent line. All of these builders had relied heavily on the normally lucrative double-deck market, increasingly so as the single-deck bus market dried up, but what had been under-supply in the early 1970s moved towards overkill just a few years later. Barely 1,000 double-deckers had been delivered to British operators in 1970, and through the decade the market called for less than 2,000 per annum. Leyland reckoned it could satisfy that alone; now it had Ailsa, Dennis, Foden and MCW to cope with as well.

To aggravate the situation further, news leaked of London Transport's XRM, an in-house project to 'overcome the

123

deficiencies, in particular unreliability, displayed by existing off-the-peg designs in intensive urban service'. The XRM would have been a short, manoeuvrable bus, perhaps with side-mounted engine, perhaps with eight small wheels and twin-steer front axles. The project was dropped in 1980 as LT settled in to large orders of two main types. There was the Leyland Titan, already mentioned, and MCW Metrobus.

Metrobus was MCW's integral double-decker, with rear-mounted Gardner 6LXB engine and Voith transmission. London bought a large Metrobus fleet, starting in 1978, and this dual-source policy, with supplies more or less in parallel, helped top up the fleet and permit Fleetline withdrawal. The Metrobus was more widely popular than the Titan, with PTEs and larger municipalities taking deliveries; it was also offered as a separate underframe, and as such was bought by Midland Scottish and other fleets.

A resurgence of interest in electric power was the Tyne & Wear Metro, the light railway system that is to all intents and purposes the equivalent of some of the modern tramway systems on the Continent; the Metro has revolutionised transport on Tyneside, and although expensive in capital outlay, has proved a resounding success in attracting passengers. And there is, of course, the famous Blackpool seafront tramway, which celebrated its centenary in 1985; in recent years the predominantly prewar tram fleet has been modernised with

123 Leyland's sophisticated Titan integral double-decker was introduced as the eventual replacement for the existing, ageing Leyland models, but it proved too advanced for many operators, and was also dogged with production difficulties that led to several cancelled orders. London Transport became the principal customer. This Titan demonstrator was on loan to West Midlands PTE, which actually bought five in 1978/79 — and sold them to London in 1985. *T. W. Moore*

heavily rebuilt single-deck and double-deck cars, and these were joined by brand-new East Lancs bodied single-deck cars in 1984 and 1985.

There were some novel approaches in the 1970s to the problems facing the bus industry, like the continued growth of private motoring.

Alternative sources
For years the boffins had been busy predicting the problems the world would face when the energy crunch eventually came. Suddenly at the end of 1973 their gloomy forebodings proved dramatically accurate. Suddenly oil was in short supply, and costing more each day, and the alternatives became more attractive.

Electric power probably had most in its favour, though we have seen how British operators abandoned first the tramcar and then the trolleybus. Britain's final trolleybus system closed down in March 1972 when the Bradford system was abandoned; ironically, that same month, only nine miles away at Leeds, the first of a number of experimental battery buses entered service. The trial, sponsored by the Department of Trade and Industry, involved small buses built by Crompton Electricars on converted BLMC 900 FG truck chassis and bodied by Willowbrook. These electric buses were used in various towns in Britain, and were fairly successful. Greater Manchester PTE took the idea a couple of stages further with the Silent Rider project, a full-size Seddon/Chloride bus to be used at peak hours and recharged in between, and a Lucas electric version of the Seddon midibuses already operating on the busy Manchester Centreline service.

The problems with electric buses include the size and weight of batteries necessary, the limited mileage range, and the slower acceleration, but many of the big manufacturers in Britain and on the Continent have projects in hand which may overcome these. A Leyland National was even converted for experimental use towing its batteries in a separate trailer which was thought to be one answer to the difficulties with size, weight and recharging time.

Some of the Continental manufacturers have also experimented with gas buses, using liquid petroleum gas (LPG). In Britain the Teesside undertaking introduced in 1976 a Daimler Fleetline fitted with a Rolls-Royce B81G engine converted to run on LPG. Four years' experience with the 'Clean Air Bus' proved that it could never be cost-effective. In 1979 Ribble fitted an Atlantean with a special Leyland 680LPG engine, but fuel consumption at 3.6 mile/gal compared with 7.4 mile/gal on a diesel bus, and fuel costs per mile were 58% more with LPG.

At the Cheshire new town of Runcorn, an unusual approach was adopted. Here a 12-mile exclusive Busway was built into the road network, allowing a rapid transit system in a basic figure-eight, but ensuring that no home is more than five minutes from a bus stop. The Crosville single-deck buses used can achieve an average running speed of 20mph, and the Runcorn Busway is the natural extension of the bus priority schemes which are now familiar in most towns and cities. The first bus lanes were in London, allowing service buses to avoid traffic snarl-ups at busy junctions, and the idea was extended to provide bus lanes running against the normal traffic-flow, thus avoiding lengthy and time-consuming one-way systems.

Park-and-ride services have been tried in many centres as an attempt to keep cars out of town and city centres by encouraging drivers to park at suburban car parks and travel into shopping or business areas by bus. A variation is the frequent city centre service, providing a useful link during business hours for short-distance passengers; these usually have a single flat fare, but Nottingham

Transport has carried things to a logical conclusion with its Central Area free services.

Small, but useful

In urban areas, smaller buses in both mini and midi size ranges appeared on dial-a-ride and similar services, where passengers could phone a central control point to request transport into town, and the driver was contacted to arrange a pick up at the most convenient point — often the caller's front door. There was normally a basic route, with some form of timetable and fixed stops for those without phones, and the driver diverted to pick up and set down passengers as near to their homes as possible. These services operated under a variety of names, and often served residential suburbs which did not otherwise have a bus service. Few survived more than a few years.

Minibuses were also used on some of the city centre shoppers' services, in some cases using pedestrian areas, but two more unusual uses are worth mentioning.

The first, postbus, appeared experimentally in 1968, a BMC minibus which carried passengers as well as mail on

a rural route in East Lothian. Four years later a postbus service on Skye marked the start of a fast-growing system operated by the Scottish Postal Board. Gradually, other services were started by the Post Office in more remote parts of the Scottish mainland and islands, and in parts of England and Wales as well.

Scotland's 50th postbus was launched in 1975, and the numbers grew annually, in some cases taking services over from established operators. The Commer PB 11-seat minibus was the most popular vehicle for this type of service, and the driver not only collected and delivered mail, but also essential supplies; the postbus has become an important part of life in many isolated rural areas, a highly practical solution to at least some of the transport problems.

124 **The new town of Runcorn incorporated a reserved busway system connecting outlying districts with the town centre, and Crosville used some of its large fleet of Seddon RU on the Busway services.** *Ian Allan Library*

124

125

126

125 A novel answer to the problems of rural bus services was the Border Courier, introduced in 1979 as a joint venture between Borders Region and Eastern Scottish. Five Bedford CF minibuses with 13-seat Reeve Burgess bodies were used on rural services which also linked health centres with the principal hospital in the area, hence the goods compartment at the rear. These buses were replaced by larger Bedford VAS models in 1981. *SBG*

126 Anticipating later minibus services, the Carterton Dial-a-Ride service operated by Oxford South Midland used this 15-seat Deansgate-bodied Ford Transit with 2-litre petrol engine. *Ford*

A quite different approach was the village bus, an experimental type of service first introduced in 1975. Its aim was to provide a self-help bus service for communities which would normally have been too small to support a conventional service. Eastern Counties provided a 12-seat Ford Transit minibus for six Norfolk villages, where residents shared the responsibility for their own public transport. The locals provided a team of volunteer drivers, and handled normal operation, though Eastern Counties and Norfolk County Council, the joint sponsors, retained overall control.

The village bus mainly provided connections with rail and bus services to larger towns, and could be used for other purposes under imposed guidelines. The County Council backed the service financially — but the costs were much less than for a service using full-size buses, a situation which would never have been considered.

It was clear that the bus industry was prepared to seek new solutions for its problems. National Bus undertook a major market research exercise, the Market Analysis Project (MAP). This involved large-scale surveys of travel patterns, which permitted new networks of services to be designed to suit identified demand. Substantial cost savings were made, including fleet reductions, which meant that a greater strain was placed on the remaining vehicles. An important aspect of the implementation of new MAP networks was the promotional effort, designed to inform bus users and non-users of the changes. Scottish Bus Group followed NBC's example with SCOTMAP, a development of the National system.

These extensive exercises shifted the two big nationalised groups from a traditional preoccupation with the supply side of the bus business, to become demand-oriented, and stood them in good stead for the uncertainties of the 1980s.

Events

1969 National Bus Company and Scottish Transport Group formed.
1969-70 First Passenger Transport Executives in business.
1970 London Country Bus Services formed from LT Country Area. London Transport DMS type Daimler Fleetline double-decker. Leyland National single-deck city bus unveiled.
1972 Last British trolleybus, Bradford.
1973 Ailsa and Metropolitan double-deck models introduced.
1974 Local government reorganisation and new PTEs, England and Wales.
1975 Leyland unveils B15 double-decker, later Titan.
1976 Dennis Dominator double-decker appears.
1978 MCW Metrobus double-decker.
1979 Leyland National 2 introduced. AEC Southall factory closes. Last London Transport RT in public service.

World Events

1969 Man lands on the moon.
1971 Decimalisation of Britain's currency.
1972 Munich Olympics massacre. Britain joins EEC.
1973 Coal strike; state of emergency; three-day week.
1974 United States President Nixon resigns.

1975 Unemployment exceeds one million.
1977 Silver Jubilee of HM Queen.
1979 Lord Mountbatten assassinated. Devolution referendum, Scotland and Wales.

Leyland National

Leyland's decision to mass-produce a rear-engined single-deck city bus in a purpose-built assembly plant was a brave one. When the project was first considered, in the mid-1960s, the single-deck bus seemed to be in the ascendant, and the future seemed bright.

The new bus was the Leyland National, an integral vehicle making use of highly standardised units to produce a small range of model options: two body lengths, one or two doors, right- or left-hand drive.

A Mk 1 Leyland National in the Midland Red fleet carries Reddibus symbols, an early NBC local identity for services in Redditch new town. *Ian Allan Library*

It was a bold concept, and although the main customer was the National Bus Company, with whom it was a joint venture, municipal, PTE, London Transport, SBG and independent fleets all bought Nationals; the bus also enjoyed some export success.

The National 2 of 1979 replaced the original 510 engine with the more familiar 680 unit, and a front-mounted radiator changed the appearance.

Demand slowed in the 1980s, and National production was run down in favour of a new underframe, the Lynx — but not before some 8,000 Nationals had been delivered, an astounding total for a bus that introduced so many new concepts.

Sign of the Times

Profile

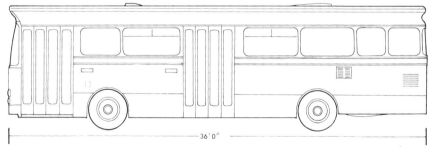

Similar to 1960s buses, but some with two doors; rear engine popular, though not universal as some operators stuck to mid-underfloor layout. 48 seats.

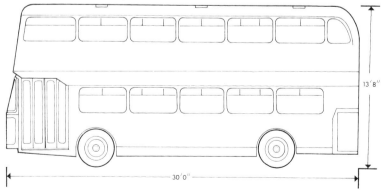

Many operators reverted to single-door double-deckers, and stuck with shorter-than-maximum -length buses; rear vertical engines and epicyclic gearboxes virtually standard. 74 seats (43/31).

NEW TYPE BUSES ON ROUTES 95 & 181
STARTING JANUARY 2

London Transport introduced one-man bus services on two south London routes with this leaflet describing the new-type buses. 'The eventual conversion of all services to one-man operation,' said the introductory text, 'will enable buses to be run with fewer but better paid staff; this will help to recruit and retain drivers.'

114

The greatest thing in coaching for years
The 1980s

127

The 1980s were barely nine months old when significant new legislation changed the whole face of the express coach business. Since the 1930 Act, express coach services had been subject to licensing controls, but in line with the policies of the Conservative Government of the time the services were deregulated to encourage free competition.

Before 1980 most of Britain's express coach services were in the hands of the two nationalised groups, as well as important independents like Barton, Grey-Green, Premier Travel and Yelloway. Services were good, but operators had not taken full advantage of the motorway system to increase speeds, and vehicles did not always offer much in the way of amenities or comfort.

The coach had been no real threat to British Rail on longer-distance routes, but after October 1980 that was to change.

Not only did existing operators respond willingly to the new opportunities offered by deregulation, but many fresh names appeared on the express scene.

The first was British Coachways, an ambitious scheme to unite independent operators from all parts of Britain under a common brand-name and livery to operate a network of services. Mike Kay, one of the architects of the scheme described the 1980 Act as 'The greatest thing in coaching for years'. British Coachways was a brave concept, but the constituent operators deserted the consortium after a relatively short time.

In their wake came a flood of new

127 **Leyland's Tiger coach chassis helped it to recover some of the business lost to Volvo, and appeared with a wide variety of coachwork. This Tiger, from the fleet of Redfern's of New Mills, has Belgian-built LAG Galaxy bodywork.**
Leyland

express services, some operated by existing operators, others by new operators. Some newcomers did not last long but others persevered and expanded their business. But as the express business settled down after the initial skirmishes, the existing big operators emerged as market leaders, and with new, fast services and reduced fares, National Express expanded dramatically.

The increased services attracted fresh public interest and operators sought vehicles that suited this new coaching era. British-made coaches could not really compete with the imported vehicles: the lighter-weight Bedfords and Fords were not ideal for fast, long-distance motorway work; the AEC Reliance was being phased out; Leyland's Leopard was a popular workhorse, but could be noisy and ponderous with a standard of ride that did not measure up to the Continental chassis. The home market bodybuilders, Duple and Plaxton, had long-running ranges that lacked the styling crispness of Belgian designs.

Express deregulation opened the doors to a general upgrading of coach standards. Volvo and DAF chassis were chosen for some of the new services, and Caetano and Van Hool bodies were joined in the 1980s by a host of new names from Belgium, Germany, Italy, Netherlands and Spain. Not all of these were just bodies. In 1980 MAN, from West Germany, introduced its SR280 model into Britain, a rear-engined integral coach, and although it has not been particularly successful in Britain it was the first of many similar models. Within a few years there was a bewildering array of imported chassis, bodies and integrals available in Britain.

The most successful imports were DAF and Volvo chassis, Jonckheere and Van Hool coach bodies, and Bova, Neoplan and Van Hool integrals. And as the imports grew, so did the coaches. They could be no longer than 12m (39ft 4in) but extra capacity — for both passengers and luggage — became the main preoccupation. First came high-floor coaches with extra underfloor luggage space, and then a rebirth of interest in double-deck coaches. For years, double-deck coaches had only a limited appeal, but several of the new express coach operators chose the Neoplan Skyliner for their services, and this was followed by similar models from Jonckheere, Setra and Van Hool. These were based on three-axle underframes and prompted the development of British-made alternatives. Leyland produced a coach version of its Olympian, with ECW bodywork, and this

128 Dutch-built DAF coaches were popular with many operators, and this MB200 underfloor-engined model with Belgian-built Van Hool Alizee body, from the fleet of Harris of Grays, is seen leaving Buckingham Palace with the Essex county cricket team. *DAF*

128

129 Imported coaches became increasingly familiar on Britain's roads in the 1980s, and NBC fleets joined the list of customers. Crosville bought this strikingly-styled Bova Futura for use on National Express Rapide services, which featured video, hostess and snacks.
Stewart J. Brown

130 With its roots in the erstwhile Ward company, the Albion Equipment Company (AEC) introduced the short-length Puma coach chassis. With another name-change, the builders emerged as Alternative Chassis Engineering (ACE), and their products found favour with independent operators like Mackie of Alloa, here using a Puma with Plaxton's Paramount body on contract work in Edinburgh in 1985.
G. R. Mills

129

130

was followed by the three-axle MCW Metroliner, and the Plaxton Paramount 4000. The Metroliner was based on an MCW bus chassis for Hong Kong, while the first Paramount 4000s used Neoplan underframes. Alexander produced the RDC coach body for SBG, and several NBC fleets ordered bus-shell Olympians with coach seating for longer-distance journeys.

A compromise between the high-floor single-decker and the double-deck coaches was the high-deck coach, with a single full-length passenger deck, sometimes stretching forward over the driver's compartment, and in many cases with an extra low-slung passenger compartment at the extreme rear increasing capacity by around a dozen seats.

Many of the new coaches were rear-engined, although Volvo resolutely stuck to the mid-engined layout for its coaches, and DAF offered both layouts.

The British response

What was the British manufacturing industry doing to meet the new coach challenge? Firstly, Leyland replaced its Leopard and AEC Reliance with a new chassis, the Tiger. This new model had a mid-mounted 218bhp TL11 engine, a choice of automatic or synchromesh gearboxes, a front-mounted radiator and air suspension. A 245bhp engine was quickly offered and later a 260bhp option appeared; this reflected a trend to more powerful engines.

The Tiger was instantly successful, competing with its nearest rival, the Volvo B10M, for a market that was moving steadily towards heavyweight coaches. Dennis introduced coach chassis, the Falcon V in 1980 and the Dorchester in 1982. The Falcon V, with rear-mounted

Perkins V8 engine, was specified for Duple-bodied coaches for National Express, but this was not a particularly successful model. The Dorchester had a mid-mounted Gardner 6HLXCT engine, filling an apparent need for a Gardner-engined coach chassis; Leyland then produced a Gardner-engined Tiger.

Leyland also took a calculated gamble with a rear-engined coach model to take on the Continentals, the Royal Tiger. It was introduced in 1982 as a separate chassis and as a complete integral vehicle, the Royal Tiger Doyen, a British answer to sophisticated models like the German

Setra. The Doyen was assembled at the Roe coachworks in Leeds, but when this factory closed in 1984 production continued at Workington. This was not the only complete new coach from a British manufacturer in 1982; MCW, long associated with double-deck bus bodies, broke into the coach market with the Metroliner range that year, including a 12m (39ft 4in) normal-height coach with rear-mounted Cummins L10 engine. Initial sales were to NBC and SBG fleets, and Strathclyde PTE. This was followed by the Metro Hiliner, an integral high-floor coach.

131 **To emphasise the integrated nature of local transport in PTE areas, some NBC company operators painted a proportion of their fleet in the livery of the PTE. This was most evident in Tyne & Wear, where Northern and United buses wore the PTE's yellow and white colours; a Northern MCW Metrobus 2 leaving the Gateshead Interchange, where buses and Metro meet.** *Ian M. Train*

Two brand-new names appeared on the model lists in the early 1980s. Ward Motors, based near Huddersfield, produced a Perkins-engined coach chassis, the Dalesman, and a few were built before the company was declared bankrupt. It re-emerged in 1984 as Albion Engineering Co (AEC!), with a range of coach chassis including underfloor and rear-engined designs. AEC resurfaced as ACE, Alternative Chassis Engineering, in 1985. Another new name, Quest 80, offered several single-deck chassis including a Ford-powered chassis, the VM, for Excelsior of Bournemouth; Quest 80 went into receivership in 1985.

Bedford and Ford were losing ground to the heavyweights, and Bedford retaliated with constant developments of its Y model range. The YNT became the top model with a 206bhp turbocharged engine, and in 1984 this was joined by the YNV, named

Venturer, with air suspension and designed for the heavier bodies. Ford's changes were largely restricted to the introduction of the improved Dover series engine, and consequent redesignation to R1015 and R1115 for its 10m and 11m chassis, respectively. With falling sales, Ford withdrew from the full-size bus market in 1985.

The home coach bodybuilding team of Duple and Plaxton had varied fortunes in the 1980s. Normally they dominated the market, with Plaxton traditionally in the lead, but Continental builders were making serious inroads into the increasingly up-market coach business, and the Duple Dominant and Plaxton Supreme ranges were beginning to look a little tired. Duple's holding action was to introduce smaller-windowed Dominant variants, one version having the trapezoid-shape windows favoured by SBG, the other simply a shallower version of the normal side windows. These were followed by high-floor versions, named Goldliner, offering increased underfloor luggage space. Plaxton's reply was the Supreme V and VI models, one with a revised rear end, the other also featuring shallower side windows.

Inevitably these models had to be replaced and in 1982 — a vintage year for British coaches — both Duple and Plaxton unveiled new ranges.

Plaxton introduced the Paramount in normal height 3200 and high-floor 3500 variants, and this range quickly became familiar on Britain's roads. Duple introduced two very different designs — the normal height Laser and high-floor Caribbean, which bore little obvious family relationship. Duple was experiencing serious problems at the time, and the firm was rescued by the Hestair Group, with Dennis already under its wing, which bought the ailing company and set about regaining lost goodwill.

The model range was revised, and the Laser 2 and Caribbean II were introduced in 1984, improved versions of the coaches of two years earlier. At the same time Duple announced an ambitious new up-market coach, the Integral 425, a dramatically-styled coach with Cummins L10 engine at the rear. Hestair exorcised all remnants of the previous designs when the Laser and Caribbean were replaced in 1985 by totally new bodies — the 320 and 340 ranges.

The only other serious contender on the home market was Wright of Ballymena, Northern Ireland. The striking Contour body, styled in conjunction with Bedford, was offered initially on Bedford chassis, and sold in small numbers. Alexander, more normally associated with service bus bodies, produced the TC type coach in 1983, a stylish development based on the

132

133

132 After the initial false start, articulated buses returned to South Yorkshire PTE in 1985 when 10 of these DAB-built Leylands were delivered for the network of Clipper services in Sheffield. These urban artics were joined later that year by three coach-seated examples for inter-urban express work. *M. Fowler*

133 The only customer other than London Transport for the Leyland Titan model in its later years was Reading Transport which bought 12 in 1979/83. Five had 66 coach seats for the municipality's post-deregulation Goldline express services to London. *Leyland*

familiar T type shell. Willowbrook, whose fortunes in the bus industry have been mixed, returned to the scene with a new coach body, the Crusader, in 1985.

Declining Market

As up-market coaches increased in popularity, the single-deck bus was on the decline. The Leyland National had fast become Britain's best-selling single-deck citybus in the 1970s; in 1978 a record 900 Nationals were sold in Britain, the great majority to NBC fleets. The National 2 was launched in 1979, with front-mounted radiator, and 680 engine in place of the fixed-head 510 unit; three years later the Gardner 6HLXB and 6HLXCT were offered as an option to Leyland's TL11 turbocharged development of the 680. By this time, though, single-deck bus sales had dropped to around 130 delivered in the year. Most were Nationals, but other models were still chosen. Production of the National ceased in 1985.

Scottish Bus Group, independent and municipal fleets bought Leyland Leopards and Tigers for bus duties, and SBG also took Seddon Pennine VIIs. Some operators chose the Volvo B58 and B10M for bus work, and other models like the Dennis Dorchester and Lancet.

The only rear-engined models to emerge to challenge the National were from Dennis, Scania and Ward. Among its plethora of new models, Dennis in 1980

introduced the Falcon H, with a rear-mounted Gardner 6HLXB engine, and this found favour with municipal customers. Previously some municipal operators had chosen the Dennis Dominator for single-deck bodywork. In addition, Scania sold nine BR112DH chassis to Newport, and Darlington took six Ward GRXI buses in 1983.

With a declining home single-deck market, and with an integral model that was not acceptable in some markets, Leyland introduced a new rear-engined single-deck citybus underframe in 1984, the Lynx. Designed for both home and export markets, the Lynx could be fitted with locally-built bodywork or sold as a complete bus with Leyland-built bodywork.

Most single-deck buses were full-length 10.6-11.6m (34ft 9in-38ft) vehicles, but there was still a limited demand for midi-size buses. Lacking a purpose-built model, manufacturers offered different solutions. Lothian took 18 Leyland Cubs in 1981, a truck-derived model, and in 1982

Portsmouth chose shortened Dennis Lancets. Leyland produced a 'midi-size' model in 1984, the Tiger Cub, an older name resurrected for a bus built in Denmark by DAB, and finished in Britain by ECW; at 9.5m long (31ft) the Tiger Cub was hardly a genuine midi, but offered operators a replacement for models like the Bristol LH. Faced with the need to replace its Seddon Midis on Centreline services, Dennis developed a low-floor rear-engined midi-length chassis, the Domino, for Greater Manchester Transport. Northern Counties bodywork was fitted and the result was the best-conceived midibus since the unfortunate Bedford JJL; South Yorkshire PTE also opted for this model and received the first examples of Optare bodywork, built in the former Roe coachworks in Leeds. At the other end of the size range South Yorkshire created a mild stir in 1984 when it announced that it was ordering more articulated buses, 13 Danish-built Leyland-DABs — an interesting development following its earlier abortive efforts.

134 **Many operators specified brighter liveries and marketing names for their services. Bristol Omnibus ran these Clippers on Bristol city services, but these have since been replaced by a new City Clipper livery. The bus is one of 55 Leyland Olympians with 76-seat Roe bodywork delivered in 1982; the electronic destination indicator was a feature that first appeared in the 1980s.** *Leyland*

The over-provision in the double-deck bus market was further aggravated in 1980 when another two models joined the lists. There was the Scania BR112DH, a model developed by the Swedish builder for the UK Market, and, more significantly the Leyland Olympian. This was Leyland's model to succeed the Atlantean/Fleetline/VRT ranges, and unlike the Titan it was offered as an underframe suitable for locally-built bodies, in lowheight or normal-height form; to cater for existing customers, engine options were the

Leyland TL11 and Gardner 6LXB. The Olympian quickly picked up orders from NBC, SBG, PTE, municipal and independent operators, and established itself with the MCW Metrobus as the best-selling models on the market. The Metrobus relied largely on two main customers, London Transport and West Midlands PTE, while Leyland's Titan relied almost entirely on London business; Reading was the only other Titan customer in later years. When London orders finished in 1984, production of the Titan ceased. Widely recognised as a good model, the Titan offered a degree of sophistication that most operators did not require.

The main customers for the Dennis Dominator were South Yorkshire PTE, Leicester City and Central and Western Scottish, though many were sold to smaller municipalities. Dennis offered another model from 1981, the Falcon V, with a rear-mounted Mercedes-Benz 0M421 V6 engine. This was available for single-deck or double-deck use, and the compact engine meant there was little intrusion into saloon space.

The Volvo Ailsa still had its following, particularly among Scottish operators, but in 1982 Volvo introduced the Citybus, an underfloor-engined double-deck chassis based on the B10M coach. This was not a new idea — AEC and BMMO had experimented with this layout — but the compact nature of the Volvo THD100E engine meant that the lower saloon floor levels were low, and the Citybus succeeded where others had failed. Like the Ailsa, the Citybus was built at the Volvo plant at Irvine. Leyland's answer was the Lion, a DAB-built chassis.

Double-deck sales started to drop in the 1980s as economic recession hit operators, and manufacturers expressed serious concern about their survival. Some relied heavily on London business, potentially the largest single customer. After its problems with the Fleetlines, London had apparently settled into a steady pattern, building up large fleets of Metrobuses and Titans. But in 1984 it started a programme of tests involving different types of double-decker, to evaluate these under identical conditions on route 170. There were to be three each of Dennis Dominator, Leyland Olympian, MCW Metrobus and Volvo Ailsa, although there were variations on each theme. The Dominators with Northern Counties bodies had Gardner 6LXB engines, one with a Maxwell gearbox, the others Voith

D851. Of the Olympians with ECW bodies, one had a Leyland TL11/hydracyclic gearbox combination, the others 6LXB/Voith. Only two of the Metrobuses entered service, one with Cummins L10 engine and Maxwell gearbox, and the other had the 6LXB/Voith combination.

But the Alexander-bodied Ailsas were probably the most interesting. Here were front-engined double-deckers for London service again, and while two had conventional two-door bodies with front entrance and centre exit, the third had front and *rear* doors — although not the familiar open rear platform of the Routemaster; platform doors were fitted, and there was no cutaway. Another Volvo, a Citybus with an experimental flywheel

135 **With the Citybus chassis, Volvo achieved what other builders had unsuccessfully attempted — a practical underfloor-engined double-decker. Municipal orders included this coach-seated example for Plymouth, with East Lancs bodywork; several operators looking for extra capacity chose normal bus shells with coach seats and fittings as a lower-price alternative to the full-specification double-deck coach.**
G. R. Mills

135

136 An early taste of urban bus service competition, and a *cause celebre* at the time, resulted from the decision to grant CK Coaches authority to run two city services in Cardiff, where previously the City Transport had enjoyed monopoly powers. CK's opposition lasted for less than a year from April 1981. It used former London Transport Daimler Fleetlines, a popular source of secondhand buses for operators of all sizes in the early 1980s. *G. R. Mills*

137 British-built double-deck buses sold well in export markets, helping to offset the decline in domestic requirements. Some, like Hong Kong, had long used British double-deckers; this Leyland Olympian with ECW body is seen in service with Kowloon Motor Bus. Other markets were totally new, and there was often fierce competition between manufacturers to win orders. *Leyland*

arrangement, joined the other test buses in 1985, but not before London placed an order for 260 Leyland Olympians.

British manufacturers traditionally had the export business to bolster home sales, and while many one-time export markets had been lost to competitors, others were discovering the benefits of the British-style double-decker. During the 1970s Hong Kong, Indonesia, Djakarta and Singapore placed substantial orders for high capacity vehicles; some were lengthened versions of home-market chassis — Dennis Dominators, Leyland Atlanteans and Olympians, MCW Metrobuses and Volvo Ailsas, sometimes three-axle versions — while others were rugged front-engined chassis from Dennis and Leyland.

This new export business from distant parts of the world was welcome, but in the meantime a once-faithful customer nearer home had turned elsewhere for its buses. Coras Iompair Eireann, Ireland's state transport operator, had principally bought Leylands for 30 years, but stopped buying buses altogether in the late 1970s while it developed a new range of buses with FFG, the West German transport consultancy. From 1980 examples of these new vehicles, built in Ireland by Bombardier, appeared in service — single-deck and double-deck

buses, and inter-city and touring coaches. Initially built around Detroit Diesel two-stroke engines and Allison automatic gearboxes, later versions had Cummins engines and Voith transmission, and were built by GAC, which had taken over production.

The British bus population at the end of 1983 stood at 70,191, 64% single-deck. The nationalised sector had the biggest total fleet — 17,731 between NBC and SBG. London Transport had a further 5,638, the seven PTEs 9,612, and the 50 local authority fleets 5,271. Roundly 46% were in private hands — 31,939 buses and coaches.

All of these vehicles were responsible for 6,185 million passenger journeys in 1983, an impressive figure, even though it has been gradually declining for some years; but buses and coaches still carried four times more than all of Britain's railways, so the importance of the bus industry in the everyday life and leisure of the country should not be underestimated.

Deregulation and privatisation
All of this was taking place against a background of new uncertainties arising from the publication in 1984 of the

Government White Paper *Buses,* proposing radical changes in the legislative structure of the industry. Complete deregulation of stage carriage services would follow the experience with trial areas where licensing had been abolished, and the doors would be reopened for competition on the streets. This legislation, coupled with the Government's intention to disband the Metropolitan Counties in England, with its implications for the future of the PTEs, threw the industry into a state of uncertainty. Added to this, the Government's plans to privatise the National Bus Company meant that the future shape of bus orders was in some doubt.

NBC was instrumental in the rediscovery of the minibus. Few larger operators had taken minibuses seriously, but following a successful experiment in Exeter, NBC

138 After a period when no new buses were bought, CIE eventually received deliveries of its new standard bus range, built initially by Bombardier, but subsequently by GAC. A distinctive family of double-deck and single-deck models, designed in Germany, has entered service, and this Bombardier is seen in 1984 passing Dublin's Busaras, the central coach station. *R. L. Wilson*

138

fleets ordered them in some quantity, and some manufacturers of full-size buses turned their attentions to smaller vehicles.

The uncertainties of deregulation aggravated the already depressed bus market of the mid-1980s. Some observers did not anticipate a return to healthier bus production levels until the end of the decade. Others wondered what future there was for the full-sized bus, anticipating a Britain over-run with minibuses. Certainly the market for new buses and coaches in Britain had dropped to only 3,379 vehicles in 1984, down on previous years and a far cry from the record 10,000 plus of 1949. And manufacturers were pessimistic about the prospects for the immediate future, as operators delayed placing large orders, partly a consequence of the uncertainty surrounding deregulation. The growing impact of imported buses and coaches in a shrinking market was a further complication. Of the 3,379 buses and coaches registered in 1984, over 20% were imported, and one of the importers, Volvo, captured 13.5% of the market, ranking third behind Leyland and MCW. The only other significant performances by British manufacturers were by Bedford (10.5%) and Dennis (3.7%).

Although the British motor bus has come a long way from the days of the Milnes-Daimler and the B-type, in most cases the ancestry can be clearly traced back. Buses have got bigger, of course, with single-deck and double-deck coaches up to 12m (39ft 4in) long, and articulated buses up to 18m (59ft) long. Engine positions have changed over the years: from being firmly set at the front from the earliest days, underfloor-mounted engines became popular in the 1950s, and rear engines in the 1960s; today, front engines are the exception in full-size buses, and Volvo's Citybus popularised the underfloor engine on double-deckers.

The power output of bus engines increased as buses grew, and noise and emission legislation prompted widespread acceptance of turbocharged engines. While double-deckers of the 1950s were adequately powered by 100-125bhp engines, 180-200bhp is more typical for the 1980s, and many modern high-specification coaches have engines of 260-290bhp output; some imported models have even more powerful units.

Epicyclic gearboxes were favoured by many operators with urban services from the 1930s, and these developed into semi-automatic and fully-automatic

139 **NCB's pre-deregulation investment in minibuses has changed the face of public transport in several towns and cities. This Ford Transit operating on South Midland's Minibus service in Oxford is typical of many, with 16-seat body conversion by Carlyle Works, former home of Midland Red's bus production unit.**
Katie Johnstone

systems in the 1950s. Few, if any, service buses have manual gearboxes today, and although automatics and semi-automatics are familiar on coaches, many drivers prefer synchromesh gearboxes like the popular ZF units. Power-assisted steering, air brakes and air suspension have become widely accepted as part of the standard specification on the majority of full-size buses and coaches.

There have been some unconventional moves to change our traditional view of bus operation. Like the guided busway projects in West Germany, France, Sweden, Australia and Britain. These have involved varying lengths of specially-built narrow concrete tracks, operated by buses which are mechanically or electronically guided in the restricted space. These systems offer the advantages of a segregated track within the flexibility and

Double-deck luxury

One of the most surprising success stories of the 1980s has been the double-deck coach. Although Ribble had dabbled with coach versions of normal double-deck models over many years, many in the manufacturing and operating industries were sceptical of their passenger appeal.

It took Auwarter, the German builder, to prove them wrong with the spectacular Neoplan Skyliner model, sold initially to Trathens for a Plymouth-London service in 1980. Other operators followed this lead, like Stagecoach of Perth, and the rather ostentatious three-axle Skyliner became gradually more familiar. Other imported double-deck coaches included the Setra Imperial and Van Hool Astromega.

To meet a demand for home-produced double-deck coaches, Leyland and ECW produced a stretched two-axle Olympian for NBC fleets in 1982; this was not the most attractive coach visually, but it was readily chosen by NBC fleets for commuter-type services. MCW followed with the three-axle Metroliner, produced initially for SBG, and subsequently for NBC and Tyne & Wear PTE. Based on a Hong Kong Metrobus chassis, it had a crispness of line that rivalled overseas designs. Leyland face-lifted its Olympian coach in 1984, with neater windows and a greatly improved front-end structure.

These British-produced models were all above the Continental maximum height of 4m (13ft 1in) restricting their use to the UK. Plaxton used a Neoplan underframe for its 1983 Paramount 4000, an attractive double-deck coach to the Continental height.

Another double-deck coach appeared in 1984, the RDC from Walter Alexander. It successfully transformed the standard R-type double-deck body into an attractive coach, and was initially built on Volvo Citybus and Leyland Olympian for SBG's Scottish Citylink services.

140

141

efficiency of the bus. Much of the development work has been carried out by manufacturers eager to promote the safety and speed and low capital costs compared with conventional light rail systems. In particular, Daimler-Benz in West Germany has its experimental O-Bahn concept, with three-part articulated trolleybuses with space for 240 passengers; other builders have developed extra-long articulated motor buses for segregated busways. In Furth, West Germany, MAN has developed an electronically-guided busway using under-road cables and on-bus sensors.

In Britain the first operational example is the West Midlands PTE Tracline system at Short Heath, Birmingham, which opened in 1984. This 600m section of route 65 uses Metrobus double-deckers with special guidewheels which allow the buses to run with the guideway, which occupies 25% less space than a conventional bus lane.

Although the Birmingham system uses motor buses, the guided busway would be equally useful for trolleybuses. There was a rebirth of interest in the trolleybus in the 1980s, first at West Yorkshire PTE and then at South Yorkshire PTE, and, following the success of the Tyne & Wear Metro, three other tramway-type light rail systems were scheduled to follow. In London, a light rail system was designed to serve the revitalised Docklands area, while in Manchester and Sheffield 'Super Tram' networks were to be developed using much existing rail track.

'Real' trams, surviving only in Britain at Blackpool, received a boost when brand new single-deck cars were built in 1984-85; Blackpool had rebuilt older single-deck and double-deck cars to produce modern-looking vehicles, but the new cars, introduced to coincide with Blackpool's tramway centenary in 1985, indicated the undertaking's continuing belief in the system.

With the distinction between buses and railed vehicles becoming blurred, some of Britain's bus builders have been positively promoting the use of railbuses, as a low-cost alternative to full-weight diesel

140 The first all-British response to the challenge of continental double-deck coaches was the MCW Metroliner, a 12-metre three-axle coach with rear-mounted Cummins engine. Examples have been built for Scottish Bus Group, Tyne & Wear PTE and NBC, whose large fleet includes Rapide specification vehicles like this National Travel West coach.
Ian Allan Library

141 Internally, the Metroliner is typical of many modern coaches, with direct glazing, soft trim and reclining seats; the video screens are part of the Rapide specification.
Ian Allan Library

142 **The West Midlands PTE Tracline system** *143*
provides a low-tech guided busway at the outer
end of route 65, at Short Heath. The buses used
are MCW Metrobus 2 painted in a special black
and silver livery. *R. L. Wilson*

143 **The return of the trolleybus. South**
Yorkshire PTE's prototype vehicle, built on
Dennis Dominator chassis with Alexander R-type
bodywork, signalled a fresh interest in this form
of traction. *M. Fowler*

multiple units. Leyland used its expertise
— and spare capacity — at Workington to
develop a National-based railbus, in
versions ranging from single units to
two-coach wider-bodied trains. West
Yorkshire PTE bought the first production
trains, for rail services in the county, and
Metro-Cammell and Walter Alexander
also won contracts. Metro-Cammell has a
long history of railway building, but this
was a new venture for Alexander.

But while the industry was tentatively
looking forward to an uncertain future, the
interest in the past continued to grow. Bus
preservation had been a restricted interest
until the 1960s, but has mushroomed since
then, with thousands of buses in private
hands, many painstakingly restored and
rallied at a growing calendar of events
throughout the summer months. Bus
operators have caught the preservation
bug, with restored buses, sometimes
operating on normal service, and, as a less
extreme concession to history, modern

buses repainted in older liveries. Several
transport museums have sprung up, many
including buses, trams and trolleybuses.
The London Transport Museum at Covent
Garden is the culmination of LT's
pioneering efforts in this field, while others
of note are at Cobham, Glasgow and
Manchester; the excellent Crich Tramway
Museum continues to flourish, and there is
the trolleybus museum at Sandtoft.

Inevitably, newer buses dominate the
preserved ranks, reflecting the oldest
vehicles that were available when the
preservation boom occurred. This means
that postwar types like the Bristol L, Guy

Arab and Leyland Titan PD2 are much in
evidence at rallies, and will be enjoyed by
future generations. Fewer older buses
survive, but, amazingly, 'new' veterans still
appear to join their longer-preserved
brethren, like the London Transport
collection. Now you can see classic models
like the LGOC B-type, Leyland PLSC
Lion and Daimler COG5 — and Bedford
OBs and AEC RTs by the score. With
more recent models to complete the
picture, it is increasingly easy to judge and
enjoy the advances in design and
sophistication that are represented by the
British motor bus.

Profile

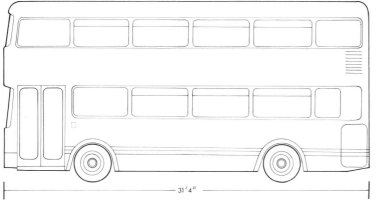

31' 4"

Slightly longer windows, though double-deckers usually only 9.5m long; rear vertical engines (often turbocharged), epicyclic gearboxes or torque converters, one door. 75 seats (43/32).

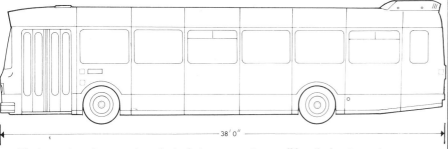

38' 0"

Most operators chose one-door single-deckers, many to overall length close to maximum; rear horizontal engine (sometimes turbocharged), epicyclic gearbox. 52 seats.

Events

Year	Event
1980	Leyland Olympian double-decker introduced. Deregulation of express coach services.
1981	Leyland Tiger coach chassis appears. Last Bristol VRT built.
1982	Volvo Citybus underfloor-engined double-decker.
1983	Closure of Bristol Commercial Vehicles.
1984	Leyland Lynx and Tiger Cub models.
1985	Transport Bill proposes deregulation of bus services and privatisation of National Bus Company.

World Events

1981	Social Democratic Party launched. Riots in Brixton and Toxteth.
1982	Falklands war. Channel 4 on the air.
1984-85	Miners' strike.

INVITATION TO TENDER

London Regional Transport Bus Services

London Regional Transport invite tenders for the operation of a new network of bus services in the Orpington area.

These services will be marketed as an integral part of the London Regional Transport network. Under the contract process, London Regional Transport will maintain a number of controls over the maintenance and financial requirements under the PSV licensing regulations.

The routes involved are:

L1	Sidcup, Queen Mary's Hosp. – Orpington – Bromley Cmn.
L3	Petts Wood – Orpington – Chelsfield – Green St. Green
L4	Locks Bottom – Orpington – Augustine Road
L5	Orpington – Cudham – Pratts Bottom – Orpington
L6	Sevenoaks – Chelsfield Village – Orpington
51	Woolwich – Orpington/Green Street Green
61	Chislehurst – Bromley
61B	Chislehurst – Eltham Well Hall
229	Sidcup – Bexleyheath/Erith
261	Bromley Common – Lewisham
261A	Green Street Green – Bromley
858	Orpington – Biggin Hill

Routes L1, L3, L4, L5, L6 and 858 will be suitable for operation by vehicles with a capacity of about 25 passengers.

In addition, separate tenders are invited for a number of journeys related to routes L5 and L6.

If you are interested, please contact Nick Newton on 01-437 8353 for specifications and a tender application form, or write to him at:

Group Planning Department, London Regional Transport
Oxford Circus House, 245 Oxford Street, LONDON W1R 1LF.

Tender closing date: 20th January 1986

LONDON
REGIONAL
TRANSPORT

A taste of things to come was provided by London Regional Transport's adverts inviting tenders for some of its less remunerative bus routes. These appeared from 1985.

127

Statistical Checkpoint

Motor Buses in Britain

1904	5,345*
1910	24,466*
1915	44,480*
1920	74,608*
1925	98,833*
1930	52,648
1935	47,215
1938	53,600
1945	98,700*
1950	77,636
1955	78,468
1960	78,722
1965	81,600
1970	78,000
1975	75,510
1980	69,136
1983	70,181

Includes taxis

London Transport Motor Buses

1933	5,700
1934	5,976
1939	6,139
1953	8,466
1954	7,617
1961	7,819
1966	8,428
1970	6,591
1976	7,013
1984	5,638

Electric Trams in Britain

1914	13,000
1920	10,594
1924	14,000
1928	12,000
1932	12,275
1939	7,900
1945	6,200
1950	4,700
1955	2,143
1960	400
1984	79

Motor Buses in London 1897-1933

1897	1
1898	0
1899	5
1900	4
1901	10
1902	29
1903	13
1904	31
1905	230
1906	783
1907	933
1908	1,066
1909	1,180
1910	1,142
1911	1,962
1913	2,000
1914	2,500
1919	1,758
1925	5,478
1933	5,350

Further reading

There is a bewildering selection of bus books available for the interested reader these days, and I would not pretend that the titles detailed here represent a comprehensive list. They are, though, the books I found most useful in preparing and updating *The British Motor Bus*, and can be recommended.

There are many books on specific makes, marques — even classes — of bus, but a good general background to the principal builders can be found in the *Buses in Camera* series published by Ian Allan Ltd. The series covers *AEC* by Robin Hannay, *Albion and Crossley* by Stewart J. Brown, *Bristol* by Martin Curtis, *Daimler* by Stewart J. Brown, *Dennis* by Robin Hannay, *Guy* by Jasper Pettie and my own *Leyland* book. Alan Townsin's titles for Transport Publishing Co provide fuller backgrounds of AEC (*Blue Triangle*), *Park Royal* (in two volumes) and *Plaxtons;* other books in the same series cover *Alexander Coachbuilders Duple, Northern Counties* and *Roe.* In addition, TPC publishes Doug Jack's epic volume *The Leyland Bus.*

More information on specific bus and coach models is contained in the Ian Allan *Bus Monographs* series. Titles so far are

Bristol K by Geoff Green, *Leyland National* by Stephen Morris, *Routemaster* by Stewart J. Brown and my own *Leyland Atlantean.* TPC's series *The Best of British Buses* by Alan Townsin includes useful titles on older models, like the AEC Regal, Regent and Q, and Leyland Tiger and Titan, and an excellent survey of wartime bus production, *The Utilities.*

Some of the more distinguished bus models over the years are covered in the Ian Allan book *The Classic Buses,* and *The British Bus Today and Tomorrow* deals in greater detail with the ups and downs of the British bus market since 1969.

The problems of operating buses from the viewpoint of the engineer and manager are entertainingly covered in Geoffrey Hilditch's two books *Looking at Buses* and *A Further Look at Buses* (Ian Allan).

The organisation of the bus and coach operating industry is a complex and fascinating story, well covered in *The History of British Bus Services* by John Hibbs (David & Charles). The early history of the bus is dealt with in Charles E. Lee's twin booklets *The Horse Bus as a Vehicle* and *The Early Motor Bus* (London Transport), and the important part played by the railway companies in the earliest

days of the motor bus is the subject of the two volumes *Railway Motor Buses and Bus Services,* John Cummings (OPC). Ray Stenning deals with the situation before and after the formation of the National Bus Company in his two attractive books *The Years Before National* (Fleetline Books) and *A National Bus Company Album* (Viewfinder). Another title from Ray Stenning is *Bus and Coach Recognition,* one of a series of Ian Allan paperback titles which also includes the *NBC and SBG Fleet List* and *The Bus Book.*
Two tramway books that are well worth reading are *The Golden Age of Tramways* by Charles Klapper (David & Charles), and *Tramway Twilight* by J. Joyce (Ian Allan); trolleybuses are well covered in *History of the British Trolleybus* by Nicholas Owen (David & Charles).

Regular publications covering current developments in bus and coach design and development include the weeklies *Commercial Motor, Motor Transport* and *Coachmart* and the monthlies *Buses* and *Coaching Journal. Buses* also includes historical features, as does its bi-monthly Ian Allan stable-mate *Buses Extra.*